THE SCHOOL MATHEMATICS PROJECT

When the SMP was founded in 1961, its main objective was to devise radical, new secondary school mathematics courses to reflect, more adequately than did the traditional syllabuses, the up-to-date nature and usages of mathematics. The first texts produced embodied new courses for O-level (*SMP Books 1–5*) and A-level (*SMP Advanced Mathematics Books 1–4*). *Books 3, 4* and *5* have now been revised to become *SMP New Book 3, Parts 1* and *2, New Book 4, Parts 1* and *2*, and *New Book 5*, while *Revised Advanced Mathematics Books 1, 2* and *3* cover the syllabus for the A-level examination in SMP Mathematics. Five shorter texts cover the material of the various sections of the A-level examination SMP Further Mathematics. There are two books for SMP Additional Mathematics at O-level. All the SMP GCE examinations are available to schools through any of the GCE examining boards.

Books A–H cover broadly the same development of mathematics as the first few books of the O-level series. Most CSE boards offer appropriate examinations. In practice this series is being used very widely across all streams of comprehensive schools and its first seven books, together with *Books X, Y* and *Z*, provide a course leading to the SMP O-level examination. *SMP Cards I* and *II* provide an alternative treatment in card form of the mathematics in *Books A–D*. The six Units of *SMP 7–13*, designed for children in that age-range, provide a course for middle schools which is also widely used in primary schools and the first two years of secondary schools. *SMP 11–16*, the latest SMP course, provides the basis for a differentiated curriculum in the secondary school, catering for most children, including the most able. Teacher's Guides accompany all these series.

The SMP has produced many other texts and teachers are encouraged to obtain each year from Cambridge University Press, The Edinburgh Building, Shaftesbury Road, Cambridge CB2 2RU, the full list of SMP publications currently available. In the same way, help and advice may always be sought by teachers from the Executive Director at the SMP Office, Westfield College, Kidderpore Avenue, London NW3 7ST. SMP syllabuses and other information may be obtained from the same address.

The SMP is continually evaluating old work and preparing for new. The effectiveness of the SMP's work depends, as it has always done, on the comments and reactions received from a wide variety of teachers – and also from pupils – using SMP materials. Readers of the texts can, therefore, send their comments to the SMP in the knowledge that they will be valued and carefully studied.

ACKNOWLEDGEMENTS

The principal authors, on whose contributions the SMP texts are largely based, are named in the annual reports. Many other authors have also provided original material, and still more have been directly involved in the revision of draft versions of chapters and books. The Project gratefully acknowledges the contributions which they and their schools have made.

This book – *Book Y* – has been written by

T. Easterbrook
D. Hale
E. W. Harper
Joyce Harris
B. Jefferson

and edited by Mary Tait.

The Project owes a great deal to its Secretaries Miss Jacqueline Sinfield and Miss Julie Baker, for their careful typing and assistance in connection with this book.

We would especially thank Professor J. V. Armitage and P. G. Bowie for the advice they have given on the fundamental mathematics of the course.

Some of the drawings at the chapter openings in this book are by Ken Vail.

We are grateful to the Oxford and Cambridge Schools Examination Board and the Southern Regional Examinations Board for permission to use questions from their examination papers, and to Frederick Parker Limited, P.O. Box 146, Leicester, for providing us with the photograph of the 'Little Giant' 150 litre/5T cement mixer and for allowing us to reproduce it.

We are very much indebted to the Cambridge University Press for their cooperation and help at all times.

THE SCHOOL MATHEMATICS PROJECT

Book Y

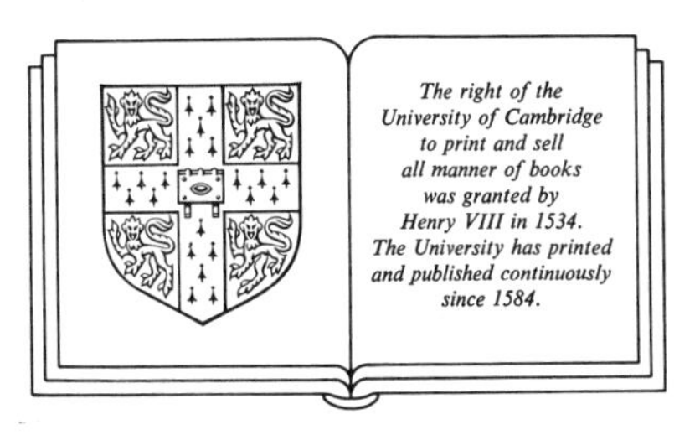

CAMBRIDGE UNIVERSITY PRESS

Cambridge
London New York New Rochelle
Melbourne Sydney

Preface

This is the second of three books designed for O-level candidates who have previously followed the *A–H* series of books. *X*, *Y* and *Z* follow on from *Book G* and cover the remainder of the course for the O-level examination in 'SMP Mathematics'. The books will also be found suitable for students following a one year revision course for O-level and for those who have previously taken the CSE examination.

Many of the topics introduced in *Books A–G* are extended in *X*, *Y* and *Z* and several new topics are also introduced. *Book Z* contains review chapters covering the complete O-level course.

Book Y commences with a graphical and algebraic approach to Rates of Change. This dual approach is also used in the chapters on Simultaneous Equations and Quadratic Functions. The chapter on Coordinates extends the work in 3D introduced in *Book X* and reviews polar coordinates. Algebraic structure is dealt with in some depth in the chapters on Looking for an Inverse, Sets of Numbers and Looking for Functions. The Slide Rule chapter introduces a method for testing for proportionality between ordered sets, and the method is applied in Looking for Functions.

The chapters on Plans and Elevations and Linear Programming form complete sections of the syllabus, and the Tangent chapter completes the work on trigonometry required for the O-level course.

The formula for the volume of a tetrahedron is established in the Mensuration chapter and this is used to deduce volumes of other solids.

Three interludes are included in the book. These are Incidence Matrices, Circle, and Units and Dimensions and they should be viewed as an integral part of the course.

Each of the three books is accompanied by a Teacher's Guide. The Teacher's Guides contain answers, teaching suggestions and ideas.

Contents

1 Rates of Change

1 The way things change

(*a*) When a bar of metal is heated, it expands, causing its length to increase. The arrow diagram in Figure 1 shows the results of an experiment in which the length of a bar of metal was measured at various temperatures.

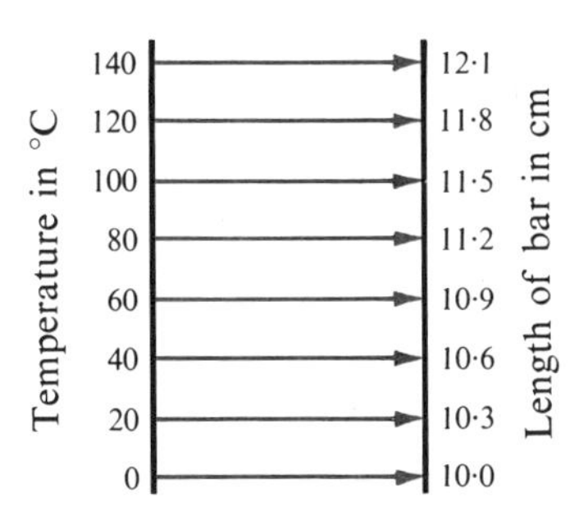

Fig. 1

Suppose that the metal bar at a temperature of 40 °C is heated until its temperature is 100 °C. Check from Figure 1 that the corresponding change in length is 0·9 cm.

We say that the *rate of change* of length with respect to temperature is

$$\frac{11{\cdot}5-10{\cdot}6}{100-40}=\frac{0{\cdot}9}{60}=0{\cdot}015\,\text{cm}/^\circ\text{C}.$$

Notice that a rate of change has units: in this case the units are cm/°C.

(*b*) Suppose that we heat the bar from 20 °C to 40 °C. What is the rate of change of length with respect to temperature for this interval?

Work out the rates of change for some more intervals of your own choice. What do you notice?

(*c*) If we graph the relation represented by Figure 1 we obtain the straight line graph shown in Figure 2.

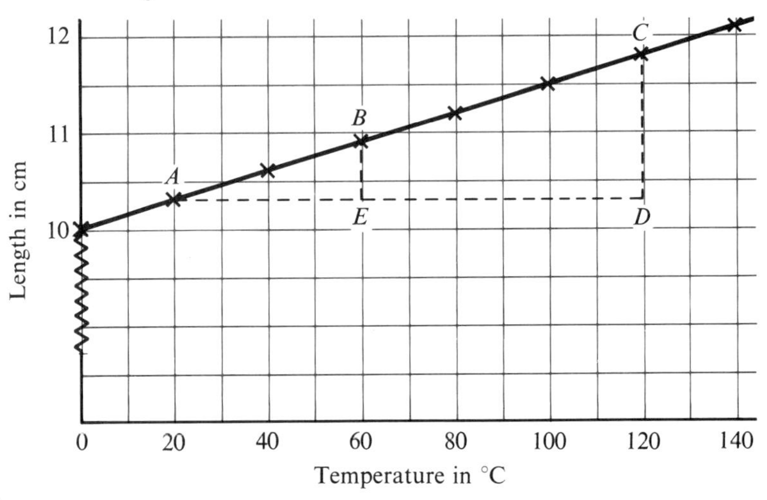

Fig. 2

Consider again the rate of change of length with respect to temperature.

In Figure 2, the distance AE represents a change of temperature of 40 °C and BE represents a change in length of 0·6 cm. Hence the rate of change for this interval is measured by $\frac{BE}{AE}$.

Now look at the triangle ACD. The rate of change for this interval is measured by $\frac{CD}{AD}$.

What can you say about triangles ABE and ACD?

Do you agree that $\frac{BE}{AE}=\frac{CD}{AD}$?

The rates of change for the two intervals are therefore equal. If you choose a different interval will you obtain the same rate of change?

(*d*) You should have found in (*b*) and (*c*) that the rate of change of length with respect to temperature is *constant* and equal to 0·015 cm/°C.

When the graph of a relation is a *straight line* then the rate of change of one quantity with respect to the other is constant.

Exercise A

1

x	0	2	4	6	8
y	1	7	13	19	25

Find the rate of change of y with respect to x for the intervals:
(i) $x = 0$ to $x = 6$; (ii) $x = 2$ to $x = 4$; (iii) $x = 4$ to $x = 8$.

2

x	$^{-}3$	0	3	6	9
y	$^{-}4$	1	6	11	16

Find the rate of change of y with respect to x for the intervals:
(i) $x = {}^{-}3$ to $x = 3$; (ii) $x = 0$ to $x = 6$; (iii) $x = 3$ to $x = 9$.

3 The distance a car has travelled from a starting point is recorded at various times and the results shown in the table. Find the rate of change of distance with respect to time for three intervals of your choice. Draw a graph of distance against time.

Time (s)	0	5	10	15	20	25	30
Distance (m)	0	$7\frac{1}{2}$	15	$22\frac{1}{2}$	30	$37\frac{1}{2}$	45

4 The temperature of oil being heated is measured at various times, and the results shown in the table.

Time (s)	0	10	20	30	40	50	60
Temperature (°C)	10	12·1	14·3	16	17·7	19·2	20

Find the rate of change of temperature with respect to time for three intervals. Comment on your results.

5 An engineering firm tests bolts to see how much they stretch under given loads. The table shows the results of a particular test.

Load (Newtons)	0	8	16	24	32
Length (mm)	500	502·5	505	507·5	510

Find the rate of change of length with respect to load for three intervals of your choice.

Draw a graph of the table to check that the rate of change is constant over the whole range.

6 (*a*)

x	0	1	2	3	4	5
y	1	3	5	7	9	11

Calculate the rate of change of y with respect to x, and draw a graph.

(*b*) Repeat (*a*) for the following table:

x	0	1	2	3	4	5
y	9·5	8	6·5	5	3·5	2

In what respect do the two graphs differ? How is this difference reflected in the rates of change?

2 Gradient

(*a*)

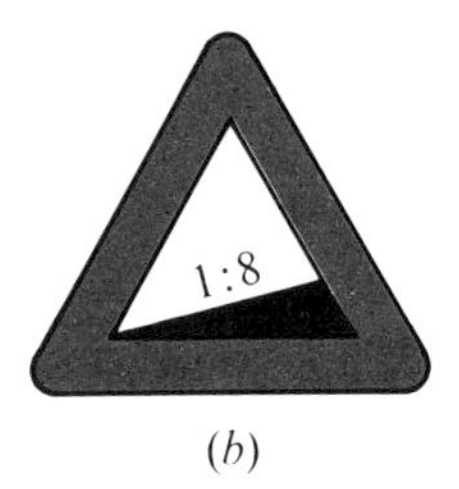

(*b*)

Fig. 3

(*a*) What do the road signs in Figure 3 tell you? Which hill is the steeper?

We say that the *gradient* of the hill represented in Figure 3(*a*) is 1 in 4, that is, the road climbs 1 m in every 4 m.

What would appear on a road sign for a road which climbs 100 m in 500 m?

Gradient measures the steepness of a road. It is the ratio of the vertical distance to the corresponding horizontal distance travelled in driving up the hill.

(*b*) In Figure 4 in going from A to B what is the vertical distance travelled? What is the horizontal distance travelled? Now write down the gradient and express it in its simplest form.

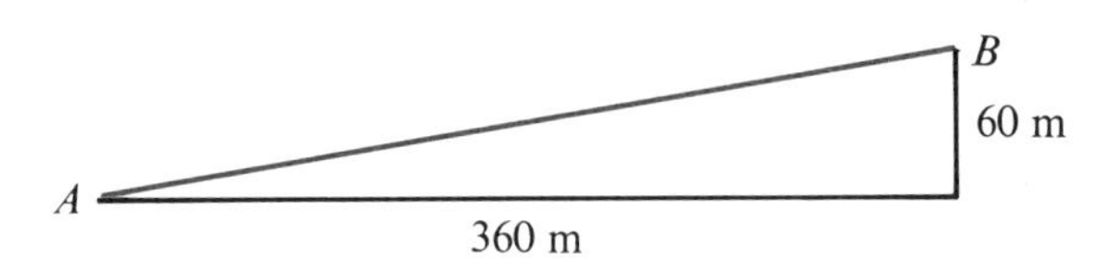

Fig. 4

(*c*) Look at the straight line graphs in Figure 5.

Suppose we wish to measure the gradient of the line in Figure 5(*a*).

What is the horizontal distance from A to B?

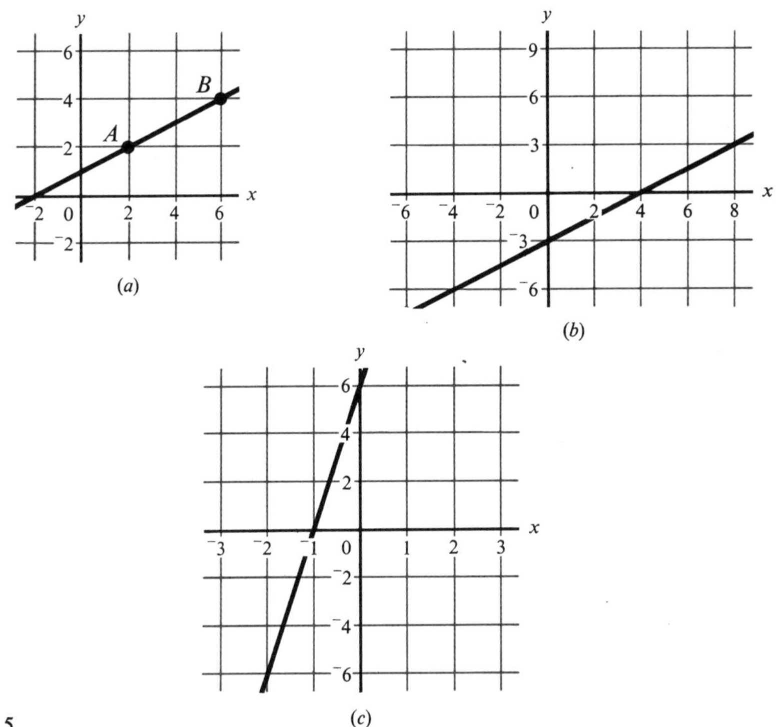

Fig. 5

What is the vertical distance from A to B?

Do you agree that the gradient of the line is 1 in 2?

The gradient of a line is generally written in fractional form and hence we would write the gradient of this line as $\frac{1}{2}$.

Now find the gradients of the lines in Figure 5(*b*) and (*c*) giving your answers in fractional form.

(*d*) Consider the graph shown in Figure 6. The horizontal distance from A to B is $^{-}2$. The vertical distance from A to B is 4.

Hence the gradient of the line is $\frac{4}{^{-}2} = {^{-}2}$.

In what way does the slope of the line in Figure 6 differ from those in Figure 5? How is this difference shown in the value of the gradient?

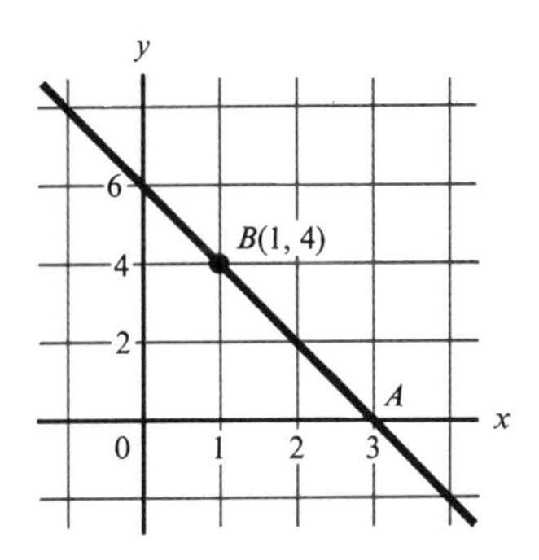

Fig. 6

3 Gradient and rate of change

Consider the relation:

distance (m)	0	3	6	9
time (s)	0	1	2	3

What is the rate of change of distance with respect to time for the time interval from 1 second to 3 seconds?

Draw a graph of the relation.

What is the gradient of the graph?

What is the connection between the gradient of the line and the rate of change?

This shows that the rate of change for a relation is the gradient of its graph together with the appropriate units.

Summary

1 The gradient of a line is the ratio of the vertical displacement to the corresponding horizontal displacement.

2 If the angle between a line and the positive x direction is greater than 90°, the gradient of the line is *negative*.

3 The rate of change for a relation is equivalent to the gradient of its graph together with the appropriate units.

Exercise B

1 Draw graphs showing examples of lines of gradients (*a*) 2; (*b*) $\frac{3}{5}$; (*c*) $^{-}\frac{1}{4}$; (*d*) 0.

2 Write down the gradients of the lines joining the following pairs of points and illustrate your answers with a sketch to check them:

(*a*) $(3, 1)$ and $(^{-}1, ^{-}2)$; (*b*) $(1, ^{-}1)$ and $(3, 1)$;
(*c*) $(^{-}4, ^{-}3)$ and $(^{-}2, 5)$; (*d*) $(4, 1)$ and $(2, 5)$;
(*e*) $(4, 1)$ and $(0, 6)$; (*f*) $(3, ^{-}2)$ and $(^{-}2, 3)$;
(*g*) $(6, ^{-}5)$ and $(0, 0)$; (*h*) $(^{-}1, ^{-}2)$ and $(^{-}6, 8)$;
(*i*) $(4, 2)$ and $(6, 2)$; (*j*) $(4, 2)$ and $(4, 8)$.

3

x	0	3	5	8	9
y	10	14	$16\frac{2}{3}$	$20\frac{2}{3}$	22

(i) Find the rate of change of y with respect to x.
(ii) Draw a graph of the relation and find its gradient.

4 Repeat Question 3 for each of the following tables:

(*a*)

x	$^-2$	0	1	3	6
y	6	5	$4\frac{1}{2}$	$3\frac{1}{2}$	2

(*b*)

x	$^-2$	$^-1$	1	5
y	7	$4\frac{2}{3}$	0	$^-9\frac{1}{3}$

5 Repeat Question 3 for each of the following tables:

(*a*)

length (cm)	10	25	30	40
mass (g)	7	$17\frac{1}{2}$	21	28

(*b*)

cost price (p)	10	15	20	25
selling price (p)	12	18	24	30

(*c*)

length (cm)	1	2	3	4
area (cm²)	0·5	2	4·5	8

4 Gradients of algebraic functions

(*a*) Consider the gradient of the graph of $f: x \rightarrow 2x + 5$ as shown in Figure 7.

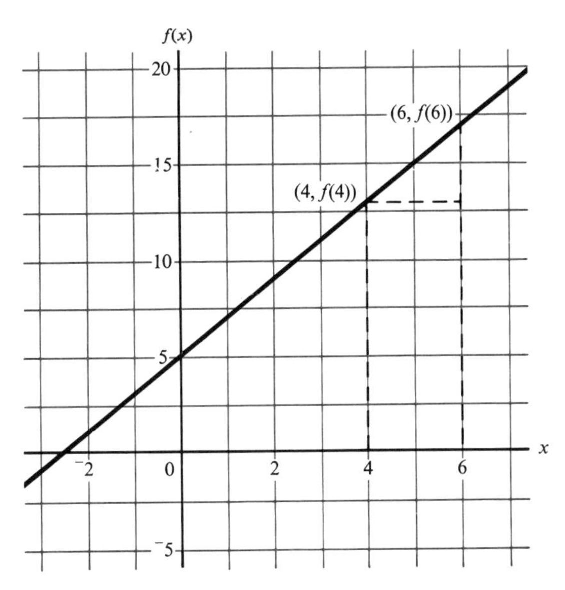

Fig. 7

Find $f(4)$ and $f(6)$.
Did you obtain 13 and 17?

Can you explain why the gradient of the line is $\dfrac{17-13}{6-4} = \dfrac{4}{2} = 2$?

Use this method to find the gradient of the graphs of the following functions:

(i) $f: x \rightarrow \frac{1}{2}x + 1$;
(ii) $f: x \rightarrow 3x - 2$;
(iii) $f: x \rightarrow {}^{-}2x + 3$.

What do you notice? Find the gradient of some more functions of the same form. Do they confirm your findings?

You should have found that a function of the form $f: x \rightarrow mx + c$ has gradient m. We say that m is *the coefficient of x in $mx + c$*. The gradients in (i), (ii), (iii) are $\frac{1}{2}$, 3 and ${}^{-}2$, respectively.

(*b*) Figure 8 shows the graph of the linear function $f: x \rightarrow f(x)$.

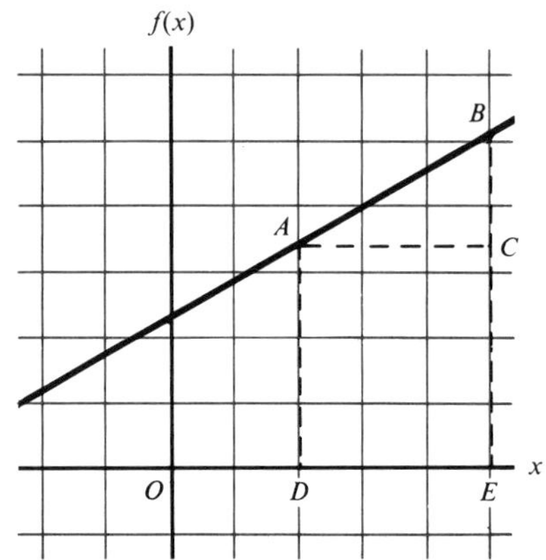

Fig. 8

If $OD = a$, then $AD = f(a)$.
If $OE = b$, then $BE = f(b)$.
What is the length of BC? What is the length of AC?

The gradient of the line is $\dfrac{BC}{AC} = \dfrac{f(b) - f(a)}{b - a}$.

Since the rate of change of a relation is measured by the gradient of its graph, we can say that the rate of change of $f(x)$ with respect to x is also $\dfrac{f(b) - f(a)}{b - a}$.

Notice that, where x and $f(x)$ are numbers, this expression is a ratio and no units are involved. But where, for example, x represents time in seconds and $f(x)$ represents distance in metres, then the expression is a rate and the units, metres per second, must be stated.

(*c*) The table shows some values which are related by an equation of the form $y = mx + c$.

x	1	2	3	4	5
y	5	7	9	11	13

What is the rate of change of y with respect to x?
Do you agree that the gradient of the graph of the relation is 2?
So we can now write $y = 2x + c$.
But when $x = 1$, $y = 5$ and therefore we can find the value of c.
Do you agree that $y = 2x + 3$?

Exercise C

1 Draw the graph that represents the function $f: x \to 3x + 1$, and find its gradient.

2 Calculate the gradient of the line $y = 1 + \frac{3}{4}x$.

3 Write down the gradients of the following functions:

(*a*) $x \to 3x + 4$; (*b*) $z \to 2 + 5z$;
(*c*) $x \to 3 - 8x$; (*d*) $t \to \frac{2}{3}t - 7$.

4 Write down the gradients of the following lines:

(*a*) $y = 4x - 3$; (*b*) $2y = 3x + 4$;
(*c*) $\frac{1}{3}y = 3 - \frac{1}{5}x$; (*d*) $\frac{3}{4}y = 7x - 1$.

5 Express y as a function of x of the form $y = mx + c$ for the following tables:

(*a*)

x	1	2	3	4
y	2	8	14	20

(*b*)

x	$^-5$	$^-3$	$^-1$	1
y	0	$^-4$	$^-8$	$^-12$

(*c*)

x	6	12	18	24
y	5	9	13	17

6 The following table shows the length of a piece of wire carrying various masses:

mass m (kg)	5	10	20	25
length l (cm)	51·5	53	56	57·5

Express l as a function of the form $l = am + b$. Use your expression to find (*a*) l when $m = 28$ and (*b*) the unstretched length of the wire (that is, the value of l when $m = 0$).

5 Rate of change at an instant

(*a*) A man drove from Manchester to Bristol, a distance of 255 km, in 3 hours. What was his average speed for the journey?

Do you think it likely that he travelled at exactly 85 km/hour for the whole of the journey?

(*b*) Here is a table giving more details of his journey:

time (hours)	0	0·4	0·68	1·18	1·68	2·18	2·37	3
distance (km)	0	20	50	100	150	200	220	255

The rate of change of distance with respect to time from 50 km to 200 km is $\frac{200-50}{2{\cdot}18-0{\cdot}68} = \frac{150}{1{\cdot}5} = 100$ km/hour. Notice that this is the average speed for the interval 50 km to 200 km.

Calculate the average speed for the following intervals:

(i) 150 km to 200 km; (ii) 0 km to 20 km;

(iii) 200 km to 255 km. Comment on your results.

(c) All the speeds calculated so far have been average speeds, but a speedometer measures speed at an instant.

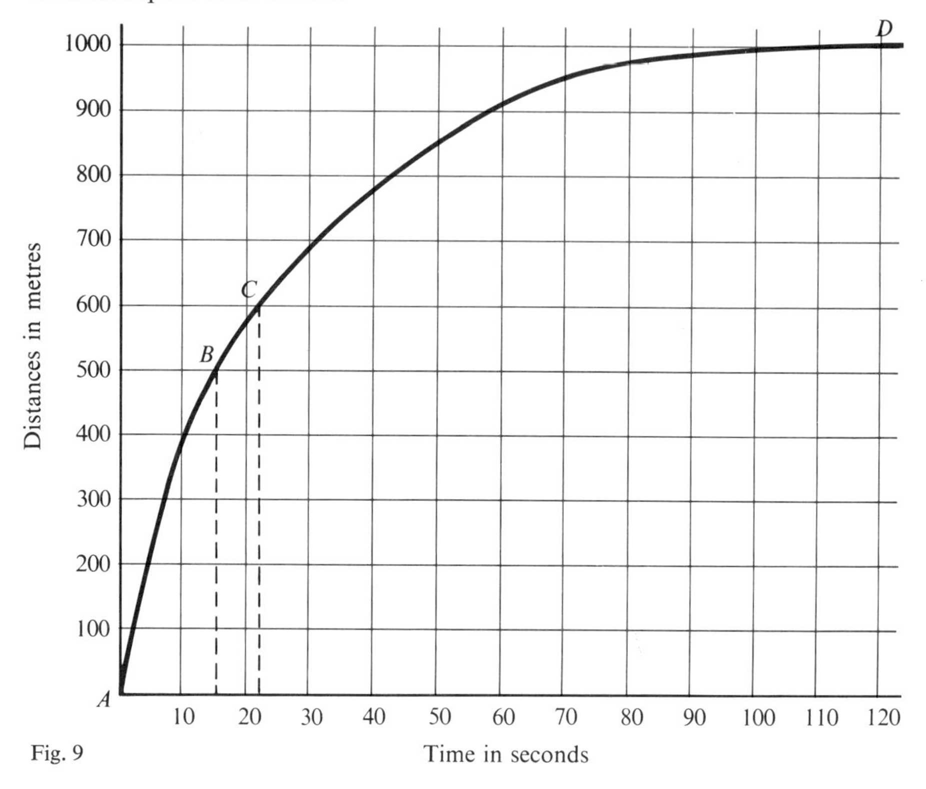

Fig. 9

Figure 9 shows a distance–time graph for a car which is slowing to rest over a distance of 1 km.

Calculate its average speed in metres per second over the whole interval from A to D.

Do you think this would be a good estimate of its speed as it passes the 500 m mark, point B on the graph?

The car was also timed from 500 m to 600 m, the interval B to C on the graph. Calculate its average speed over this interval.

Do you think this would be a better estimate of its speed at B?

How might we improve on our estimate of the speed at B?

In general, the shorter the distance over which the car is timed, the more accurate will be our estimate of its speed at B.

This is shown in Figure 10. The lines BC_1, BC_2, . . ., are chords all passing through B. As the point C gets closer to B, our idea that the curve possesses a direction at B suggests that there is exactly one line which 'just touches' the curve there and that the chords get closer to it in the sense of having the same direction

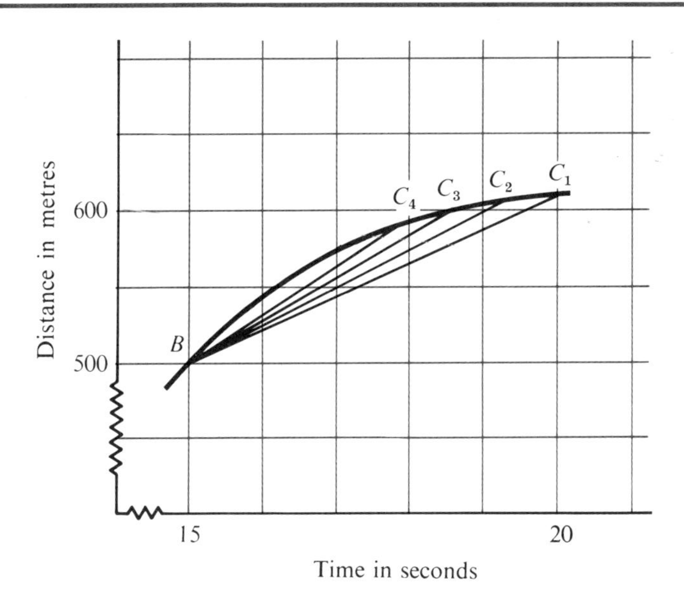

Fig. 10

at B. If there is such a line it is called the *tangent* at B. So the gradient of the chord BC approaches the gradient of the tangent as C approaches B.

We say that the speed at a given instant is the gradient of the tangent to the graph at that instant with appropriate units, that is the rate of change of the function at that instant.

To find the rate of change of distance with respect to time at a point we

(i) draw the tangent to the curve at that point;
(ii) calculate the gradient of the tangent;
(iii) state the units.

Figure 11 shows a distance time graph of a particle over an interval of 4 s.

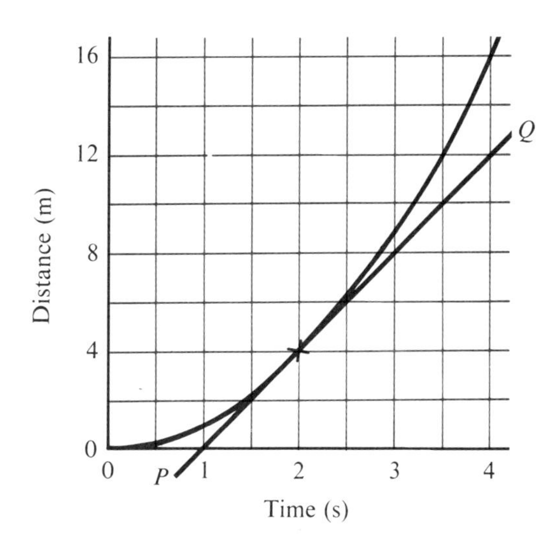

Fig. 11

The line PQ is the tangent to the curve at (2,4). Calculate the gradient of PQ. Do you agree that the speed of the particle after 2 s is 4 m/s?
Copy Figure 11 and find the speed of the particle after 3 s.
Your answer should be approximately 6 m/s.

Exercise D

1 Draw the graph of the function $y = x^2 + 2x$ for $^-1 \leqslant x \leqslant 3$.
(*a*) Draw the tangent to the curve at $x = 1$.
What is the gradient of the tangent?
(*b*) By drawing the tangent at $x = 0$, estimate the gradient of $y = x^2 + 2x$ at $x = 0$.
(*c*) Find the gradient of $y = x^2 + 2x$ at $x = 2$.

2 Use a graph to estimate the gradient of $y = x^2 - 3x + 5$ at
(*a*) $x = 0$; (*b*) $x = 2$; (*c*) $x = 0{\cdot}5$.

3 Draw the graph of $R = v^3 - 2v$ for the range $v = {}^-3$ to $v = 3$.
Find the approximate gradient of the graph at
(*a*) $v = 1$; (*b*) $v = {}^-2$; (*c*) $v = 0$.

4 A sledge slides down a slope and its distance travelled, s metres, at time t seconds is given by

$$s = 10t + 2t^2.$$

Draw a graph of s against t for $0 \leqslant t \leqslant 4$. Estimate the speed of the sledge at
(*a*) $t = 1$; (*b*) $t = 3$; (*c*) $t = 2{\cdot}4$.
What are the units of your answer?

5 Draw the curve $y = 2 - \frac{1}{x}$ for $\frac{1}{4} \leqslant x \leqslant 4$. Plot at least 8 points. Estimate the gradient of the graph at $x = \frac{1}{2}$ and at $x = 2$.

6 Graph the function $g: x \to x + \frac{1}{x}$ for $0{\cdot}2 \leqslant x \leqslant 3$. Find the smallest value of $g(x)$ in this range and the value of x for which it occurs. What is your estimate of the gradient of the curve at this point?

7 A pig is being fattened for market. The table shows its mass at ten-day intervals.

Day	0	10	20	30	40	50	60	70	80	90
Mass (kg)	2	16	20	28	39	49	56	70	84	101

Represent this information graphically, and find the rate of increase of mass on the 20th day. Would the farmer be sensible to keep the pig longer? Explain your answer.

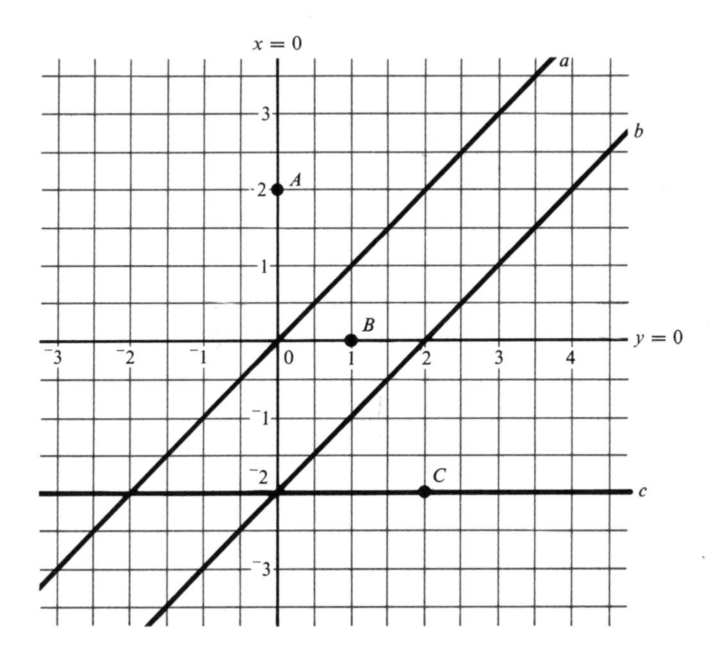

2 Coordinates

1 Coordinates in two dimensions

(*a*) A review

Make a copy of the diagram at the head of this chapter and use it to answer the following:

(i) What are the coordinates of A, B and C?

(ii) Draw the line through A, B, C. What is its gradient? If the equation of this line is $y = mx + c$, what are the values of m and c? (Check that the coordinates of A, B and C really do satisfy your equation.)

(iii) Write down the equations of the lines a, b and c.

(iv) Mark with a cross all points belonging to the set

$$\{(x,y)\colon y < x - 2;\ x, y \text{ are whole numbers}\}.$$

(v) What values of x and y satisfy both $y = {}^{-}2x + 2$ and $y = x - 2$? Check by substitution.

(*b*) Cartesian coordinates

The (x,y) system of coordinates for describing the position of a point was invented by the seventeenth century mathematician René Descartes. For this reason, they are generally called *Cartesian coordinates*.

It is important to remember that the axes used in a Cartesian coordinate system may be labelled in one of two ways (Figure 1).

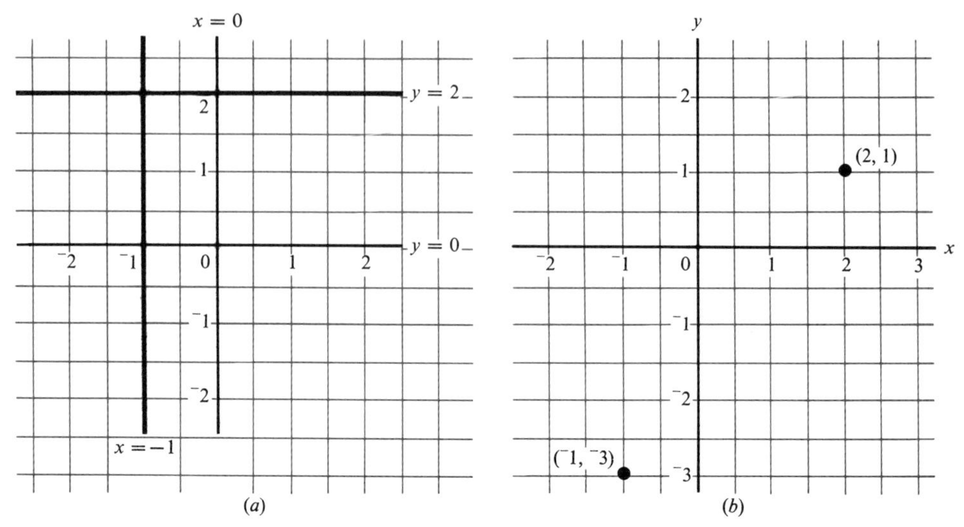

Fig. 1

Figure 1(a) reminds us that lines parallel to $y = 0$ have equations of the form $y =$ constant and lines parallel to $x = 0$ have equations of the form $x =$ constant. Figure 1(b) shows that the x and y coordinates of a point are read on the x and y axes.

(c) Distance on a graph

What are the coordinates of A and B in Figure 2? How can you obtain the length of AP from the x coordinates? How long is BP?

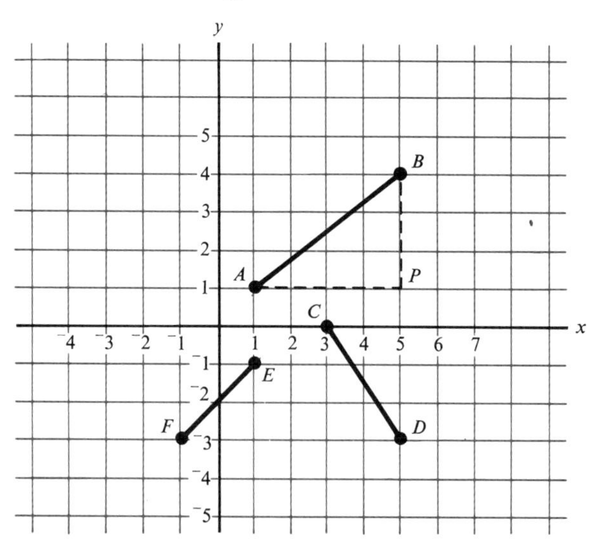

Fig. 2

Now use Pythagoras' rule to work out the distance from A to B. Copy Figure 2 and draw suitable right angled triangles to help you find the lengths CD and EF correct to 2 S.F.

Exercise A

1 Write down the equation of the line through $(0,3)$ which has a gradient of $^{-}2$. Which of the following points lie on this line?

$$(1,2), (1,1), (2,{}^{-}1), ({}^{-}1,5), (3,{}^{-}2).$$

2 Show on a graph the set of points $\{(x,y): y > 2x\}$.

3 What is the gradient of the line joining $(1,2)$ and $(4,{}^{-}1)$?

4 A is the point $(1,0)$ and B is the point $(5,0)$. Write down the coordinates of three points which belong to the set $\{P: PA = PB\}$.

5 Find the area of the region bounded by the x and y axes and the line $4x + 3y = 12$.

6 If $A = \{(x,y): x > 2\}$ and $B = \{(x,y): y < x\}$, show clearly on a diagram the set $A \cap B$.

7 A pentagon $ABCDE$ is symmetrical about the line $y = x$. A is $(3,0)$, C is $(6,6)$ and D is $(3,6)$. What are the coordinates of B and E?

8 State a set of inequalities satisfied by the coordinates of all the points of the shaded region in Figure 3. (The boundary is included.)

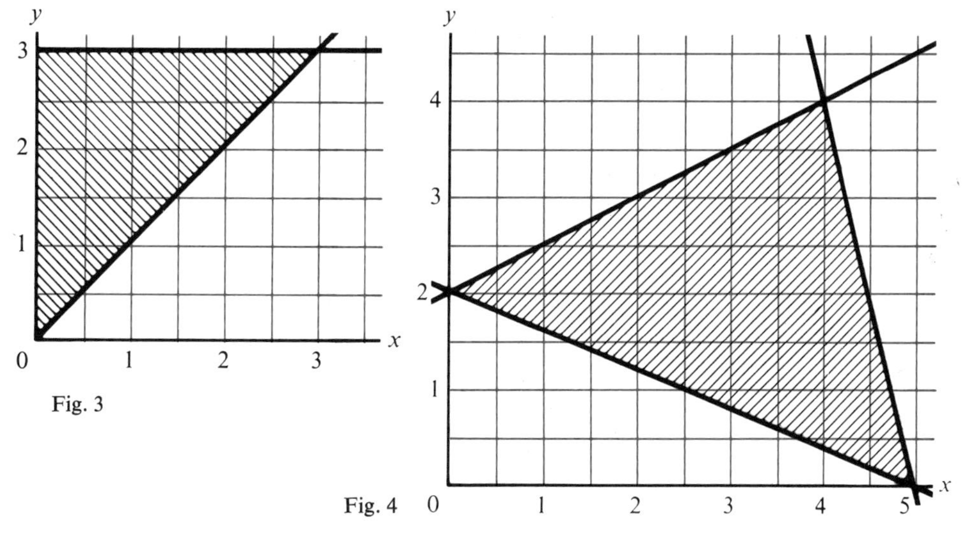

Fig. 3

Fig. 4

9 Two sides of the shaded triangle (Figure 4) have equations $2x + 5y = 10$ and $4x + y = 20$. What is the equation of the third side? Say whether the following points are inside the triangle, outside the triangle, or on its boundary.

$$(2,2), (3,2), (1,4), (2\tfrac{1}{2}, 1), (1, 1), (3, 1).$$

10 What are the coordinates of the point $(3,2)$ after reflection in the x axis? Find the image of $(3,2)$ under the composite transformation – 'reflection in the x axis followed by a half-turn about the origin'.

11 If O is the origin and A, B are the points $(3,4)$, $(7,1)$ respectively, calculate the lengths OA, OB and AB. Show that the triangle OAB is right-angled.

12 Show that the points with coordinates $(7,10)$, $(^-5,^-6)$ and $(7,^-6)$ lie on a circle with its centre at $(1,2)$. What is the radius of this circle?

13 Check that $(0,2)$ belongs to the set of points $\{(x,y): x^2+y^2=4\}$ and find three other members of this set. Draw a graph to show the complete set.

14 P is the point $(2,0)$, Q is the point $(1,2)$ and P', Q' are their images under a transformation whose matrix is $\begin{pmatrix}1 & 0\\ 2 & 1\end{pmatrix}$. Calculate the lengths PQ and $P'Q'$ and explain why the transformation cannot be a reflection or rotation.

2 Coordinates in three dimensions

(*a*) Fred in space

Fred, the mathematical fly, has landed at the centre of the floor, F_1 (Figure 5). His position on the floor is given by $(3,4)$. If Fred decides to land on a wall or ceiling, how can we describe his position? Fred's second landing place, F_2, is in the middle of a wall (Figure 6).

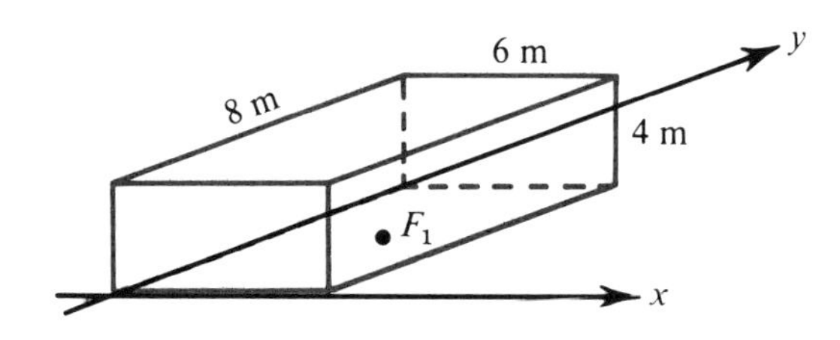

Fig. 5

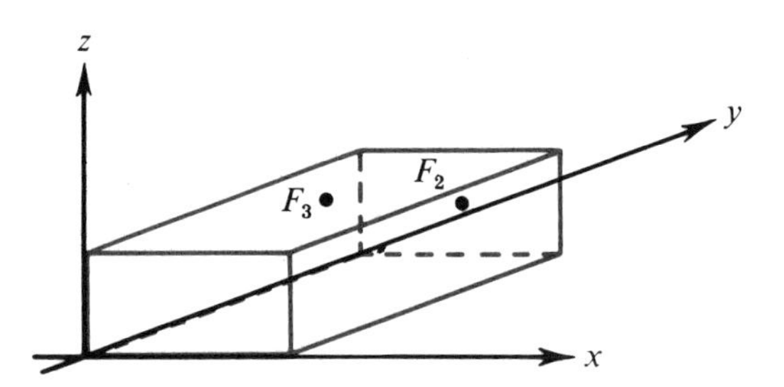

Fig. 6

Do you agree that his position is given by the three coordinates $(3,8,2)$? We can say that F_2 has x-coordinate 3, y-coordinate 8 and z-coordinate 2. What are the coordinates of Fred's third landing place in the centre of the ceiling (F_3 in Figure 6)?

We can now look again at F_1. Its position can be given by three coordinates. Do you agree that the z-coordinate of F_1 is 0? Write down all three coordinates of F_1.

In three dimensions, we establish three axes perpendicular to each other. Provided each axis has a scale, we can define the position of any point by giving three coordinates.

Make two cubes and label them as in Figure 7.

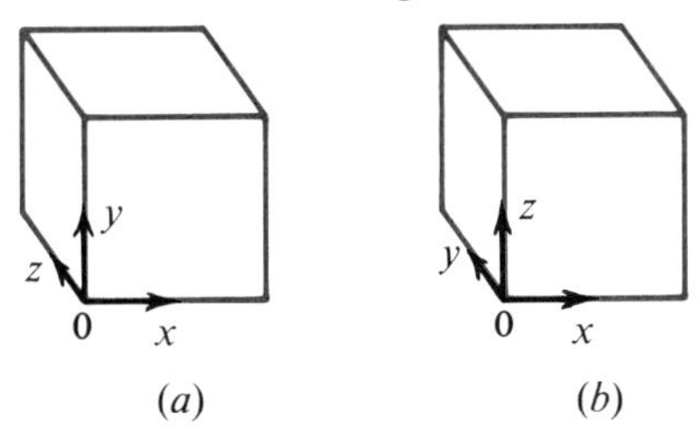

Fig. 7

Look at the set of axes shown in Figure 7(a). Is it possible to rotate them about O into the position shown in Figure 7(b)? Do you agree that the two sets of axes are not equivalent? They are related to one another as right-handed and left-handed gloves are. Figure 7(a) shows the left-handed set and Figure 7(b) the right-handed set. In practice, a right-handed set of axes is always used.

Exercise B

1 Write down the coordinates of the points A, B, C, D, E, F, G, H in Figure 8.

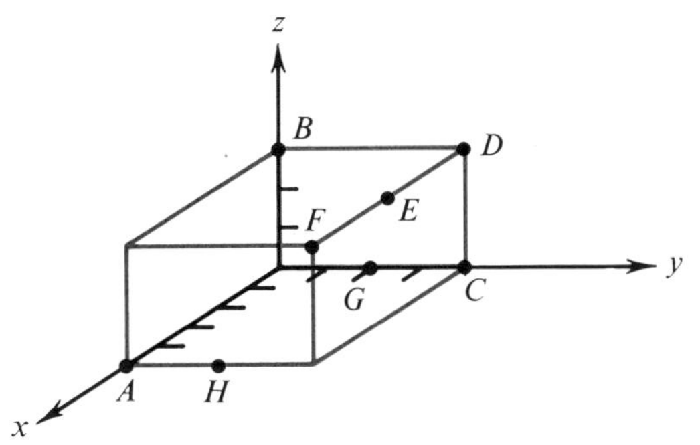

Fig. 8

2 Which sets of axes in Figure 9 are right-handed? (It will probably help to make and label some cubes.)

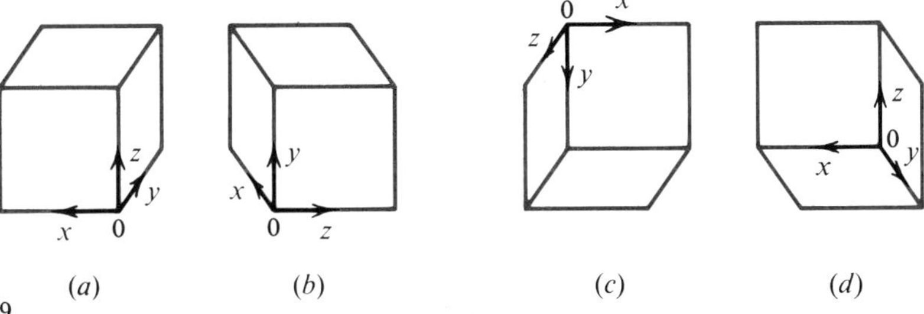

Fig. 9

3 $ABCDPQRS$ is a cuboid (Figure 10). The origin is at its centre and the axes are parallel to its edges. If A is the point $(3, 2, 1)$, find the coordinates of the other seven vertices.

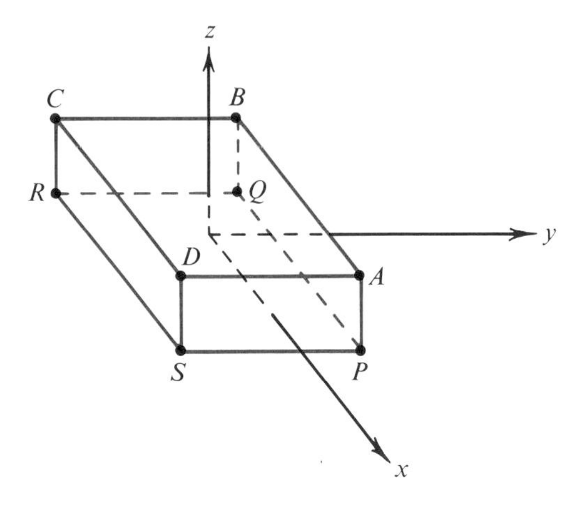

Fig. 10

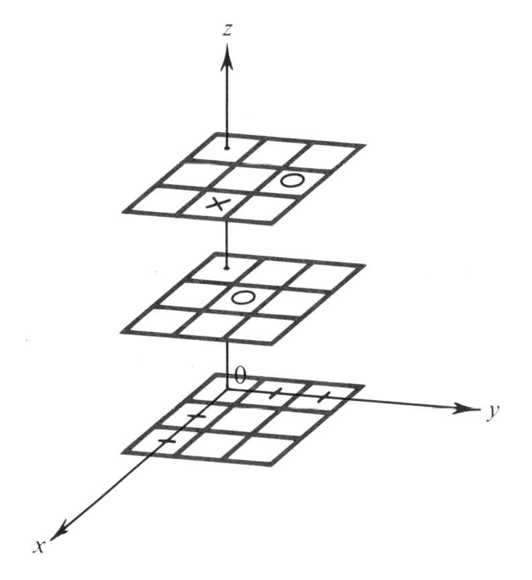

Fig. 11

4 *3D noughts and crosses*

The position of the cross in Figure 11 can be written $(2, 1, 2)$ and one of the noughts is at $(1, 1, 1)$.

(*a*) What is the position of the other nought?
(*b*) Where would a third nought have to be placed to complete a winning line?

5 In 3D noughts and crosses, where would crosses have to be placed to make winning lines if there were already crosses at the following pairs of points?

(*a*) (2,0,2), (1,0,2); (*b*) (0,0,0), (0,0,1);
(*c*) (0,2,2), (1,1,1); (*d*) (1,0,2), (1,2,2);
(*e*) (0,1,2), (2,1,0); (*f*) (1,1,1), (1,1,2).

(*b*) Planes

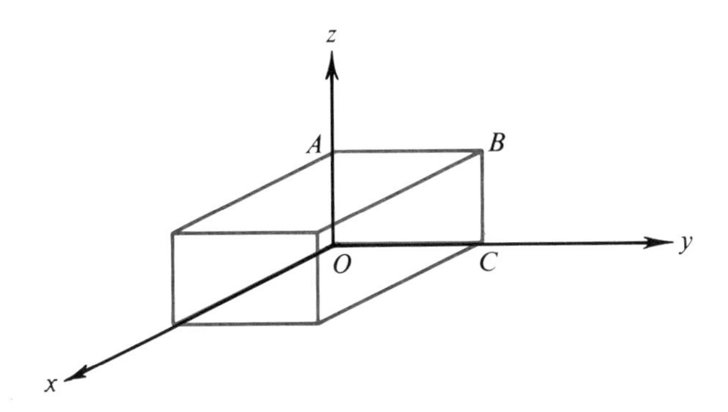

Fig. 12

In Figure 12,

O is the point (0,0,0),
A is the point (0,0,4),
B is the point (0,6,4),
C is the point (0,6,0).

These four points lie in a plane. Can you visualize this plane; it also contains the y and z axes? Write down the coordinates of two other points in the plane $OABC$.

Can you describe the set of points in space which satisfy the relation $x = 0$? Does your description agree with Figure 13?

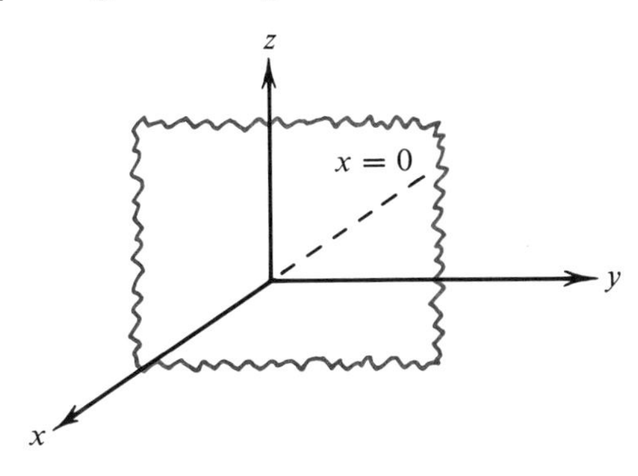

Fig. 13

$x = 0$ is the equation of a plane which contains the origin and is perpendicular to the x axis. Describe the planes $y = 0$ and $z = 0$ in a similar way.

(*c*) A model

In answering the questions of Exercise C, it will be useful to have a model of the three planes $x = 0$, $y = 0$ and $z = 0$ (Figure 14).

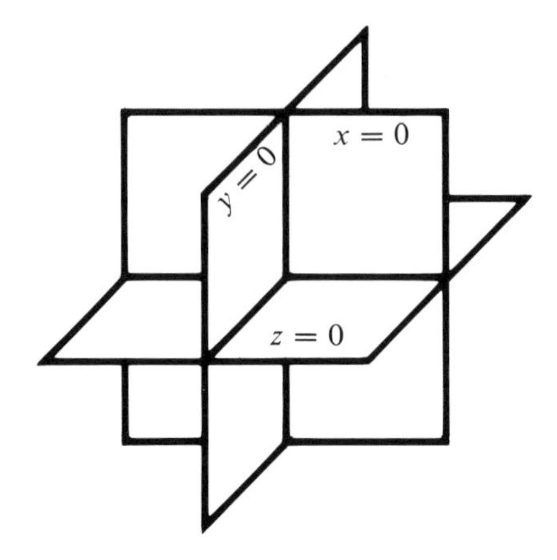

Fig. 14

To make the model you will need three squares (with sides about 15 cm long) of thin card. Two of these are cut as shown in Figure 15(*a*) and the third as in Figure 15(*b*).

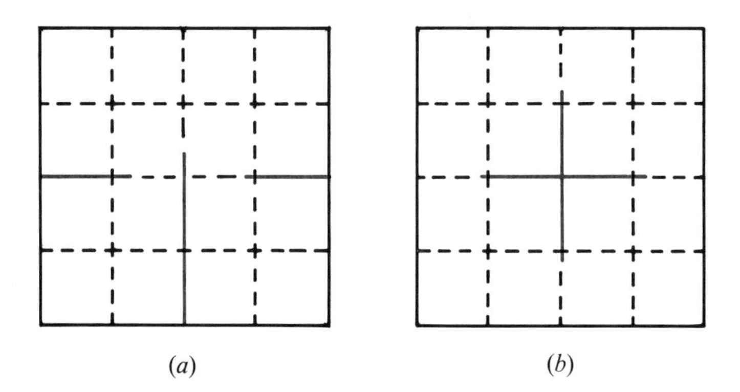

Fig. 15

Fit the two identical pieces together (Figure 16(*a*)) and then fold as shown in Figure 16(*b*).

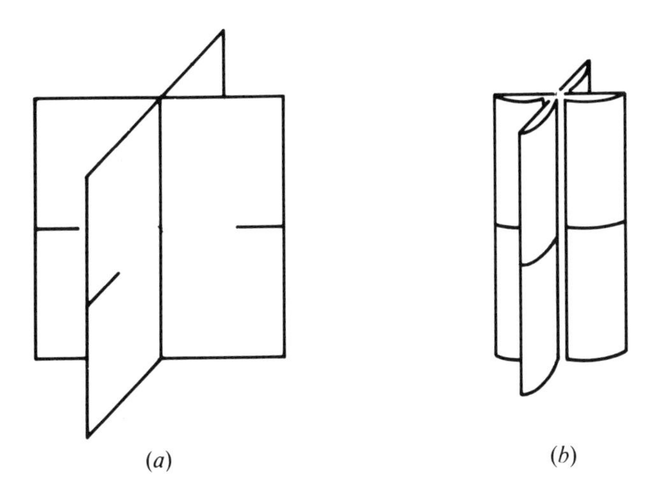

Fig. 16

The third square can now be placed half way down and when unfolded the model should appear as in Figure 14. Label the planes and the x, y and z axes.

Exercise C

1 In Figure 17, the shaded plane is parallel to the plane $z = 0$ and 3 units above it. Write down the equation of the shaded plane. What is the equation of a plane parallel to $z = 0$ and 3 units below it?

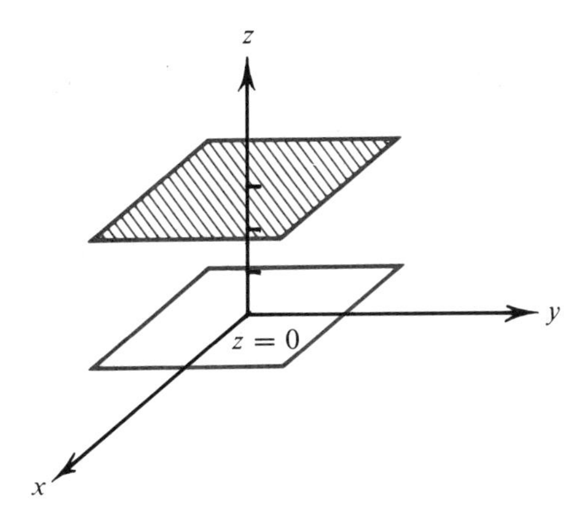

Fig. 17

2 Say which of these statements is true;

(a) the planes $x = 1$, $x = 5$ are parallel;
(b) the planes $x = 2$, $y = 3$ are perpendicular;
(c) the planes $x = 2$, $z = 3$ are perpendicular.

3 Put a suitable scale on the axes of your model. Mark four points on your model which have a y-coordinate, 0, and a z-coordinate, 1. Describe the set $\{(x,y,z): y=0, z=1\}$.

4 Draw and label on your model the following sets of points:

(*a*) $A=\{(x,y,z): y=0, z=2\}$;
(*b*) $B=\{(x,y,z): x=1, z=0\}$;
(*c*) $C=\{(x,y,z): x=0, z=2\}$;
(*d*) $D=\{(x,y,z): x=0, y=2\}$.

5 What does the equation $x=y$ represent in three-dimensional space?

6 Find $\{(x,y,z): x=y, z=0\}$. Draw it on your model, and label it with the letter E.

7 Find the angles between these pairs of planes:

(*a*) $x=0, y=0$;
(*b*) $x=0, y=x$;
(*c*) $y=0, y=x$;
(*d*) $z=0, y=x$;
(*e*) $x=3, y={}^{-}100$.

8 Give the coordinates of four points which satisfy the equation $x+y+z=2$. What do you think this equation represents?

If $$P=\{(x,y,z): x+y+z=2\}$$

and

$$Q=\{(x,y,z): x+y+z=3\},$$

what can you say about $P \cap Q$?

(*d*) Distance from the origin

Can you do a calculation to show that the point $(2,3,6)$ is 7 units from the origin? Do you remember Pythagoras' rule in 3D? Look at Figure 18 for a reminder.

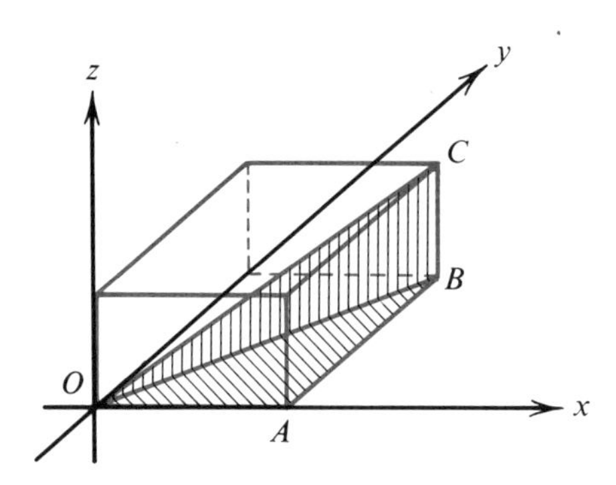

Fig. 18

$$OC^2 = OB^2 + BC^2 \quad \text{and} \quad OB^2 = OA^2 + AB^2$$

therefore

$$OC^2 = OA^2 + AB^2 + BC^2$$

or

$$OC = \sqrt{(OA^2 + AB^2 + BC^2)}.$$

With the axes shown, the lengths of OA, AB, BC are respectively the x, y, z coordinates of the point C. So if C is the point (x, y, z), its distance from the origin O is

$$\sqrt{(x^2 + y^2 + z^2)}.$$

The point (4, 5, 20) is also a whole number of units from the origin. Can you find this distance?

(*e*) **Distance between two points**

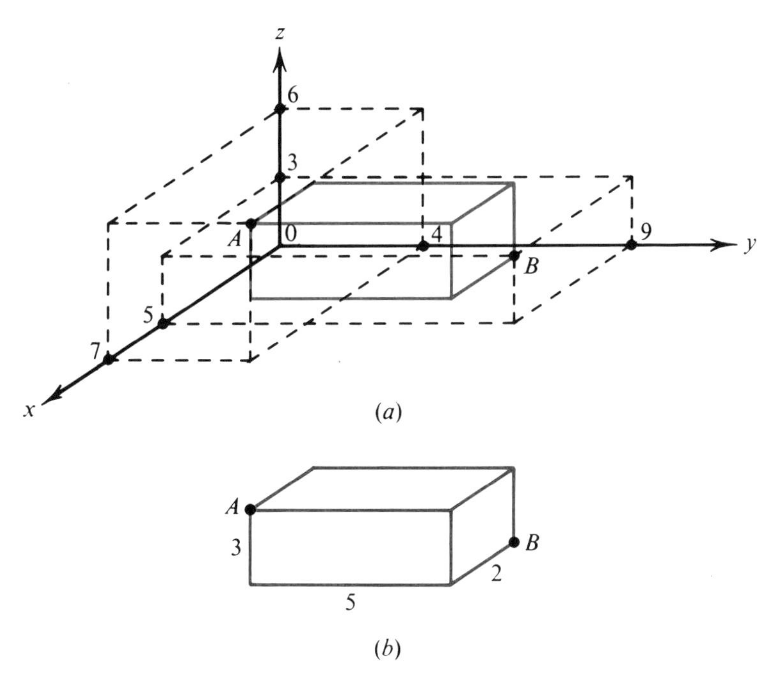

Fig. 19

In Figure 19(*a*), A is the point (7, 4, 6) and B is (5, 9, 3). Figure 19(*b*) shows a box with A and B at opposite corners and its edges parallel to the axes. How are the dimensions of this box obtained from the coordinates of A and B? Check by a calculation that $AB \approx 6{\cdot}2$.

The method used in this particular case will enable us to find the distance between any two points in space whose coordinates are known. We visualize a box with edges parallel to the axes and with the two points at opposite corners.

The dimensions of the box are obtained by taking the numerical difference between each pair of coordinates in turn. Finally, the 3D version of Pythagoras' rule is used to calculate the required distance. Special care is needed if some of the co-ordinates are negative numbers. For example,

$$\left.\begin{array}{l} P \text{ is } (^-2, 1, 5) \\ Q \text{ is } (^-3, ^-1, 2) \end{array}\right\} \Rightarrow \text{box dimensions are } 1, 2, 3$$

$$\Rightarrow PQ \approx 3{\cdot}7.$$

Exercise D

1 How far from the origin are the points:

(*a*) $(3, 4, 12)$;
(*b*) $(1, 0, 1)$;
(*c*) $(^-1, 4, 8)$;
(*d*) (a, b, c)?

2 Find the distance between the points:

(*a*) $(1, 1, 1)$ and $(4, 5, 13)$;
(*b*) $(^-1, ^-2, ^-3)$ and $(2, 2, 9)$;
(*c*) $(0, ^-1, 4)$ and $(^-2, 3, 4)$.

3 A is the point (a, a, a) and $OA = 15$ units. Calculate a correct to 1 D.P.

4 Check that $(0, 3, 4) \in \{(x, y, z)\colon x^2 + y^2 + z^2 = 25\}$. Find six other members of the set and describe the surface which is formed by the set of points.

5 Give the equation of the sphere with its centre at the origin and with a radius of 4 units.

6 C is the set of points $\{(x, y, z)\colon x^2 + y^2 + z^2 = 9\}$ and D is the set $\{(x, y, z)\colon x = 4\}$. Describe the sets C and D. What can you say about $C \cap D$?

7 Describe the surface formed by the set of points

$$\{(x, y, z)\colon x^2 + y^2 = 4\}.$$

(First consider what $x^2 + y^2 = 4$ represents in 2D.)

8 Find p if the points $(p, 1, 2)$, $(2, 3, 5)$, $(4, 7, 11)$ are in a straight line.

3 Polar coordinates

(*a*) A reminder

If you have a long memory, Figure 20 may be familiar. It is a drawing of a radar screen which appeared in *Book B*.

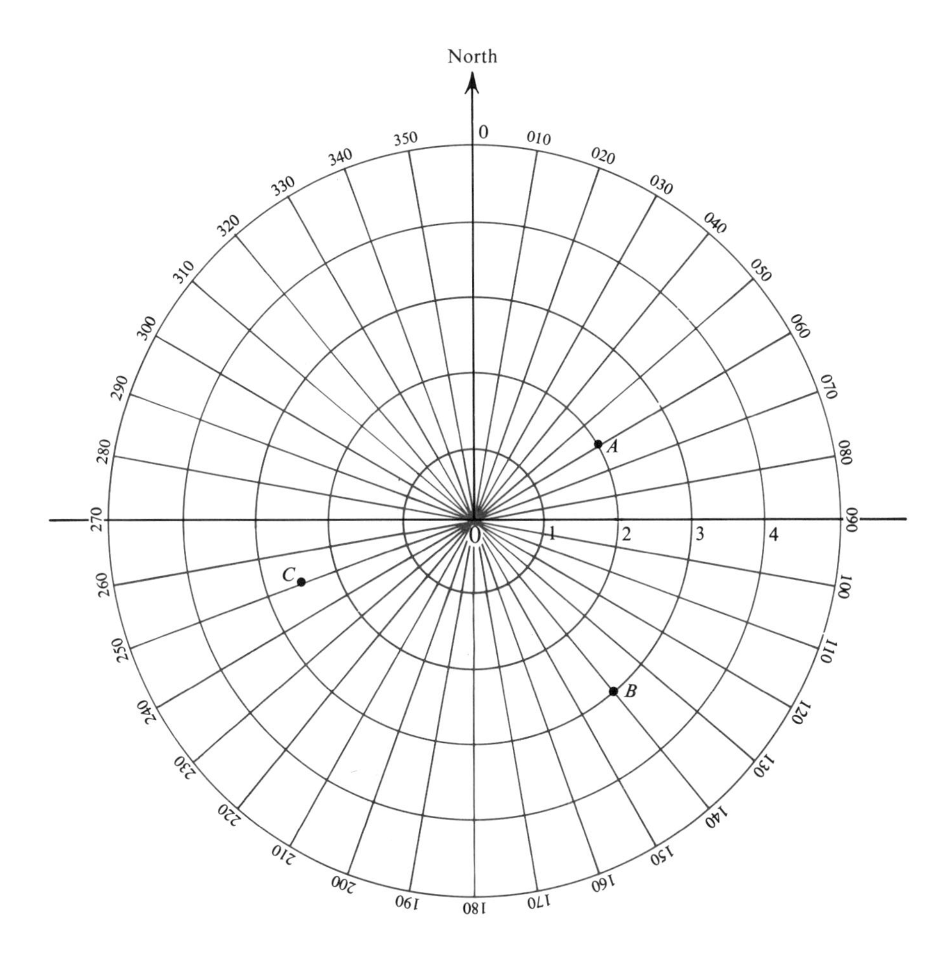

Fig. 20

The position of A is given by the two numbers 2 and 060°. We could refer to A as the point (2, 060°) remembering that the first number is a *range* and the second a *bearing*. Write B and C in a similar way.

This provides another example of two numbers specifying the position of a point in a plane. The numbers are known as the *polar coordinates* of the point.

When bearing is not specifically involved, it is customary to use the convention 'anti-clockwise is positive' in measuring angles. The starting line for angle measure is sometimes referred to as the *initial direction* or central direction.

Figure 21 shows some points plotted on polar graph paper. What are their polar coordinates?

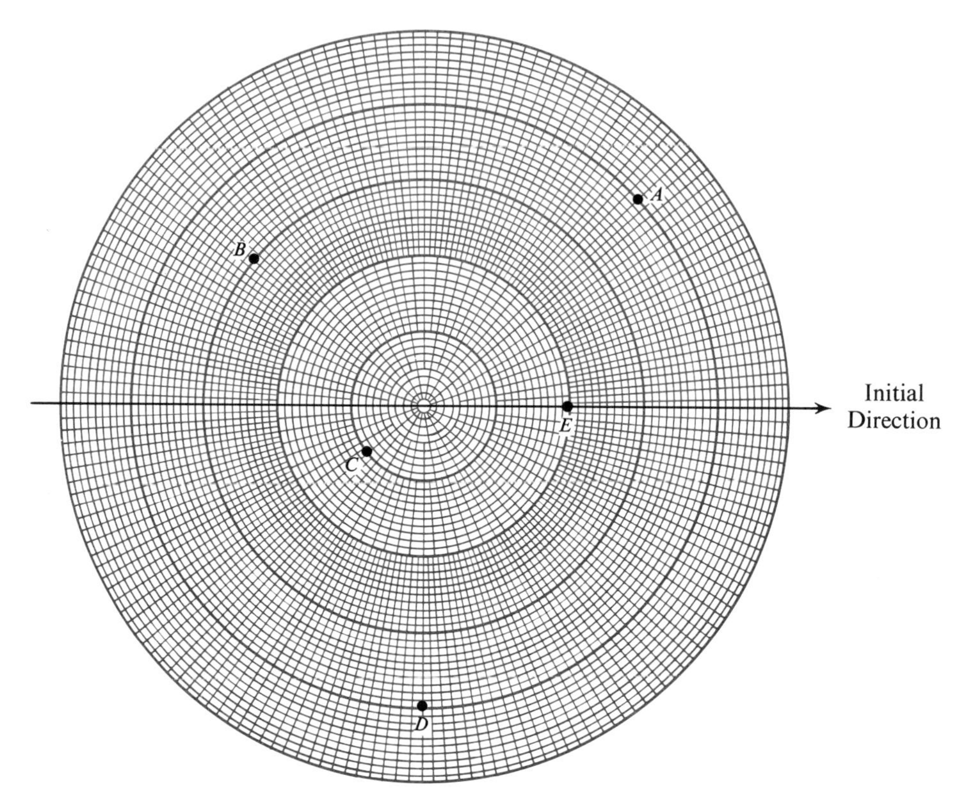

Fig. 21

Did you decide that the polar coordinates of A are $(4, 45^\circ)$?

Where is the point $(4, {}^{-}315^\circ)$? Check that it is the same point A. Try to write the polar coordinates of B, C, D and E in at least two different ways. In this system, therefore, it is possible to write the coordinates of a particular point in many different ways. To avoid possible confusion we will normally use the coordinates (r, α°) of a point which satisfy the following inequalities:

$$r \geqslant 0$$
$$0 \leqslant \alpha < 360.$$

(*b*) **Polar and Cartesian**

We now have two ways of giving the position of a point in a plane: polar coordinates and Cartesian coordinates.

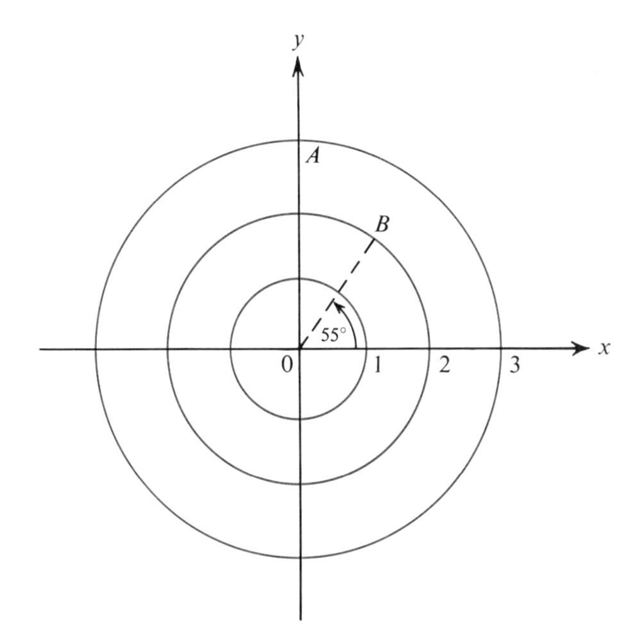

Fig. 22

How are the two types of coordinates related? In Figure 22, A has Cartesian coordinates $(0,3)$ and polar coordinates $(3,90°)$. In polar coordinates, B is $(2,55°)$. What are its (x,y) coordinates? Figure 23 helps to answer this using trigonometry.

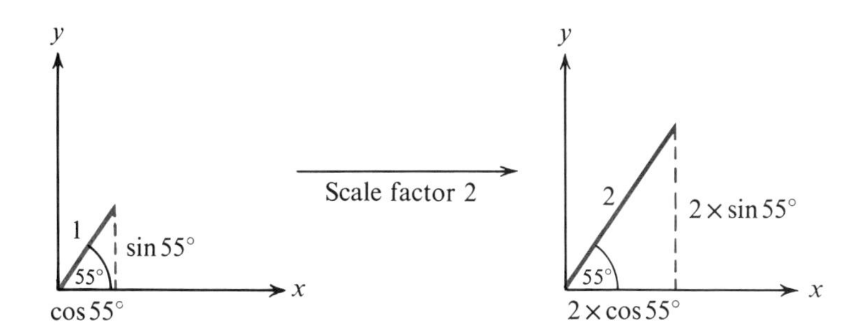

Fig. 23

The x coordinate of B is $2 \times \cos 55° \approx 1{\cdot}15$.

The y coordinate of B is $2 \times \sin 55° \approx 1{\cdot}64$. B has Cartesian coordinates $(1{\cdot}15, 1{\cdot}64)$.

Figure 24 shows a general point P *in the first quadrant*.

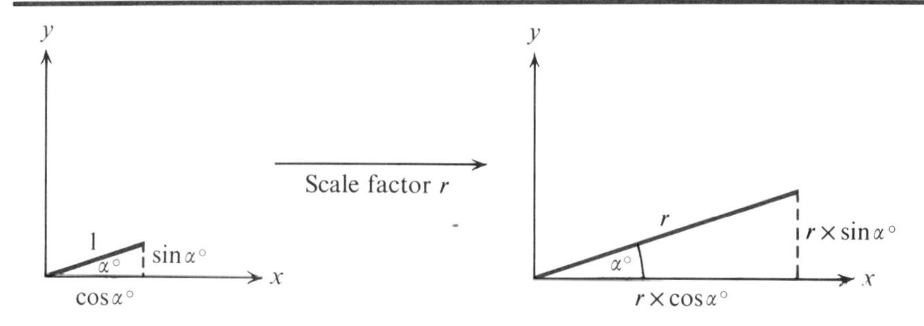

Fig. 24

From it we can see that the Cartesian coordinates of P are

$$(r \cos \alpha°, r \sin \alpha°).$$

This means that (x, y) and $(r, \alpha°)$ are related by:

$$x = r \cos \alpha°$$

and

$$y = r \sin \alpha°.$$

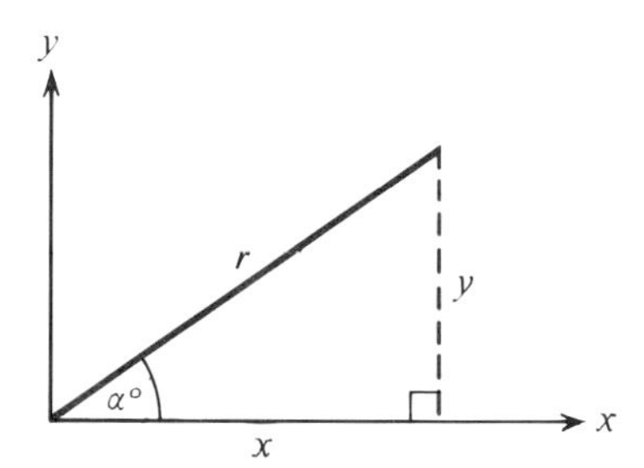

Fig. 25

Look at Figure 25 and complete the following:

$$x^2 + y^2 =$$

Exercise E

1 Write down the Cartesian coordinates of the points which have these polar coordinates:

$$(5, 90°), (2, 270°), (1, 180°).$$

2 Write down the polar coordinates of the points which have the following Cartesian coordinates:

$$(0, 2), (^-3, 0), (5, 0), (0, ^-1), (0, 0), (1, 1).$$

3 Describe the sets of points $\{(r, \alpha°): r = 2\}$ and $\{(r, \alpha°): r = 3\}$. If $A = \{(r, \alpha°): 2 < r < 3\}$ and $B = \{(r, \alpha°): 30 < \alpha < 60\}$, show shaded in separate diagrams the sets of points, A, B, $A \cup B$, $A \cap B$.

4 Calculate, correct to 2 S.F., the Cartesian coordinates of points which have polar coordinates:

$$(1, 20°), (10, 75°), (2{\cdot}5, 45°).$$

5 What are the polar coordinates of points which have Cartesian coordinates:

$$(1, 1), (3, 3), (3, 4), (4, 3), (1, 2)?$$

6 Use your tables to find $\sin 140°$ and $\cos 140°$ and then work out $5 \times \sin 140°$ and $5 \times \cos 140°$. The point $(5, 140°)$ is shown in Figure 26. What are its Cartesian coordinates?

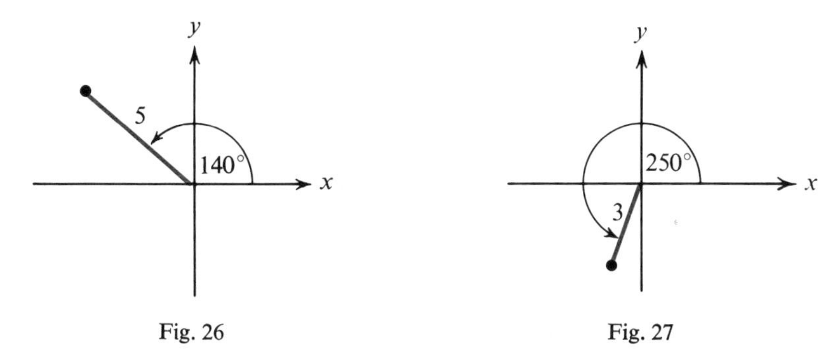

Fig. 26

Fig. 27

7 Work out $3 \times \sin 250°$ and $3 \times \cos 250°$. What are the Cartesian coordinates of the point $(3, 250°)$ shown in Figure 27?

8 Work out the Cartesian coordinates of the point with polar coordinates $(10, 330°)$.

9 We have seen that the equations $x = r\cos\alpha°$, $y = r\sin\alpha°$ relate the Cartesian and polar coordinates of any points in the first quadrant. Do you think that they apply to points in the other three quadrants?

10 Work out the polar coordinates of the points A, B, C in Figure 28.

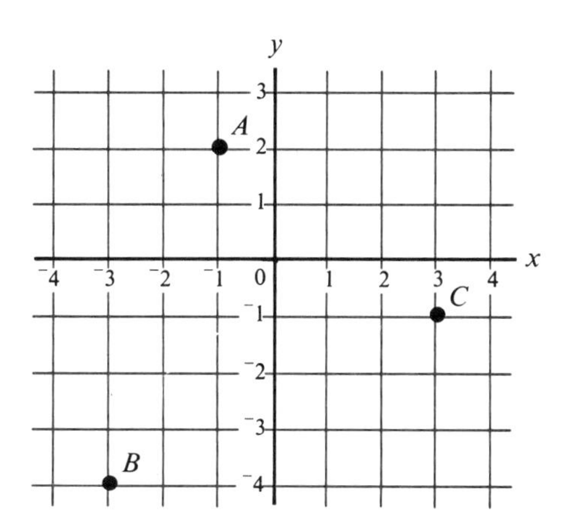

Fig. 28

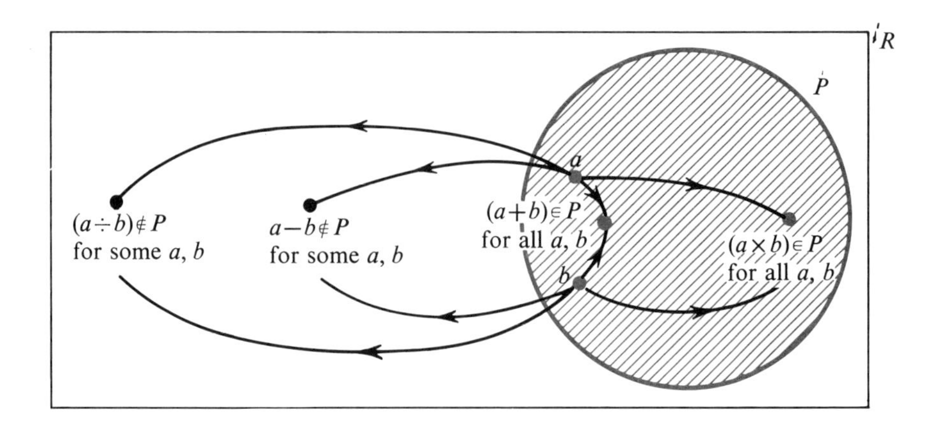

3 Sets of numbers

1 The integers

(*a*) Let us denote the set of positive whole numbers by P:

$$P = \{\text{Positive whole numbers}\} = \{^+1, ^+2, ^+3, \ldots\}.$$

Because these numbers behave like the counting numbers, we usually omit the upper positive and write, for example, $^+2$ as 2.

If a number system consists of only the positive whole numbers (i.e. if $\mathscr{E} = P$), which of the following equations have solutions:

(i) $x + 3 = 2$; (ii) $x + 2 = 3$; (iii) $x + 2 = 2$?

If the equation $x + a = b$ has a solution, what can you say about a and b?

(*b*) You should have found that $x + a = b$ has a positive whole number solution only if $b > a$. Check that this is true for equations (i)–(iii) in (*a*).

Now suppose a number system consists of the integers. These numbers form the set Z:

$$Z = \{\text{Integers}\} = \{\ldots, ^-3, ^-2, ^-1, 0, ^+1, ^+2, ^+3 \ldots\}.$$

Remembering now that $\mathscr{E} = Z$, which of the equations in (*a*) have solutions? What about $x + a = b$?

(*c*) If we take Z as our universal set, then $x + a = b$ always has a solution. This is precisely the reason that the negative whole numbers and zero were introduced into our number system. Without them we could not possibly solve, for example, equations (i) and (iii) in (*a*).

(*d*) If a and b are positive whole numbers which of the following are *necessarily* positive whole numbers:

(i) $a + b$; (ii) $a - b$; (iii) $a \times b$; (iv) $a \div b$?

If a and b are integers which of the above are *necessarily* integers?

(*e*) For each pair of positive whole numbers (a,b), $a+b$ is always a positive whole number. The same is true of $a \times b$, but not of $a-b$ and $a \div b$.

We say that P is *closed* under the operations of addition and multiplication. P is *not closed* under the operations of subtraction and division. The diagram at the head of the chapter attempts to represent the idea of closure for P.

Under which operations is the set of integers closed? Draw a diagram like the heading diagram to illustrate your answer.

Summary

1 $P = \{\text{Positive whole numbers}\} = \{^+1, ^+2, ^+3, \ldots\}$.
$Z = \{\text{Integers}\} = \{\ldots, ^-3, ^-2, ^-1, 0, ^+1, ^+2, ^+3, \ldots\}$.
We usually omit the upper positives and write the members of P as 1, 2, 3, ...

2 P is closed under addition and multiplication, i.e. if a, $b \in P$ then $a+b \in P$ for all a, b, and $a \times b \in P$ for all a, b.
Z is closed under addition, multiplication and subtraction.

Exercise A

1 Draw a Venn diagram to represent the relationship between P and Z.

2 If (*a*) $\mathscr{E} = Z$; (*b*) $\mathscr{E} = P$, which of the following equations have solutions?

(i) $x+1=2$; (ii) $2x-1=3$; (iii) $x+1=2x+1$;

(iv) $3x=9$; (v) $\frac{x}{4}=2$.

3 If (*a*) $\mathscr{E} = Z$; (*b*) $\mathscr{E} = P$, which of the following problems always have a solution?

(i) A boy buys x identical pens for n pence. How much did he pay for each?
(ii) Find the number of cm in p metres.
(iii) Solve the inequality $x+a \leqslant b$.
(iv) The temperature at 12.00 hours was n °C. If it fell by t deg C per hour what was the temperature at 15.00 hours?

4 If $\mathscr{E} = P$, when has the equation $ax=b$ a solution? What if $\mathscr{E} = Z$?

5 If the domain of the functions (i) $f\colon x \to x$; (ii) $g\colon x \to 2x$; (iii) $h\colon x \to x^2$; (iv) $m\colon x \to 2x-1$ is P, what is the range of each function? What if the domain is Z?

6 State whether P and Z are closed or not closed under the operations $*$, $\oplus$, $\ominus$, @ defined below:

(i) $a * b = a \times 2b$; (ii) $a \oplus b = 2a+3b$;
(iii) $a \ominus b = 2a-3b$; (iv) a @ $b = \pm\sqrt{ab}$.

7 Graph the functions (i) $f\colon x \to x+2$; (ii) $g\colon x \to 2-x$ when the domains of f and g are (*a*) P; (*b*) Z. In each case describe the range of the functions.

2 The rational numbers

(*a*) Solve the equations (i) $4x = 2$; (ii) $3x = {}^{-}2$; (iii) $ax = b$ $(a \neq 0)$.

(*b*) The solution to (i) is $x = \frac{2}{4}$. You might have written $x = \frac{1}{2}$, which is equally correct. In fact, any one of the members of the set of equivalent fractions

$$\left\{\ldots, \frac{^{-}2}{^{-}4}, \frac{^{-}1}{^{-}2}, \frac{1}{2}, \frac{2}{4}, \ldots\right\}$$

could be given as the solution. It is usual, however, for us to write as the representative of such a set the fraction which is in its lowest terms – in this case $\frac{1}{2}$. $\frac{1}{2}$ is an example of a *rational* number. The rational numbers are the set Q of numbers of the form p/q where p and q are integers with no common divisor, and $q \neq 0$:

$$Q = \left\{\text{numbers } \frac{p}{q} \text{ such that, } p, q \in Z \text{ and have no common divisor, and } q \neq 0\right\}.$$

Which rational numbers represent the sets of equivalent fractions of which

(i) $\frac{10}{15}$; (ii) $\frac{^{-}17}{51}$; (iii) $\frac{10}{2}$

are members?

Would you say that $Z \subset Q$ is a true statement?

(*c*) The solution to $ax = b$ is $x = \frac{b}{a}$. Without the rational numbers as a further extension to our number system the equation would only have a solution if a was a factor of b. (Did you obtain this answer for Question 4, Exercise A?) This is one reason why the rational numbers are very important to us. Without them we would not be able to solve such simple problems as 'Divide 18 into 24 equal parts', i.e. 'Solve the equation $24x = 18$'.

(*d*) If a and b are rational which of the following are rational (if necessary after 'cancelling down'):

(i) $a + b$; (ii) $a - b$; (iii) $a \times b$; (iv) $a \div b$?

(*e*) Your answer to (*d*) should suggest to you an important property of the rational numbers; the set is closed under all four simple arithmetical operations, so long as we do not allow division by zero. This means that we can apply each operation and always obtain an answer which is rational.

Summary

1 $Q = \{\text{Rationals}\} = \{p/q$ such that p and q are integers with no common divisor, and $q \neq 0\}$.

2 Q is closed under addition, subtraction, multiplication and division (so long as we do not allow division by zero).

Exercise B

1 Draw a Venn diagram to represent the relationship between P, Z and Q.

2 If you were measuring (i) the diameter of a piston for a car engine; (ii) the length of a garden ready for turfing, to which particular set of numbers would your answer probably belong?

3 Which of the problems in Question 3, Exercise A always have a solution if $\mathscr{E} = Q$?

4 Write down the rational number which is representative of the following sets of equivalent fractions:

$$\text{(i)}\left\{\ldots, \frac{^-1}{^-2}, \frac{1}{2}, \frac{2}{4}, \frac{3}{6}, \ldots\right\}; \qquad \text{(ii)}\left\{\ldots, \frac{^-3}{^-18}, \frac{^-2}{^-12}, \frac{^-1}{^-6}, \frac{1}{6}, \frac{2}{12}, \ldots\right\}.$$

5 Which rational number is representative of the set of equivalent fractions of which

$$\text{(i)}\,\frac{3}{9}; \quad \text{(ii)}\,\frac{^-4}{20}; \quad \text{(iii)}\,\frac{^-9}{^-27}; \quad \text{(iv)}\,\frac{20}{20}$$

are members?

6 Express the following as rational numbers – i.e., in the form $\frac{p}{q}$:

(i) 0·25; (ii) 0·0018; (iii) 2·5; (iv) 0·03.

7 Write down a rational number $\frac{p}{q}$ such that:

(i) $\frac{1}{12} < \frac{p}{q} < \frac{1}{13}$; (ii) $\frac{p}{q} + \frac{1}{2} = \frac{1}{7}$;

(iii) $2p = 4q$; (iv) $2p - 3q = 0$.

8 Write down the identity element for Q under the operations of (i) addition; (ii) subtraction; (iii) multiplication; (iv) division. (If an identity element does not exist, say so.)

3 More about the rationals

(*a*) Convert the rational numbers (i) $\frac{1}{2}$; (ii) $\frac{1}{3}$; (iii) $\frac{1}{8}$ to decimals.

(*b*) You will have used the method shown at the top of p. 34 to convert $\frac{4}{7}$ to a decimal.

We can see that $\frac{4}{7} = 0{\cdot}\dot{5}7142\dot{8}$ which is a *recurring* decimal. $\frac{1}{3} = 0{\cdot}\dot{3}$ is also a recurring decimal, but if we express $\frac{1}{2}$ and $\frac{1}{8}$ as decimals we obtain: $\frac{1}{2} = 0{\cdot}5$ and $\frac{1}{8} = 0{\cdot}125$. These are examples of *terminating* decimals.

(*c*) *All* rational numbers can be expressed as terminating or recurring decimals. The reason for this can be seen by studying the remainders [ringed in (*b*)] after each successive division. The remainders must always be less than the divisor (7 in this case). At some stage during the division one of the remainders will be

```
      0·5714285...
    7|4·0000000000
      3 5
      ⑤0
       49
       ①0
         7
         ③0
          28
          ②0
           14
           ⑥0
            56
            ④0
             35
             ⑤0
              ⋮
```

repeated (in which case the decimal begins to recur), or the remainder will become zero (in which case the decimal terminates). Notice that when the divisor is 7, not more than seven successive divisions could be made without one of these two results being true, because the remainders can only be 0, 1, 2, 3, 4, 5, or 6.

(*d*) Now let us consider the reverse process of converting decimals to rational form.

To convert a terminating decimal to rational form we have only to express it as a fraction and then 'cancel down'. For example,

$$0\cdot204 = \frac{204}{1000} = \frac{51}{250}, \text{ which is rational.}$$

Convert the following to rational form:

(i) 0·6; (ii) 0·888; (iii) 0·41.

(*e*) Now consider the recurring decimal $0\cdot\dot{6}\dot{4}$.
To convert this to rational form we proceed as follows:
Let $D = 0\cdot64646464\ldots.$
Multiply by 100,
$100D = 64\cdot646464\ldots.$
Subtract the first equation from the second:
$99D = 64.$
Hence $D = \frac{64}{99}$, which is rational.
Now convert $0\cdot\dot{5}8\dot{2}$ to rational form (multiply by 1000).
What multiplier would you use to convert $0\cdot\dot{5}54\dot{2}$ to rational form?

Summary

1 Rational numbers, when expressed as decimals, either terminate or recur.

2 Terminating and recurring decimals can be expressed in rational form.

3 To convert $0{\cdot}\dot{a}_1 a_2 a_3 \ldots \dot{a}_n$ to rational form use the multiplier 10^n.

Exercise C

1 Convert the following to decimal form:

(i) $\frac{1}{2}$; (ii) $\frac{3}{8}$; (iii) $2\frac{1}{7}$; (iv) $\frac{13}{27}$.

2 What rationals are represented by:

(i) $0{\cdot}875$; (ii) $7{\cdot}5$; (iii) $6{\cdot}002$; (iv) $0{\cdot}\dot{7}$;
(v) $0{\cdot}\dot{8}8\dot{0}$; (vi) $1{\cdot}\dot{1}$; (vii) $3{\cdot}345$; (viii) $0{\cdot}\dot{4}24\dot{5}$?

3 If the denominator of a rational number is 2 or 5, what can you say about the decimal representation of the number? Can you find other examples of denominators for which the same is true? Can you generalize?

4 Divide 4 by the primes in turn up to 13. After how many places of decimals does each begin to recur? Try some more primes as divisors. Is there a general rule about the length of the recurring sequence?

5 Simplify (i) $\frac{1}{2}+\frac{1}{4}$; (ii) $3\frac{1}{4}+4\frac{1}{16}$; (iii) $2\frac{1}{8}-\frac{7}{16}$; (iv) $\frac{3}{7}-\frac{2}{21}$; (v) $\frac{13}{27}-\frac{4}{31}$; (vi) $\frac{3}{7}\times 1\frac{1}{8}$; (vii) $\frac{5}{8}\times 2\frac{1}{4}$; (viii) $\frac{3}{8}\div\frac{1}{4}$; (ix) $\frac{5}{7}\div 2\frac{1}{2}$.

6 Place the following in order of size, the smallest first: $\frac{1}{2}, \frac{3}{7}, \frac{5}{8}, \frac{4}{9}, \frac{6}{13}$.

7 If $a=\frac{1}{2}$, $b=\frac{1}{3}$, draw a number line and mark a and b on it. Calculate $\frac{a+b}{2}$ and mark this number on the number line. Calculate a number lying between (i) a and $\frac{a+b}{2}$; (ii) $\frac{a+b}{2}$ and b, and mark it on the number line.

8 $\frac{a}{b}$ and $\frac{p}{q}$ are two rational numbers, and $\frac{a}{b}<\frac{p}{q}$. Place these and $\frac{aq+pb}{2bq}$ in order of size, the smallest first. Explain why it is impossible to say that two numbers 'lie next to each other' on the number line.

4 The irrational numbers

(*a*) Consider the number $0{\cdot}070070007000070000007\ldots$

If the sequence of 0's and 7's is continued in this way the decimal obviously does not terminate. Does it recur?

(*b*) Numbers which do not terminate or recur when expressed as decimals $\left(\text{i.e., numbers which cannot be expressed in the form } \frac{p}{q}\right)$ are called *irrational* numbers. Write down two more examples of irrational numbers. We will denote the set of irrational numbers by I.

(c) Two examples of irrational numbers which you will have used are π and $\sqrt{2}$. $\sqrt{2}$ is the solution to the equation $x^2 = 2$. $\sqrt{2}$ units is also the length of the hypotenuse of a right-angled isosceles triangle with its equal sides of length 1 unit (see Figure 1).

We can prove that $\sqrt{2}$ is irrational by using a powerful mathematical technique known as an 'indirect proof'. We first of all assume that $\sqrt{2}$ is a rational number and then show that our assumption leads us to contradict ourselves. This being so, our original assumption must have been wrong. Try to follow the argument below.

Assume $\sqrt{2}$ is a rational number $\frac{p}{q}$, where p and q are integers with *no common divisor*. Then

$$\frac{p^2}{q^2} = 2.$$

Hence $$p^2 = 2q^2.$$

This tells us that p^2 must be an even number. Since p^2 is even then p must be even, and we can write

$$p = 2t.$$

Hence $$p^2 = 4t^2.$$

However, since $$p^2 = 2q^2$$

then $$2q^2 = 4t^2$$

so $$q^2 = 2t^2.$$

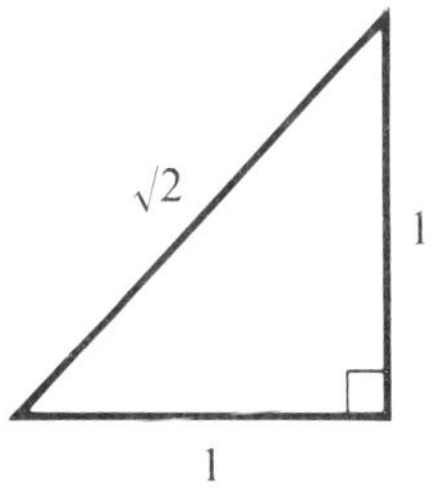

Fig. 1

This means that q is also an even number. Since both p and q have been shown to be even numbers they have a common factor 2. This contradicts our original assumption. Therefore $\sqrt{2}$ cannot be rational. By definition it must therefore be irrational.

Now try to prove $\sqrt{3}$ is irrational.

(d) The rational numbers and the irrational numbers taken together form the set of REAL NUMBERS, R. Can you think of a number which is not a real number?

Summary

1 The irrational numbers cannot be expressed in the form $\frac{p}{q}$, where p and q are integers.

2 {Rational numbers} $\cup$ {Irrational numbers} = {Real numbers}.

Exercise D

1 Draw a Venn diagram to show the sets of numbers described in this chapter. ($\mathscr{E}$ = {Real numbers}).

2 Simplify (i) Q'; (ii) I'; (iii) $R \cap Q$; (iv) $Z \cap Q$; (v) $Q' \cap I$.

3 Explain why $2 + \sqrt{2}$ is irrational.

4 If x is irrational is x^2 always irrational?

5 Multiply $(2 + \sqrt{2})$ by $(2 - \sqrt{2})$. If a and b are irrational is ab necessarily irrational?

6 Give an example to show that the irrationals are not closed under (i) addition; (ii) subtraction; (iii) division; (iv) multiplication.

7 Write down two irrational numbers whose (i) sum; (ii) product; (iii) difference is 2.

8 To which particular number sets do the solutions to the following belong? (i) $x^2 = 3$; (ii) $x^2 + 1 = 3$; (iii) $x^3 = 8$; (iv) $x^2 + x = 0$; (v) $x^2 = 8$.

5 Solution sets

(*a*) Figure 2 shows the set $A = \{^-1, 0, 1, 2, 3\}$ represented on the number line.

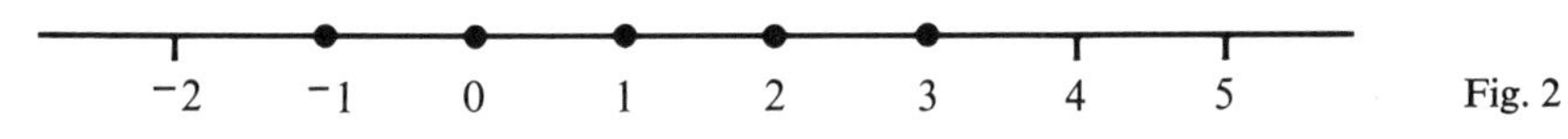

Fig. 2

Represent the sets

$$B = \{^-2, ^-1, 0, 1, 2\},$$
$$C = \{0, 1, 2\}$$

on the number line. List the members of $A \cap B \cap C$. What is $n(A \cap B \cap C)$?

(*b*) Suppose $\mathscr{E} = \{\text{Real numbers}\}$. Check that the solution to the inequality $2x + 1 > 3$ is $x > 1$.

The solution to the inequality is an infinite set of numbers which we call the *solution set*. We can write this set as

$$\{x : x > 1\}$$

(i.e. the set of numbers x 'such that' x is greater than one).

Figure 3 shows the solution set represented on the number line.

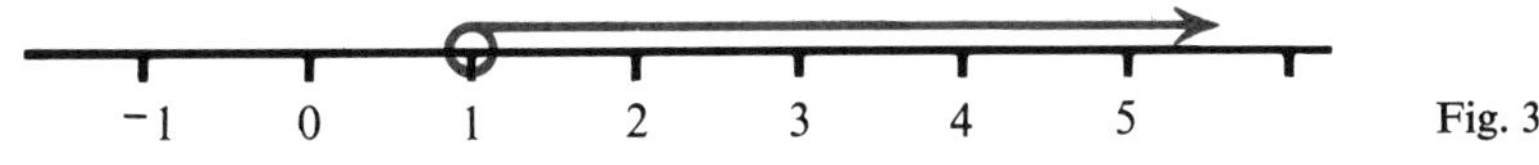

Fig. 3

Notice that the 'end point', 1, is ringed. This signifies that 1 is not, in fact, a member of the set. How do you think we would represent the solution set to the inequality $2x + 1 \geqslant 3$ on the number line (notice that the 'end point' *is* included in the set)?

(*c*) The solution set of the equation $2x + 3 = 0$ has only one member. Write the solution set in the form $\{x : x = \quad\}$.

(*d*) Solve the inequality $2x + 1 \leqslant 7$. Write the solution set in the form $\{x : x \leqslant \quad\}$, and represent it on the number line.

(*e*) We would solve the double inequality

$$3 < 2x + 1 \leqslant 7$$

in two stages:

(i) solve $$3 < 2x + 1,$$

and

(ii) solve $$2x + 1 \leqslant 7.$$

The solution sets to the two parts are respectively $\{x\colon x > 1\}$ and $\{x\colon x \leqslant 3\}$ (did you obtain this second answer in (*d*)?). Figure 4 shows the two sets represented on one number line. The numbers which satisfy the original inequality are members of each of these sets. The solution set is therefore

$$\{x\colon x > 1\} \cap \{x\colon x \leqslant 3\}.$$

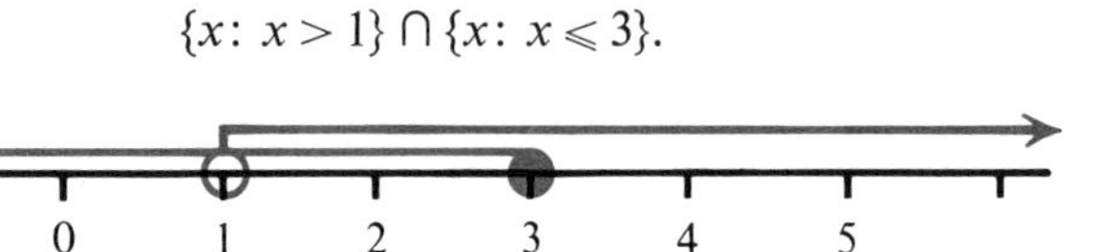

Fig. 4

Figure 4 helps to show that this expression simplifies to

$$\{x\colon 1 < x \leqslant 3\}.$$

(*f*) $\{(x, y)\colon x + y = 3\}$ is a set of *points*. Figure 5 shows the set plotted on a graph. Copy the diagram and plot the points

$$\{(x, y)\colon x = 2y\}.$$

Use your graph to help you simplify

$$\{(x, y)\colon x + y = 3\} \cap \{(x, y)\colon x = 2y\}.$$

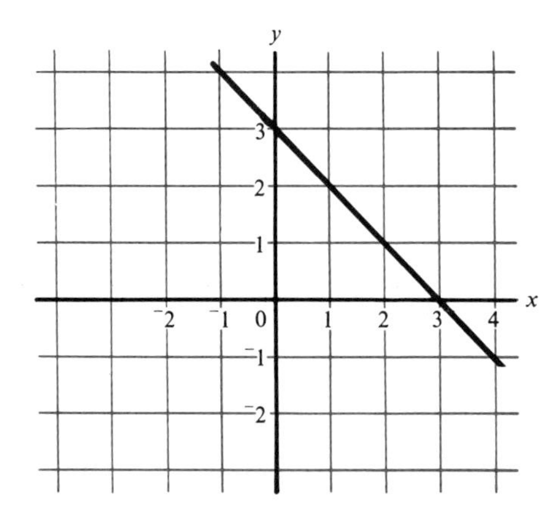

Fig. 5

Write the solution set to the simultaneous equations

$$\begin{cases} x + y = 3 \\ \quad x = 2y, \text{in the form} \{(x, y)\colon x = \quad , y = \quad \}. \end{cases}$$

Exercise E

1 Represent the following sets on the number line in the cases when (*a*) $\mathscr{E} = \{\text{Reals}\}$; (*b*) $\mathscr{E} = \{\text{Integers}\}$.

(i) $A = \{x\colon x = 1\}$; (ii) $B = \{x\colon x \leqslant 1\}$; (iii) $C = \{x\colon 1 \leqslant x < 4\}$.

List the members of $A \cap B \cap C$ in each case.

2 $\mathscr{E} = \{\text{Reals}\}$. Represent the solution sets of the following in the form $\{x\colon x \quad \}$ and on the number line:

(i) $3x + 7 = 4$; (ii) $4 - x = 9$; (iii) $x + 8 > 2$; (iv) $4x - 1 < 5$;
(v) $1 - x \leqslant x$; (vi) $x^2 = 4$; (vii) $x^2 + 3 = 4$.

3 $\mathscr{E} = \{\text{Integers}\}$. Represent the solution sets of the inequalities:

(i) $^-6 < 3x - 1 \leqslant 4$; (ii) $2 \leqslant 1 - x < 4$ on the number line.

Take $\mathscr{E} = \{\text{Reals}\}$ for the questions which follow, unless stated otherwise.

4 Plot the following sets on the number line:

(i) $\{A = x\colon x \leqslant 4\}$; (ii) $B = \{x\colon x > 5\}$; (iii) $C = \{x\colon x \geqslant 4\}$.

What is (*a*) $A \cap B$; (*b*) $A \cap C$; (*c*) $A \cup C$; (*d*) $B \cup C$?

5 Graph the sets of points:

$A = \{(x, y)\colon 2x = y\}$; $B = \{(x, y)\colon x = 6\}$.

What is $A \cap B$?

6 Draw a diagram to show the sets of points:

$A = \{(x, y)\colon x > y\}$ and $B = \{(x, y)\colon x + y \leqslant 6\}$.

(Use your own notation to denote whether a boundary line is included or is not included in the set.) Shade in the region $A \cap B$. Which of the following points are members of $A \cap B$: (i) $(2, 0)$; (ii) $(3, 3)$; (iii) $(3, 4)$; (iv) $(0, 2)$?

7 B is a fixed point. Draw diagrams to represent the sets:

(i) $\{P\colon PB = 2 \text{ units}\}$; (ii) $\{P\colon PB \leqslant 2 \text{ units}\}$; (iii) $\{P\colon PB \geqslant 2 \text{ units}\}$.

8 $A(2, 1)$ and $B(4, 1)$ are fixed points. Draw diagrams to show the sets of points:

(i) $\{P\colon PA = PB\}$; (ii) $\{P\colon PA > PB\}$; (iii) $\{P\colon PA < PB\}$.

9 $\mathscr{E} = \{x\colon 0 \leqslant x \leqslant 90\}$. Write down the solution sets of each of the following:

(i) $\sin x^\circ = 1$; (ii) $\sin x^\circ \leqslant 0{\cdot}5$; (iii) $\cos x^\circ > 1$; (iv) $0 \leqslant \sin x^\circ \leqslant 0{\cdot}5$.

10 $P = \{(x, y)\colon x^2 + y^2 = 1\}$; $Q = \{(x, y)\colon x + y = 1\}$. Plot P and Q on a graph. List the members of $P \cap Q$.

11 $P = \{(x, y)\colon x^2 + y^2 = 1\}$; $Q = \{(x, y)\colon x + y = k\}$.

(*a*) If $n(P \cap Q) = 1$, what values can k take?
(*b*) If $n(P \cap Q) = 2$, what range of values can k take?
(*c*) If $n(P \cap Q) = 0$, what range of values can k take?

4 Linear programming

1 Introduction

We often need to consider problems involving large numbers of variables (unknowns) which have to obey many conditions. For example, the production manager of a car firm may have to decide on the number of each type of vehicle his firm should manufacture over a given period of time (the unknowns here are the numbers of each type of vehicle to be produced), and in doing this he will have to take into account not only public demand but also such factors as the number of craftsmen he needs, the time required for each manufacturing process on each type of vehicle, the production costs, and so on. Each condition of this kind will impose some restriction on the number of cars he can produce, and in the final event he will be concerned with minimizing production costs and maximizing profits. We will see in this chapter that the production manager can use a process called 'linear programming' to help him make his decision. In real life, linear programming usually involves the use of computers, because of the vast number of variables and conditions involved. However, problems can be solved graphically provided that no more than two variables are involved.

2 Processes of elimination

(*a*) In many of our everyday activities we consciously, or unconsciously, use a process of elimination to select items from a particular universal set. For example, suppose you are buying a record from a shop as a present for one of your friends.

Already in your mind you might have set various conditions on your eventual choice – these will depend largely upon the kind of music your friend enjoys, and your present financial state. You might therefore have decided that the record must be

(i) 'pop',
(ii) 'an L.P.',
(iii) 'vocal'.

By considering each condition in turn you can eliminate a certain section of the stock from your search, and eventually you will arrive at a solution set – which may have more than one member, or may even be empty! If it is empty then you will obviously have to select a new universal set (go to another shop), or relax some of your conditions.

Can you think of other everyday examples in which you use a process of elimination to select objects from sets? Try to list the conditions you impose in each case.

(*b*) List the members of the set $\{x\colon 2 \leqslant x < 20,\ x \text{ an integer}\}$.

Consider each of the following conditions in turn, and for each one strike out members of the set which do not satisfy the condition. Hence find the solution set of numbers which are:

(i) not multiples of 4;
(ii) factors of 30;
(iii) not primes;
(iv) even.

If you had considered (i)–(iv) in a different order, would your solution set still be the same?

Notice that the solution set is $\{x\colon x \text{ is not a multiple of } 4\} \cap \{x\colon x \text{ is a factor of } 30\} \cap \{x\colon x \text{ is not prime}\} \cap \{x\colon x \text{ is even}\}$.

(*c*) Suppose you are playing a game of dice which involves throwing a red die and a blue die simultaneously. To win on any particular throw you must satisfy the following conditions:

(i) the total score must be less than 8;
(ii) the score on the red die must not be greater than 4;
(iii) the score on the blue die must be greater than 2;
(iv) the score on the blue die must be not more than twice the score on the red die.

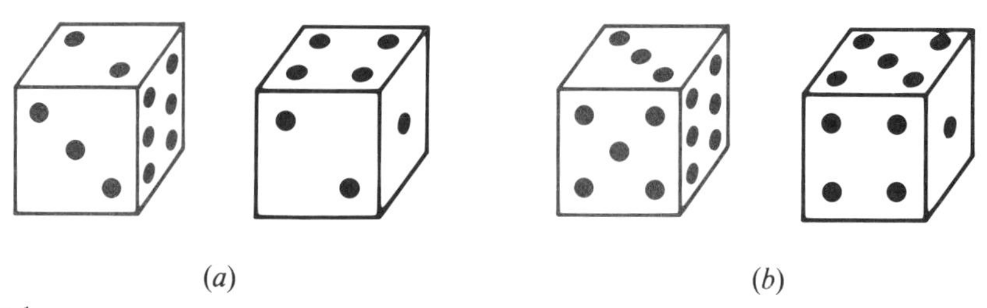

Fig. 1

Do Figures 1(*a*) and (*b*) represent winning combinations? List all the possible winning combinations. What is the probability you will win on any particular throw?

(*d*) Figure 2 shows how the set of winning combinations can be found graphically by eliminating combinations which do not satisfy each condition in turn (the 'ringed dots' are the unsatisfactory scores at each stage).

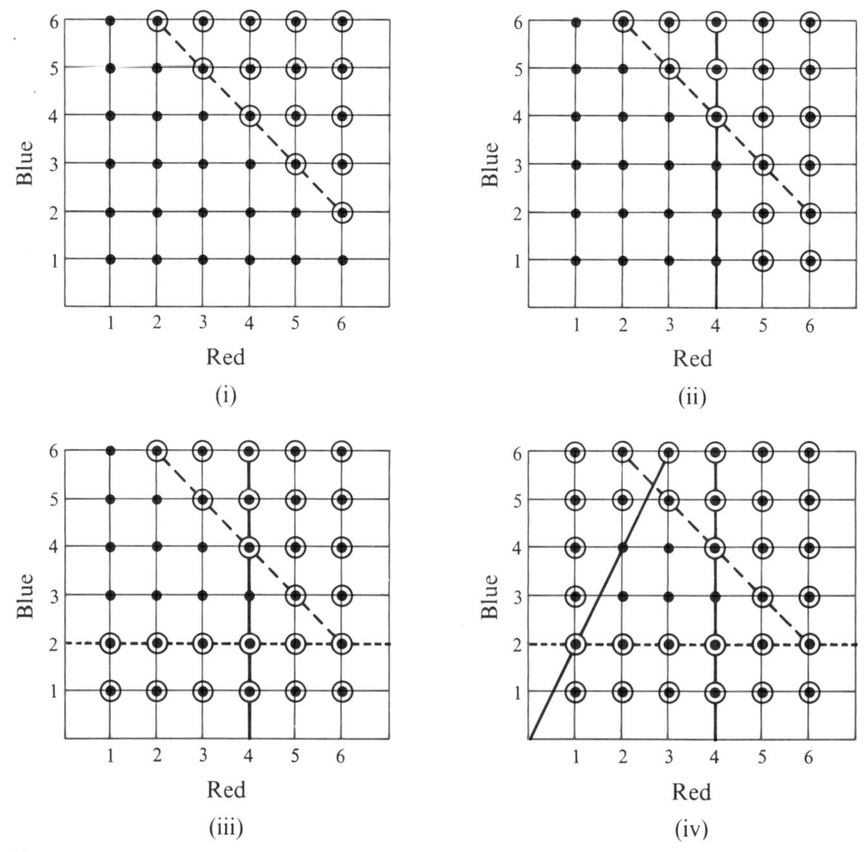

Fig. 2

We can see from (iv) that the winning combinations are represented by the ordered pairs (2, 3); (3, 3); (4, 3); (2, 4); (3, 4).

The ordered pairs (4, 2) and (4, 3) both appear to be on the 'boundary' of the solution set. Why is (4, 3) a possible solution, but not (4, 2)?

What does a broken line used as a boundary indicate? What does a continuous line indicate?

(*e*) On a diagram of the (x, y) plane *leave unshaded* the region which satisfies the conditions:

(i) $x + y < 8$;
(ii) $x \leqslant 4$;
(iii) $y > 2$;
(iv) $y \leqslant 2x$;

(that is, find the solution set

$$\{(x, y): x + y < 8\} \cap \{(x, y): x \leqslant 4\} \cap \{(x, y): y > 2\} \cap \{(x, y): y \leqslant 2x\}).$$

Compare your diagram with Figure 2(iv). What do you notice? Are the algebraic conditions equivalent to those stated in (*c*)?

In what ways are the two solution sets (i) the same (ii) different?

(*f*) We will now use the processes described above to help us solve a problem which, although artificial, helps to explain how 'linear programming' can be used to help us make decisions. Our main concern will be

(i) to express statements algebraically as relations;
(ii) to graph these relations (use a process of elimination to obtain the solution set).

(*g*) A car firm has contracted to deliver at least 60 cars per day to Dover over a long period of time, ready for export. The firm uses two types of carriers: (i) Type *A* which can carry 10 cars, and (ii) Type *B* which can carry 8 cars. There are 4 Type *A* carriers and 6 Type *B* carriers, but only 8 drivers available for the work. The carriers can only make one journey per day and each one carries a full load.

(i) How should the transport manager organize his carriers to meet the delivery demand?
(ii) What is the minimum number of drivers he needs?
(iii) What is the maximum number of cars he can deliver per day?

The two unknown quantities (variables) are:

(i) the number of Type A carriers to be used – call this x;
(ii) the number of Type B carriers to be used – call this y.

Because of the limitations on the number of carriers and drivers available we know that:

(i) $x \leqslant 4$;
(ii) $y \leqslant 6$;
(iii) $x + y \leqslant 8$.

Also, x Type A carriers can carry $10x$ cars, and y Type B carriers $8y$ cars. At least 60 cars have to be delivered, so that

(iv) $10x + 8y \geqslant 60$
(or, $5x + 4y \geqslant 30$).

The graphs of the inequalities (i) and (iii) are shown in Figure 3. Copy this figure and add graphs of the inequalities (ii) and (iv) shading the unrequired region.

(i) List the six number pairs which satisfy all four inequalities (remember that you can only have a whole number of carriers).

You should have found that the transport manager can use any of the following solutions to meet the delivery demand:

$$(2, 5); (2, 6); (3, 4); (3, 5); (4, 3); (4, 4).$$

(ii) If the first solution above is decided upon then 7 drivers will be needed. How many drivers are needed if the other solutions are used? Do you agree that a minimum of 7 drivers is needed?

(iii) If 2 Type A carriers and 5 Type B carriers are used, then $(2 \times 10) + (5 \times 8) =$ 60 cars can be delivered. Find the number of cars that can be delivered for the other five solutions that meet the delivery demand. What is the maximum number of cars that can be delivered?

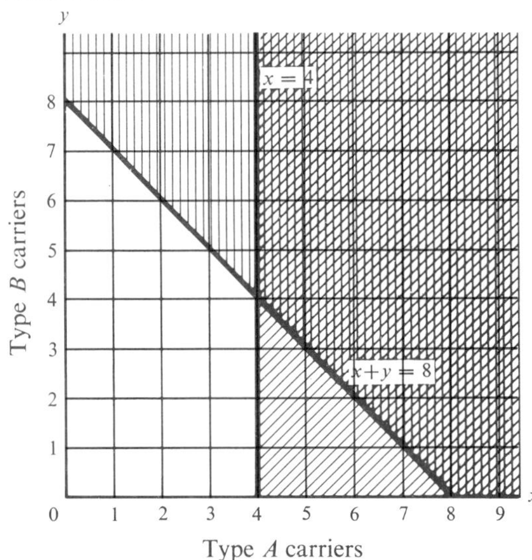

Fig. 3

Exercise A

1 On separate diagrams leave unshaded the regions representing the following inequalities:

(i) $x > 2$; (ii) $y \leqslant 6$; (iii) $x + y \geqslant 3$;
(iv) $2x + 3y \leqslant 12$; (v) $y + 2x \leqslant 50$; (vi) $xy \leqslant 144$;
(vii) $y \geqslant 2x$; (viii) $x \leqslant 2y$.

2 List the special kinds of polygons which belong to the set satisfying the following conditions:

(i) the polygons have four sides;
(ii) the polygons have half-turn symmetry;
(iii) the polygons have no lines of symmetry.

3 Leave unshaded the region of points whose coordinates satisfy all five of the following inequalities:

(i) $x \geqslant 0$; (ii) $y \geqslant 0$; (iii) $2x + y > 4$;
(iv) $x + 3y > 9$; (v) $x + y < 6$.

If x, y are integers mark each point of the solution set with a dot.

4 To make a 'perfect' cup of tea you must (i) make it in cups of capacity 50 cm³; (ii) use at least ten times as much water as milk; (iii) use not more than 12 times as much water as milk; (iv) at least half fill the cup.

Express the four statements above as algebraic inequalities and then graph the information (use w, m to represent the number of cm³ of water and milk respectively in a 'perfect' cup of tea).

Which of the following amounts of water and milk would make a 'perfect' cup of tea?

(i) 40 cm³ of water and 5 cm³ of milk;
(ii) 50 cm³ of water and 5 cm³ of milk;
(iii) 30 cm³ of water and 11 cm³ of milk;
(iv) 32 cm³ of water and 3 cm³ of milk.

5 A hotel caters for school parties of less than 30 people, and has the following rules: All parties must

(i) comprise more than 20 people;
(ii) include at least three adults;
(iii) include not more than six adults.

Take p to represent the number of pupils in the group and a to represent the number of adults. Write the four statements above in algebraic form and graph the information. If a school party includes 15 pupils, how many adults will there be in the party? What is the maximum number of pupils there can be in a party which includes only 4 adults?

6 A post office has to transport 900 parcels using lorries, which can take 150 at a time, and vans which can take 60.

(*a*) If l lorries and v vans are used, write down an inequality which must be satisfied.

(*b*) The costs of each journey are £5 by lorry and £4 by van and the total cost must be less than £44. Write down another inequality which must be satisfied by l and v.

(*c*) Represent these inequalities on a graph and dot in the members of the solution set.

(*d*) What is:

(i) the largest number of vehicles which could be used;
(ii) the arrangement which keeps the cost to a minimum;
(iii) the most costly arrangement?

7 In an airlift it is required to transport 600 people and 45 tons of baggage. Two kinds of aircraft are available: the Albatross which can carry 50 passengers and 6 tons of baggage, and the Buzzard which can carry 80 passengers and 3 tons of baggage.

(*a*) If a Albatrosses and b Buzzards are used, explain why

$$5a + 8b \geqslant 60 \qquad \text{and} \qquad 2a + b \geqslant 15.$$

(*b*) Only 8 Albatrosses and 7 Buzzards are available. Represent, on a graph, the possible arrangements of aircraft which can supply the necessary transport. Dot in the members of the solution set.

(*c*) What is the smallest number of aircraft that can be used?

3 Maximizing and minimizing

(*a*) We found in Section 2(*g*) that the maximum number of cars that could be transported to Dover per day could be found by considering each member of the solution set in turn. When the solution set contains a large number of elements, however, this method becomes impractical. We will now look again at the question 'what is the greatest number of cars that can be delivered' and answer it by a method which can be applied to solution sets with any number of elements.

(*b*) The number of cars that can be transported by x Type A carriers and y Type B carriers is given by the expression

$$10x + 8y.$$

The ordered pairs of whole numbers (x, y) which are solutions to the equation

$$10x + 8y = 60$$

tell us how many of each type of carrier could be used to transport 60 cars. If you look at the graph in Figure 4, you will see that the only two solutions are given by the ordered pairs $(6, 0)$ and $(2, 5)$. However, $(6, 0)$ is not in the solution set and so $(2, 5)$ is the only possible solution.

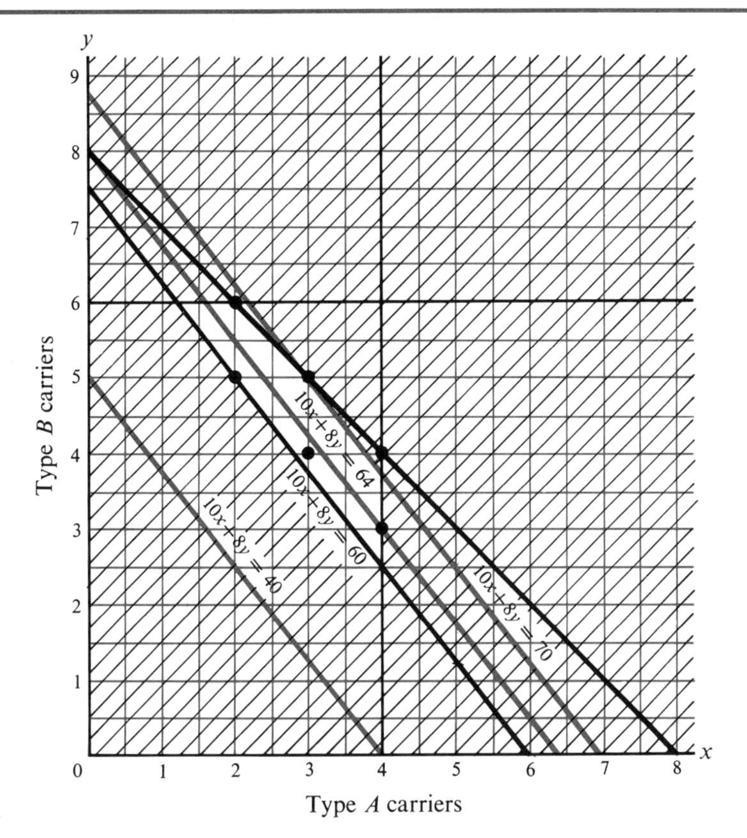

Fig. 4

The red lines in Figure 4 have equations

$$10x + 8y = 40; \qquad 10x + 8y = 64; \qquad 10x + 8y = 70.$$

How many of each type of carrier must be used to transport exactly

(i) 64 cars; (ii) 70 cars?

Can 40 cars be carried?

(*c*) Notice that the family of lines $10x + 8y = c$, for different values of c are parallel.

Place the edge of your ruler along the line $10x + 8y = 80$. Can 80 cars be delivered per day?

(*d*) What is the value of c for the lines which pass through

(i) $(3, 4)$; (ii) $(2, 6)$?

How many cars can be transported by (i) 7; (ii) 8 carriers?

(*e*) Place your ruler along the line of the family which passes through the point $(4, 4)$. What is the equation of this line?

What does the value of c in this equation tell you?

Do you agree that the maximum number of cars which can be transported is given by this value of c?

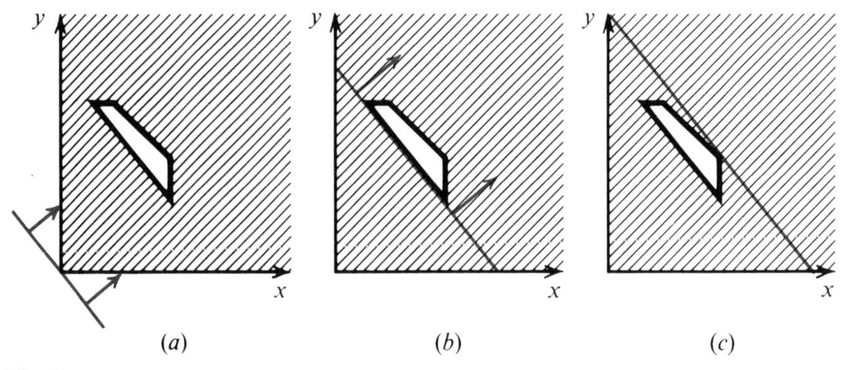

Fig. 5

(f) Translate your ruler as suggested by Figure 5. Notice that its edge always lies along one of the family of lines

$$10x + 8y = c.$$

You should find that $10x + 8y = 72$ is the last of the family of lines along which the edge of your ruler lies before it moves out of the solution set 'to the right'. This means that the *maximum* value of $10x + 8y$ for the solution set is 72. That is, the maximum number of cars that can be transported is 72.

What is the minimum number of cars that can be transported?

Example 1

A toy-firm manufactures two kinds of toy soldiers on a machine which can work for 10 hours per day. The 'Guard' takes 8 seconds to make and 8 g of metal is used to make it. The 'Cavalryman' takes 6 seconds to make and 16 g of metal is used to make it. Altogether 64 kg of metal is available per day.

If the profit on the 'Guard' is 5p and on the 'Cavalryman' is 6p, how many of each should be made to maximize the profits? What is the maximum profit that can be made per day?

The variables are

(i) the number of 'Guards' to be made – call this x;
(ii) the number of 'Cavalrymen' to be made – call this y.

The machine can work for $60 \times 60 \times 10$ or 36 000 s per day, so that

(i) $8x + 6y \leqslant 36\,000$.

Since 64 kg of metal is available,

(ii) $8x + 16y \leqslant 64\,000$.

If we now graph these relationships we obtain Figure 6.

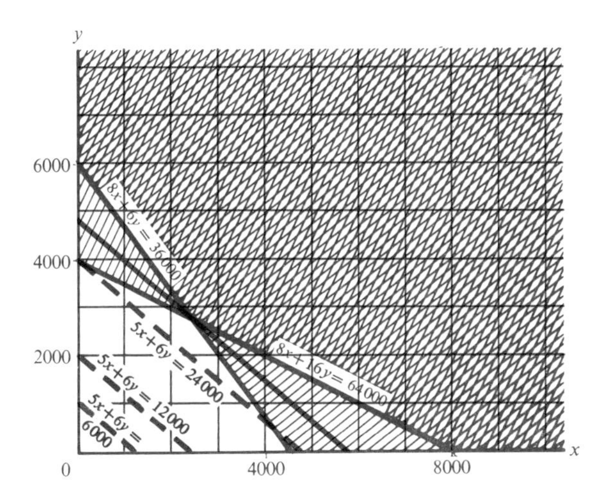

Fig. 6

Since the profit on the 'Guard' is 5p and that on the 'Cavalryman' is 6p, then the profit on making x 'Guards' and y 'Cavalryman' is given by the expression

$$(5x + 6y)\text{p}.$$

The integral points on the broken red lines in Figure 6 will tell us how many of each toy should be made to make a profit of (i) 6000p; (ii) 1200p; (iii) 24 000p. These lines are called 'lines of equal profit'.

The points on the continuous red line will tell us the number of each kind of toy that should be made to give us a maximum profit (why?). The only point of the solution set which lies on this line is (2400, 2800).

Hence, to make a maximum profit, 2400 'Guards' and 2800 'Cavalrymen' should be manufactured.

The maximum profit is then

$$\begin{aligned}(5 \times 2400)\text{p} + (6 \times 2800)\text{p} &= (12\,000 + 16\,800)\text{p} \\ &= £288.\end{aligned}$$

Exercise B

1 Leave unshaded the set which satisfies all the following five inequalities:

(i) $x \geqslant 0$; (ii) $y \geqslant 0$; (iii) $x + y \geqslant 5$;
(iv) $x + y \leqslant 7$; (v) $x \geqslant 3y$.

Find (*a*) the maximum and (*b*) the minimum value of each of the following expressions for this set:

(i) x; (ii) y; (iii) $x + y$; (iv) $x - y$;
(v) $x + 2y$; (vi) $2x + y$; (vii) $3x + 2y$.

2 Two detergent factories pour their waste products into a river. Factory *A* always produces at least twice as much waste as Factory *B* and together they always produce at least 9000 litres of waste per week. Scientists estimate that if the total amount of waste entering the river per week was greater than 15 000 litres then the population of fish in the river would be in danger.

Write down three inequalities and graph the information. (Use x for the number of litres of waste from Factory *A* and y for the number of litres from Factory *B*.)

What is the maximum amount of waste that should be produced in any week by (i) factory *A*; (ii) factory *B* if the fish are to survive?

Despite the suggested restrictions the scientists believe that for every 1000 litres of waste from factory *A* two fish die every week and every 1000 litres from factory *B* three fish die every week. What is (i) the maximum; (ii) the minimum number of fish that die per week due to pollution?

3 A haulage contractor has 7 six-tonne lorries and 4 ten-tonne lorries. He has 9 drivers, each of whom stays with the same lorry once it has been allocated to him. The six-tonne lorries can make 8 journeys per day, but the ten-tonne lorries only 6 journeys per day. He has contracted to move at least 360 tonnes of coal from a pit-head to a power station each day.

If x denotes the number of six-tonne lorries in use, and y the number of ten-tonne lorries in use, explain the meaning of the expressions

(i) $48x + 60y \geqslant 360$
(ii) $x + y \leqslant 9$.

Write down two more inequalities involving x and y.

(i) What possible combinations of lorries can the contractor use to meet the delivery demand?
(ii) Which combination of lorries uses the smallest number of drivers?
(iii) Which combination of lorries carries the maximum tonnage?

4 For a camp of 70 children two types of tent are available on hire. The Patrol tent sleeps 7 and costs £5 a week; the Hike tent sleeps 2 and costs £1 a week. The total number of tents must not exceed 19.

Write down two inequalities connecting the number of Patrol tents (p) and the number of Hike tents (h); and an expression for the cost of hiring these numbers of tents for a week. Using a scale of 1 cm to 2 units, find the most economical cost of hire and the number of each kind of tent required.

5 Ten men are available to unload 7 lorries, but not more than two men can work together on a lorry. If x denotes the number of lorries being unloaded by one man at any time, and y the number of lorries being unloaded by two men at any time, write down the two inequalities satisfied by x and y (other than $x \geqslant 0$, $y \geqslant 0$) and graph the information.

Each lorry carries a tonne of goods. Experience shows that two men together can unload three times as fast as one man by himself. If one man can unload 2 tonnes per hour, show that the rate of unloading is $2x + 6y$ tonnes per hour. Use your graph to find x and y so that the first tonne of goods is unloaded as quickly as possible.

6 A bicycle manufacturer makes two models, a sports cycle and a racing cycle. The sports model takes 8 man-hours to make and the racing model 12 man-hours. There are 20 men available for the work and they work a 35-hour week, (so that the total number of man-hours available per week is 700). The sports model costs £5 in materials and the racing model £6, and the manufacturer has £400 worth of material for use per week. The firm has a contract to supply at least 30 of each type of bicycle per week. How many of each type of bicycle should be made to obtain the maximum profit if the profit on the sports model is £6 and that on the racing model £9?

7 A farmer wishes to stock his farm with cows and sheep. Cows cost £20 each and sheep £15 each. The farmer has accommodation for not more than 40 animals and he has £700 with which to buy the animals. When he resells the animals for slaughter he expects to make an overall profit of £12 per cow and £8 per sheep. How many cows and how many sheep should he purchase to maximize his profits? What is the maximum profit?

8 Two types of screw, A and B, are made on an automatic machine which takes 5 seconds to make a screw A and 4 seconds to make a screw B. Screw A requires 8 g of metal and screw B 16 g of metal. The profit from making screw A is 0·2p and from screw B 0·2p. If the machine can work for a maximum of 7 hours per day and 96 kg of metal is available, how many of each type of screw should be made to make the manufacturer's daily profit as large as possible? What is the maximum profit per day?

4 Non-linear conditions

So far we have only dealt with conditions which are linear (i.e. conditions which, when graphed, have straight lines as their boundaries).

However, the process we have described is easily extended to non-linear conditions as the following example shows:

Example 2

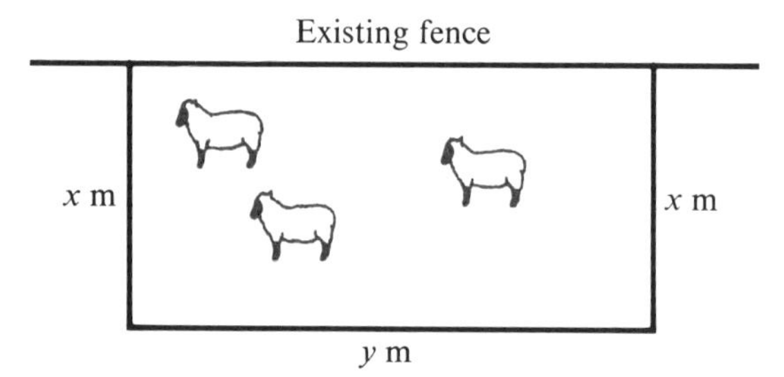

Fig. 7

A farmer wishes to make a rectangular enclosure of area 144 m^2. The enclosure is to be built against an existing straight fence (see Figure 7), and the farmer has 50 m of wire netting. What is the minimum amount of wire netting he can use to make the enclosure? What is the maximum length the existing fence needs to be? What is the minimum length it needs to be?

Suppose that the length of sides of the enclosure are x and y metres (see Figure 7). Then the area to be enclosed is xy m^2, so that

(i) $xy = 144$ (note that this is an *equation*).

The amount of wire netting to be used must not exceed 50 m, so that

(ii) $2x + y \leqslant 50$.

If we now graph these two relations, we obtain Figure 8.

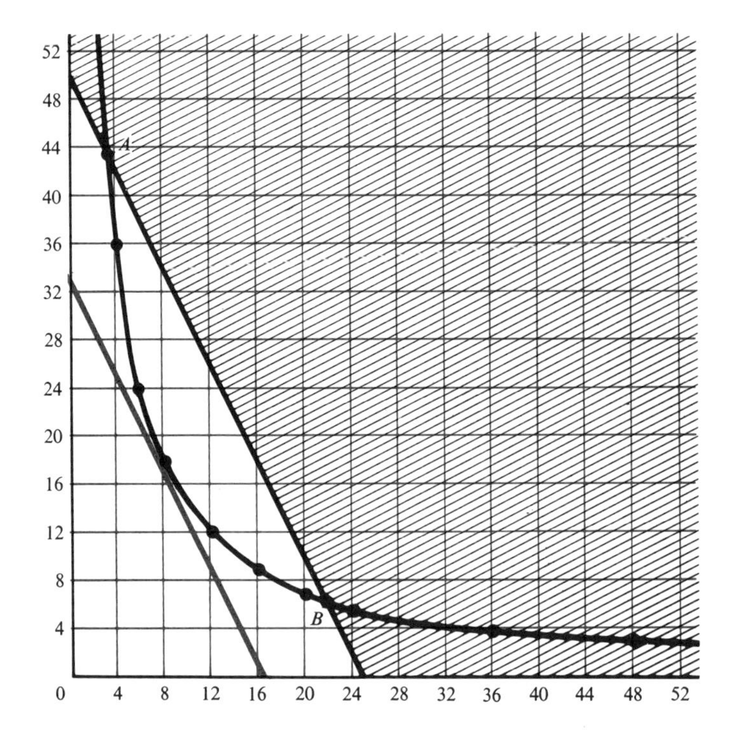

Fig. 8

The solution set for these two conditions is the set of points on the hyperbola $xy = 144$, for $3 \leqslant x \leqslant 22$.

The amount of wire netting required is given by the expression

$$(2x + y) \text{ m}.$$

This is a minimum when $2x + y = 34$ (see the red line in Figure 8), and in this case $x = 9$, and $y = 16$. Therefore the minimum amount of netting is 34 m.

The maximum length the existing fence needs to be is given by the y-co-ordinate of point A – that is, 44 m.

The minimum length the existing fence needs to be is given by the y-co-ordinate of point B – that is, 6 m.

Exercise C

1 (*a*) Calculate the values of y when x equals 1, 2, 3, 4, 5, 6 for each of the following equations:

(i) $xy = 64$; (ii) $x^2 = y$; (iii) $y = x^2 + 4$.

(*b*) On separate axes draw the graphs of (i), (ii) and (iii) above. Shade in the regions $xy \geqslant 64$, $x^2 \leqslant y$, $y \geqslant x^2 + 4$.

2 Draw the graphs of $xy = 16$ and $x + y = 10$ on the same axes. Leave unshaded the region, R, where $R = \{(x,y)\colon x + y \leqslant 10\} \cap \{(x,y)\colon xy \geqslant 16\}$.

What is the maximum value of (i) x; (ii) y for the region R? What is the minimum value of $x + y$ for the region R?

3 A farmer wants to enclose a rectangular area for sheep. They require at least 480 m^2. For one side he will use a straight fence and for the other three sides he can use 'hurdles', each 2 m long, of which he has 40. Using x for the number of hurdles he uses for each of the equal sides, and y for the number of hurdles he uses for the remaining side, write down two algebraic inequalities satisfying the above information. Graph the information and hence find the smallest number of hurdles he needs.

4 A biscuit-container manufacturer wishes to make cylindrical containers. The curved surfaces of the containers are to be made from rectangular sheets of metal of area 900 cm^2. Taking x cm to be the circumference of the base of a container, and y cm the height of the container, write the second sentence as an algebraic equation, and represent it on a graph.

The manufacturer requires that the circumference of the container be less than 60 cm and the height less than 30 cm. By graphing two more relations find the range of values within which (*a*) the circumference and (*b*) the height of the containers must lie. What is the circumference and height of the container when the rectangular sheet has maximum perimeter?

5 The distance d km that can be travelled by a motor boat at a steady speed of v km/h without refuelling is given by the formula

$$d \leqslant 12v - v^2.$$

Draw up a table of values and plot $d = 12v - v^2$ for the domain $0 \leqslant v \leqslant 12$.

Taking suitable scales, shade the area representing distances impossible at various speeds. What is special about 12 km/h? How do you account for this?

A trip round the bay is to last 3 hours. Express the relation between d and v for such a trip and plot it on your graph. What is the greatest distance that can be covered in this time and what will be the speed?

Find also the greatest distance that can be covered at any speed. How long will a trip of this distance take?

6 A stationery firm is going to market an envelope which will take paper measuring 30 cm by 20 cm folded twice, and once at right-angles, and paper 24 cm by 14 cm folded into four (along the dotted lines in Figure 9).

If this envelope is to measure x cm long, y cm wide, write down inequalities for x and y. The designer considers that the length should not be more than $1\frac{1}{2}$ times the width. Express this by an inequality and also write the perimeter of an envelope in terms of x and y. Find a solution which satisfies all the conditions and makes the perimeter as small as you think possible. Is such a solution acceptable, do you think?

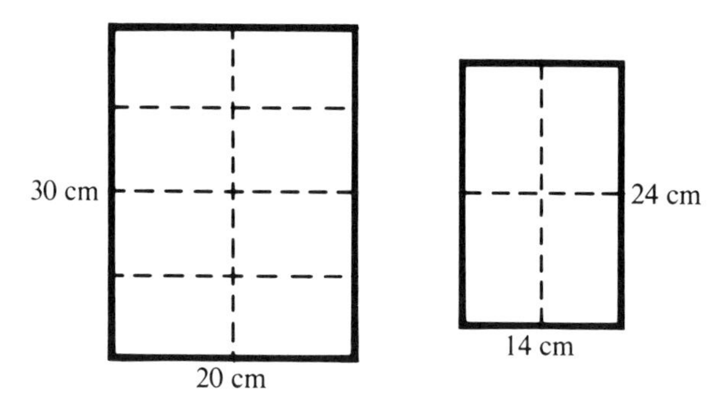

Fig. 9

Incidence matrices

(*a*) Write down the one-stage route matrix for the network in Figure 1. Call it **M**.

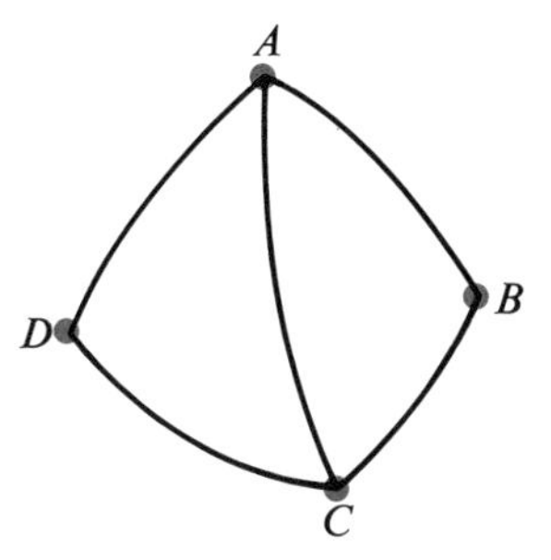

Fig. 1

(*b*) There is another way of compiling matrices to describe a network.

In Figure 1, we labelled the nodes. Suppose we now label the arcs as well:

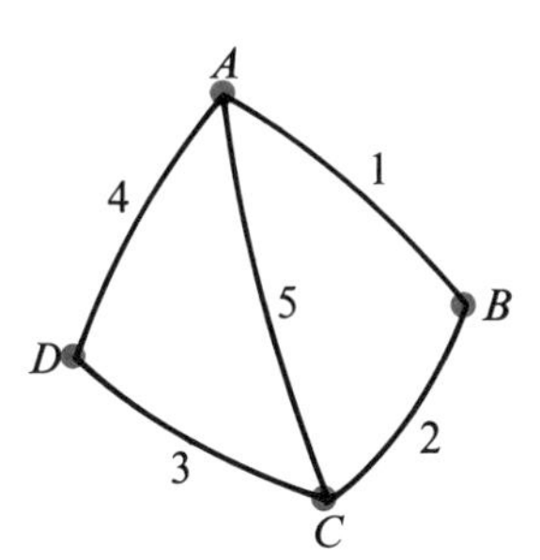

Fig. 2

Node A lies on arcs 1, 4 and 5 but not on arcs 2 and 3. We say that node A is *incident* on arcs 1, 4 and 5.

Copy and complete the matrix **R** to show which nodes are incident on which arcs.

$$\mathbf{R} = \begin{array}{c} \\ A \\ B \\ C \\ D \end{array}\begin{array}{c} \begin{array}{ccccc} 1 & 2 & 3 & 4 & 5 \end{array} \\ \begin{pmatrix} 1 & 0 & 0 & 1 & 1 \\ & & & & \\ & & & & \\ & & & & \end{pmatrix} \end{array}.$$

Now write down the 5 by 4 matrix $\mathbf{R}'$ which shows the incidence of arcs on nodes.

How are the matrices **R** and $\mathbf{R}'$ related?

Work out $\mathbf{RR}'$.

R could be described as 'a nodes by arcs' matrix and **R**′ as 'an arcs by nodes' matrix. How would you describe **RR**′? How would you describe the route matrix **M**?

Compare **RR**′ with **M**. What features do they have in common?

The result of combining the second row of **R** with the third column of **R**′ is shown below.

$$\begin{array}{c} \\ A \\ B \\ C \\ D \end{array}\!\!\begin{array}{c} \begin{matrix} 1 & 2 & 3 & 4 & 5 \end{matrix} \\ \begin{pmatrix} \cdot & \cdot & \cdot & \cdot & \cdot \\ 1 & 1 & 0 & 0 & 0 \\ \cdot & \cdot & \cdot & \cdot & \cdot \\ \cdot & \cdot & \cdot & \cdot & \cdot \end{pmatrix} \end{array} \begin{array}{c} \\ 1 \\ 2 \\ 3 \\ 4 \\ 5 \end{array}\!\!\begin{array}{c} \begin{matrix} A & B & C & D \end{matrix} \\ \begin{pmatrix} \cdot & \cdot & 0 & \cdot \\ \cdot & \cdot & 1 & \cdot \\ \cdot & \cdot & 1 & \cdot \\ \cdot & \cdot & 0 & \cdot \\ \cdot & \cdot & 1 & \cdot \end{pmatrix} \end{array} = \begin{array}{c} \\ A \\ B \\ C \\ D \end{array}\!\!\begin{array}{c} \begin{matrix} A & B & C & D \end{matrix} \\ \begin{pmatrix} \cdot & \cdot & \cdot & \cdot \\ \cdot & \cdot & 1 & \cdot \\ \cdot & \cdot & \cdot & \cdot \\ \cdot & \cdot & \cdot & \cdot \end{pmatrix} \end{array}.$$

$$(1 \times 0) + (1 \times 1) + (0 \times 1) + (0 \times 0) + (0 \times 1) = 1.$$

We obtain a '1' in the second row and third column of **RR**′ because node B is incident on arc 2 which is incident on node C, that is, because there is a route from B to C.

Check that the other elements of **RR**′ which are not on the leading diagonal also count the number of routes between pairs of nodes.

The elements on the leading diagonal of **RR**′ are different from the corresponding elements of **M**. What do these elements count? Try to explain why this happens.

(*c*) Suppose we now label the regions as well as the nodes and the arcs. See Figure 3.

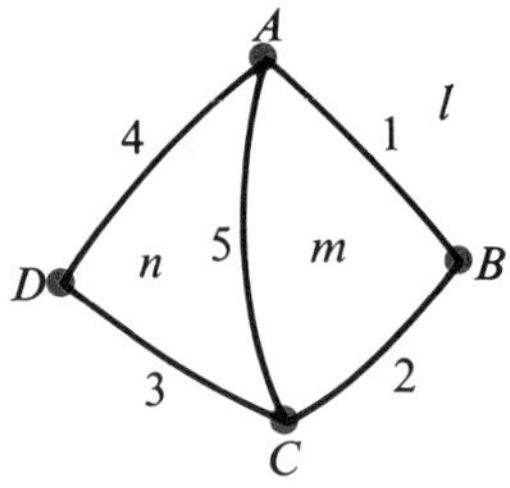

Fig. 3

Copy and complete the matrix **S** to show the incidence of arcs on regions and the matrix **T** to show the incidence of nodes on regions.

$$\mathbf{S} = \begin{array}{c} \\ 1 \\ 2 \\ 3 \\ 4 \\ 5 \end{array}\!\!\begin{array}{c} \begin{matrix} l & m & n \end{matrix} \\ \begin{pmatrix} 1 & 1 & 0 \\ 1 & & \\ 1 & & \\ 1 & & \\ 0 & & \end{pmatrix} \end{array}; \qquad \mathbf{T} = \begin{array}{c} \\ A \\ B \\ C \\ D \end{array}\!\!\begin{array}{c} \begin{matrix} l & m & n \end{matrix} \\ \begin{pmatrix} & & \\ 1 & 1 & 0 \\ & & \\ & & \end{pmatrix} \end{array}.$$

Work out **RS**.

Compare **RS** with **T**. What do you notice? Try to explain why this happens.

(*d*) Why is it impossible to form the product $\mathbf{S}^2$?

Write down the transpose of **S** and call it **S**′. What does **S**′ show?

Is it possible to form the products **SS**′ and **S**′**S**?

Work out the product **S**′**S** and explain the meaning of the elements in the product.

Exercise A

1 Draw the networks described by the following incidence matrices:

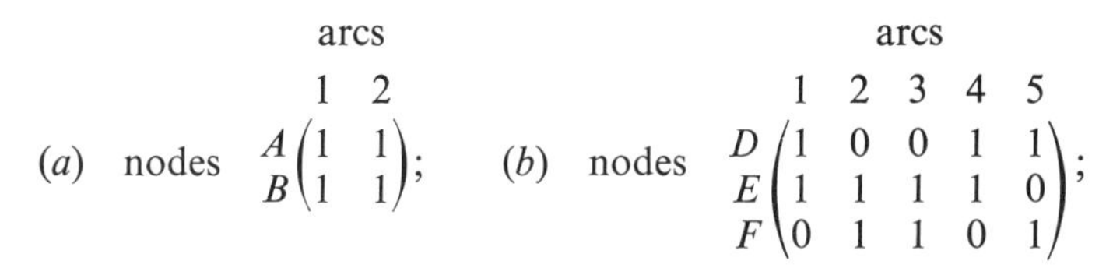

(*a*) nodes $\begin{matrix} & \text{arcs} \\ & \begin{matrix}1 & 2\end{matrix} \\ \begin{matrix}A \\ B\end{matrix} & \begin{pmatrix}1 & 1 \\ 1 & 1\end{pmatrix}\end{matrix}$; (*b*) nodes $\begin{matrix} & \text{arcs} \\ & \begin{matrix}1 & 2 & 3 & 4 & 5\end{matrix} \\ \begin{matrix}D \\ E \\ F\end{matrix} & \begin{pmatrix}1 & 0 & 0 & 1 & 1 \\ 1 & 1 & 1 & 1 & 0 \\ 0 & 1 & 1 & 0 & 1\end{pmatrix}\end{matrix}$;

(*c*) arcs $\begin{matrix} & \text{regions} \\ & \begin{matrix}a & b\end{matrix} \\ \begin{matrix}1 \\ 2 \\ 3\end{matrix} & \begin{pmatrix}1 & 1 \\ 1 & 1 \\ 1 & 1\end{pmatrix}\end{matrix}$; (*d*) nodes $\begin{matrix} & \text{regions} \\ & \begin{matrix}p & q & r & s\end{matrix} \\ \begin{matrix}X \\ Y \\ Z\end{matrix} & \begin{pmatrix}1 & 1 & 1 & 0 \\ 1 & 1 & 1 & 1 \\ 0 & 1 & 0 & 1\end{pmatrix}\end{matrix}$.

2 Find the matrices **R**, **S** and **T** for the network in Figure 4 and check that **RS** = 2**T**.

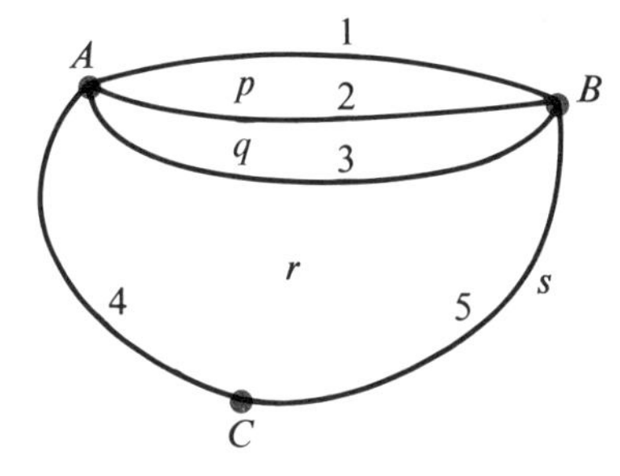

Fig. 4

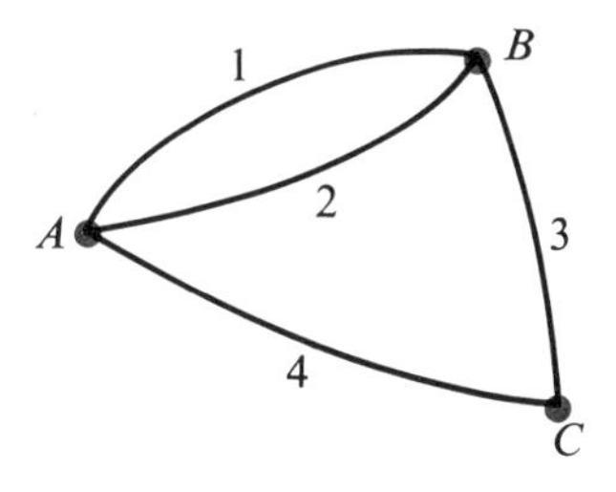

Fig. 5

3 (*a*) Find the product **R′R** for the network in Figure 2. Is it the same as **RR′**?
(*b*) What is the meaning of the elements on the leading diagonal?

4 (*a*) Find the product **R′R** for the network in Figure 5.
(*b*) Explain the meaning of the elements which are not on the leading diagonal.

5 (*a*) For the network in Figure 6, write down
(i) the matrix **P** showing how many routes there are between any two nodes;
(ii) the 3 by 6 incidence matrix **X** showing which arcs end at which nodes;
(iii) the corresponding incidence matrix **Y** showing which nodes are at the end of which arcs.
(*b*) How are the matrices **X** and **Y** related?
(*c*) Calculate (i) **XY**; (ii) **XY** – **P**.
(*d*) State what information is given by the matrix **XY** – **P**.

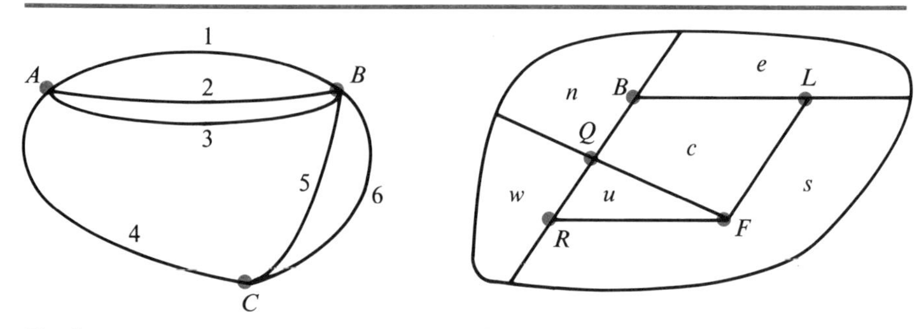

Fig. 6

Fig. 7

6 For administrative purposes one of the English counties is divided into six regions (n, e, s, w, u, c) by trunk roads joining the five towns B, F, L, Q, R. See Figure 7.

(*a*) Copy and complete the route matrix **M** for the direct routes between the five towns:

$$\mathbf{M} = \begin{array}{c} \\ B \\ F \\ L \\ Q \\ R \end{array} \begin{array}{c} \begin{array}{ccccc} B & F & L & Q & R \end{array} \\ \left(\begin{array}{ccccc} 0 & 0 & 1 & 1 & 0 \\ 0 & 0 & & & \\ 1 & & & & \\ 1 & & & & \\ 0 & & & & \end{array}\right) \end{array}.$$

(*b*) Write down the 5 by 6 matrix **T** showing incidence of towns on regions and the 6 by 5 matrix **T**′ showing incidence of regions on towns.

(*c*) Calculate the product $\mathbf{U} = \mathbf{TT}'$. Describe what information is given by the entry 2 of **U** relating B to Q.

(*d*) Explain why the entry relating Q to F in **U** is twice the corresponding entry in **M**.

7 (*a*) Look at the network in Figure 8. We say that node B is incident on region l, three times, and that arc 1 is incident on region l, twice. Use this information to help you write down the matrices **R**, **S** and **T** for this network and check that $\mathbf{RS} = 2\mathbf{T}$.

(*b*) Now find out whether $\mathbf{RS} = 2\mathbf{T}$ for the network in Figure 9. Explain how you can overcome any difficulties that arise.

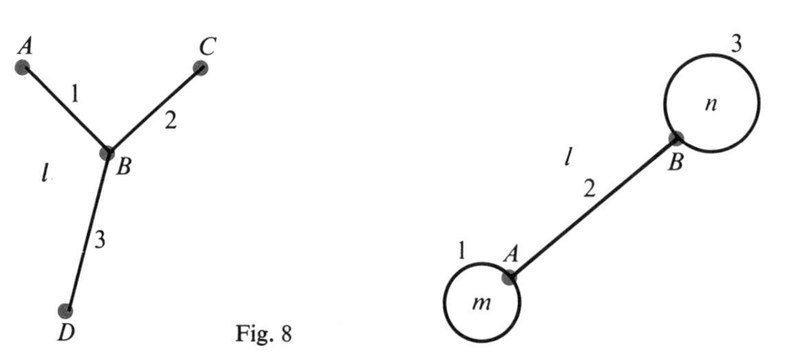

Fig. 8

Fig. 9

Revision exercises

Slide rule session

Give the answers to the following as accurately as you can.

1 $2{\cdot}17 \times 19{\cdot}4$.

2 $37{\cdot}5 \div 6{\cdot}2$.

3 $\sqrt{174}$.

4 $(1{\cdot}62 \times 54) + (17{\cdot}7 \times 0{\cdot}8)$.

5 $(14{\cdot}8)^2 \div 7{\cdot}4$.

6 $\pi \times (1{\cdot}5)^2$.

7 $\dfrac{79}{16{\cdot}8 \times 4{\cdot}2}$.

8 $\sqrt{(36{\cdot}5 \times 2{\cdot}9)}$.

9 $(14{\cdot}2 \times 0{\cdot}9)^2$.

10 $45{\cdot}4 \times 3{\cdot}7 \times 0{\cdot}095$.

11 $\dfrac{8}{7{\cdot}4}$.

12 $\frac{1}{8} \div 43$.

13 $0{\cdot}7 \times \dfrac{1}{9{\cdot}2}$.

14 $(41 \div 23) \times \frac{1}{5} \div 5$.

15 $\sqrt{28{\cdot}4} \times \dfrac{1}{4{\cdot}6} \times (19{\cdot}4)^3$.

Computation 1

Estimation of answers.

Never perform a computation without considering whether your answer is reasonable. The following examples will give some practice at making reasonable estimates. Say which answers you consider are reasonable estimates, and in the case of the others, write what you think would be better.

1 $12{\cdot}3 \times 2{\cdot}9 = 36$ approx.

2 $0{\cdot}105 \times 0{\cdot}1 = 0{\cdot}1$ approx.

3 $9{\cdot}6 \times 26{\cdot}2 = 250$ approx.

4 $1023 \times 19 = 2000$ approx.

5 $(20{\cdot}2)^2 = 400$ approx.

6 $\sqrt{170} = 13$ approx.

7 $\sqrt[3]{0{\cdot}08} = 0{\cdot}2$ approx.

8 $\dfrac{16 \times 1{\cdot}1}{3{\cdot}4} = 5$ approx.

9 $\sqrt{(3{\cdot}1^2 + 6{\cdot}9^2)} = 10$ approx.

10 $62{\cdot}9 \times 0{\cdot}9 \times 0{\cdot}49 = 3$ approx.

Exercise A

1 If $ax > bx \Leftrightarrow a < b$, what can you say about x?

2 Express 0·0056 in standard index form.

3 What can you say about the sets A and B if $A \cup B = B$?

4 Find the value of t if $\frac{3}{4}(2t + 7) = 0$.

5 Find $f(^-2)$ if $f(x) = x^2 + x$.

6 State the area of a circle whose diameter is 6 cm, leaving π in your answer.

7 What is the probability of obtaining a single head when two coins are tossed?

8 Add the fractions $\frac{2}{5}$ and $\frac{3}{4}$.

Exercise B

1 Write down 63_{10} as a number in the scale of 8.

2 Write down the median of the numbers, 34, 36, 12, 23, 29, 87, 56.

3 In triangle ABC, angle $A = 45°$, angle $B = 90°$ and $BC = 6$ cm. Find AB.

4 List the set of prime numbers between 90 and 100.

5 What single transformation is equivalent to two successive reflections in two parallel mirror-lines?

6 Give the probability of throwing a total larger than 10 when 2 dice are thrown.

7 Simplify $\frac{1}{2} - \frac{2}{3} + \frac{5}{6}$.

8 Give the inverse of the function $x \rightarrow 3x + 1$.

Exercise C

1 State the point of intersection of the lines $y = x$ and $x + y = 4$.

2 Give the image of the point $(3, 4)$ when it is reflected in the line $y = x$.

3 (*a*) What is the probability that a card, drawn at random from a pack of 52 well-shuffled cards, is a black 2?
(*b*) Two boys pick their favourite colour from red, blue, yellow. Write down the probability that:
   (i) both choose the same colour,
   (ii) both choose yellow,
   (iii) one chooses yellow, but not the other.

4 Find the coordinates of the vertices of the unit square after it has been enlarged by scale factor 3, centre the origin, followed by a half turn about the origin.

5 (*a*) Draw the lines $y = 2x - 1$, $x + y = 2$ and $y = {}^-1$ on the same graph taking values of both x and y from $^-2$ to 4.
(*b*) Give all the points with integral coordinates which satisfy all the inequalities $y \leqslant 2x - 1$, $x + y < 2$, $y > {}^-1$.

6 A certain reflection maps $(0, 1)$ onto $(4, 1)$ and $(2, {}^-2)$ onto itself. Give the equation of the mirror line.

7 Find the gradients of $2x - 3y = 6$, $4x - 6y = 9$, $2x - 3y = {}^-15$. What do you notice? Write down the equation of another member of the set of such lines.

8 Find the result if, within the set of integers, you:
(*a*) think of a number; (*b*) add the next largest number;
(*c*) add 9; (*d*) divide by 2;
(*e*) subtract the original number.

Exercise D

1 Find the points with integral coordinates that satisfy the orderings

$$^-2 \leqslant x + y < 2; \qquad 0 \geqslant 3x - y; \qquad y - 3x \leqslant 2.$$

2 Draw a network for which this incidence matrix relates nodes and arcs:

$$\text{nodes}\quad \begin{array}{c} \\ A \\ B \\ C \\ D \end{array}\!\!\begin{array}{c} \text{arcs} \\ \begin{array}{ccccc} 1 & 2 & 3 & 4 & 5 \end{array} \\ \begin{pmatrix} 1 & 0 & 0 & 1 & 1 \\ 1 & 1 & 0 & 0 & 0 \\ 0 & 1 & 1 & 0 & 1 \\ 0 & 0 & 1 & 1 & 0 \end{pmatrix} \end{array}.$$

3 Find the area of the triangle whose vertices are $(^-1, 2)$, $(1, 2)$, $(0, 4)$.

4 Simplify $\{(x, y)\colon y = 0\} \cap \{(x, y)\colon y = 1\}$.

5 An African boy has 15p in his pocket. He wants to spend his money on pineapples (60 cents each) and oranges (30 cents each). A pineapple takes $7\frac{1}{2}$ minutes to eat, an orange $2\frac{1}{2}$ minutes; the boy has 30 minutes to spare in which to consume his fruit (5p = 100 cents).

He wants to eat at least as many pineapples as oranges, and he also wants the total number of fruit eaten to be as large as possible.

If he eats x pineapples and y oranges, write down the orderings which x and y must satisfy. Find the solution satisfying all the conditions.

6 A box contains several hundred black pins and white pins – three times as many black pins as white pins. Two pins in succession are taken out in the dark. What is the probability that they are both black?

7 What angle does the plane $y = x$ make with the plane $x = 0$?

8 Give the equations of the planes which are determined by the following sets of points:

(*a*) $(0,0,0)$, $(0,1,2)$, $(0,7,9)$;
(*b*) $(1,2,3)$, $(3,2,1)$, $(5,2,4)$;
(*c*) $(5,4,3)$, $(4,4,3)$, $(5,5,3)$.

Exercise E

1 Find the distance between points with coordinates $(5,6)$ and $(^-3,0)$. Write down the coordinates of a point whose distance from $(5,6)$ is twice this.

2 Find the distance between the points $(9,^-1,7)$ and $(10,1,9)$.

3 If the line $y = 3x + c$ passes through $(1,2)$, find c.

4 What positive values of x satisfy $4 < 12/x < 6$?

5 Find the gradients of the following lines:

(*a*) $3y = ^-2x + 4$; (*b*) $2x - y = 5$;
(*c*) $x + y = 1$; (*d*) $y - 3x - 6 = 0$.

6 A triangle has vertices at $(2,1)$, $(5,2)$, $(3,3)$. Show that it is right angled and calculate its area.

7 Describe with the aid of a rough sketch the set of points $\{(x,y): x^2 + y^2 = 25\}$.

8 Find the Cartesian coordinates of points with the following polar coordinates:

$$(1,30°),\ (10,30°),\ (10,150°),\ (5,210°).$$

5 Tangents

1 Sine and cosine

(*a*) In *Book G* we defined the sine and cosine of an angle θ as the y and x co-ordinates respectively of a point P lying on the circumference of a unit circle, centre O, where OP made an angle $\theta°$ with the positive direction of the x axis.

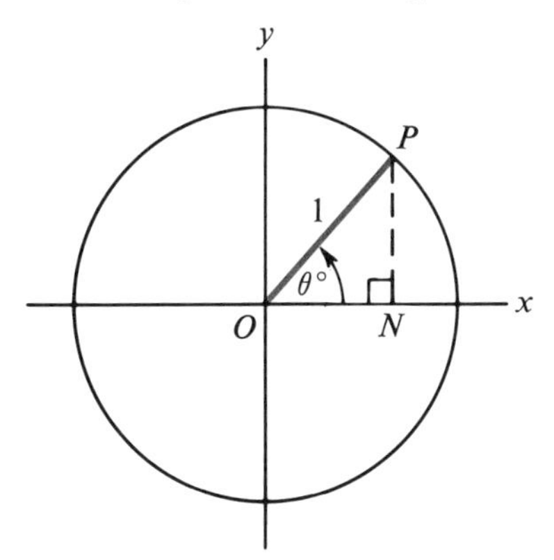

Fig. 1

Thus in Figure 1,

$$\cos \theta° = ON$$

and

$$\sin \theta° = PN.$$

The values of ON and PN for $0 \leqslant \theta \leqslant 90$ are tabulated for you in your cosine and sine tables, and you will see, for example, that when $\theta = 46{\cdot}5$, $\cos\theta° = 0{\cdot}688$ and $\sin\theta° = 0{\cdot}725$.

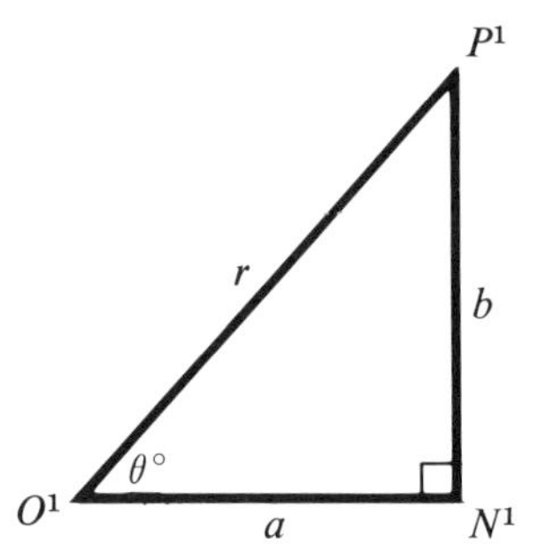

Fig. 2

(*b*) Figure 2 shows a triangle similar to triangle OPN. Figure 3 shows that this triangle has been obtained by enlarging triangle OPN with scale factor r.

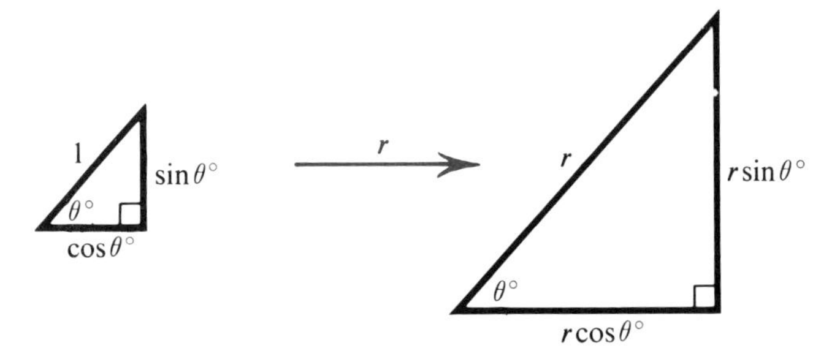

Fig. 3

By direct comparison we can see that

(i) $b = r\sin\theta°$,

(ii) $a = r\cos\theta°$.

This means that both $\sin\theta°$ and $\cos\theta°$ can be expressed as a ratio of two sides of a right-angled triangle:

$$\sin\theta° = \frac{b}{r},$$

$$\cos\theta° = \frac{a}{r}.$$

Sometimes the side opposite the angle $\theta°$ is called the *opposite* side, and the side adjacent to $\theta°$, which is not the hypotenuse, the *adjacent* side. We can therefore write:

$$\sin\theta° = \frac{\text{opposite}}{\text{hypotenuse}},$$

$$\cos\theta° = \frac{\text{adjacent}}{\text{hypotenuse}}.$$

(See Figure 4.)

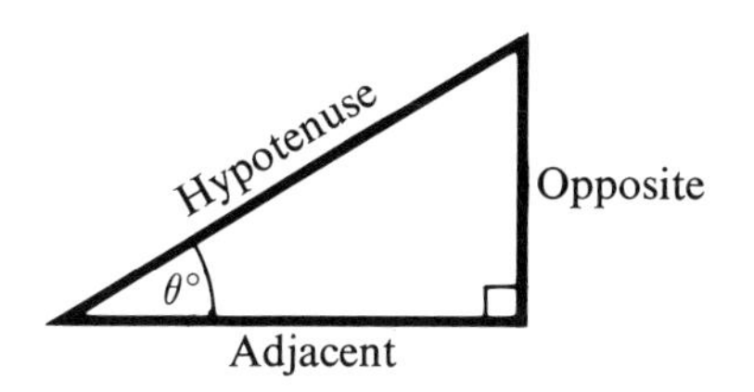

Fig. 4

(*c*)

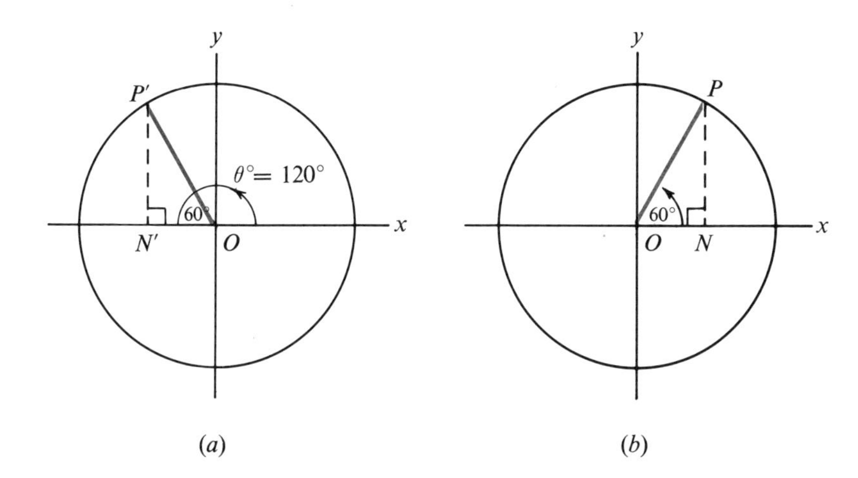

Fig. 5

Look at Figure 5(*a*) in which $\theta = 120$ and at Figure 5(*b*) in which $\theta = 60$. The y coordinates of P and P' in each figure are the same because the triangles OPN, $OP'N'$ are congruent (that is, they have the same shape and size).

Hence, $\sin 120^\circ = P'N' = \sin 60^\circ = 0{\cdot}867$.

However although the lengths ON and ON' are equal, the x coordinate of P' in Figure 5(*a*) is negative. Hence we have

$$\cos 120^\circ = {}^-\cos 60^\circ = {}^-0{\cdot}5.$$

Calculate:

(i) $\sin 150^\circ$; (ii) $\cos 150^\circ$;
(iii) $\sin 135^\circ$; (iv) $\cos 135^\circ$.

Do you agree that for $90 \leqslant \theta \leqslant 180$,

$$\sin \theta^\circ = \sin(180^\circ - \theta^\circ)$$

and

$$\cos \theta^\circ = {}^-\cos(180^\circ - \theta^\circ)?$$

(See Figure 6.)

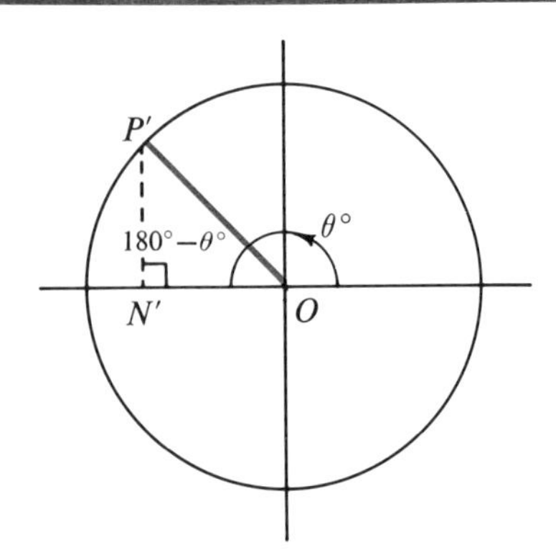

Fig. 6

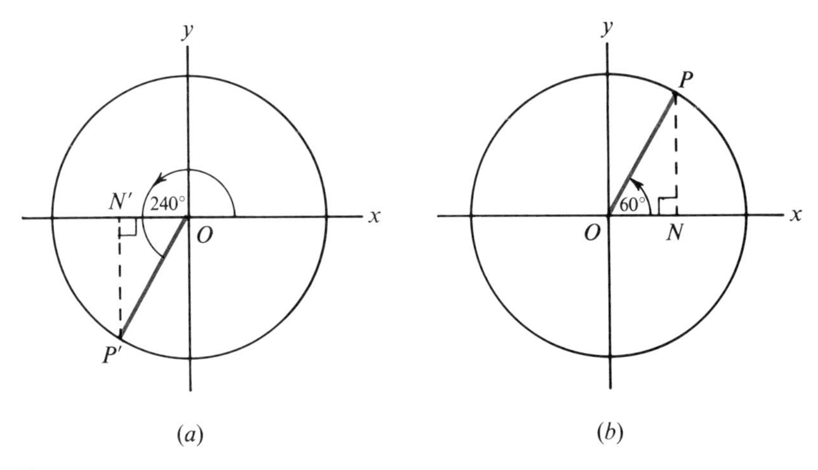

Fig. 7

(d) Look at Figure 7(a) in which $\theta = 240$, and at Figure 7(b) in which $\theta = 60$. In this case the triangles OPN and $OP'N'$ are again congruent but *both* coordinates of P' are negative.

Hence

$$\sin 240^\circ = {}^-\sin 60^\circ = {}^-0{\cdot}867$$

and

$$\cos 240^\circ = {}^-\cos 60^\circ = {}^-0{\cdot}5.$$

Do you agree that if $180 \leqslant \theta \leqslant 270$, then

$$\sin \theta^\circ = {}^-\sin(\theta^\circ - 180^\circ)$$

and

$$\cos \theta^\circ = {}^-\cos(\theta^\circ - 180^\circ)?$$

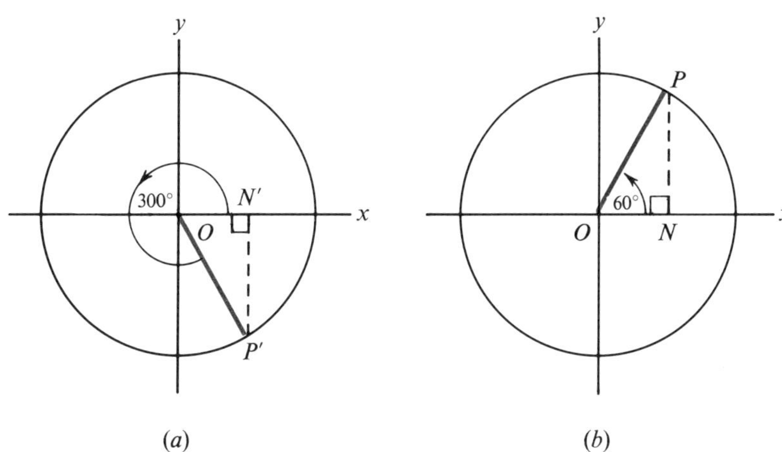

Fig. 8

Are the triangles $OP'N'$ and OPN in Figure 8 congruent? Use Figure 8 to help you find (i) sin 300°, and (ii) cos 300°.

Check that if $270 \leqslant \theta \leqslant 360$ then

$$\sin\theta^\circ = {}^{-}\sin(360^\circ - \theta^\circ)$$

and

$$\cos\theta^\circ = \cos(360^\circ - \theta^\circ).$$

(*f*) Figure 9 summarizes what we have found about the sign of sines and cosines of angles between 0° and 360°.

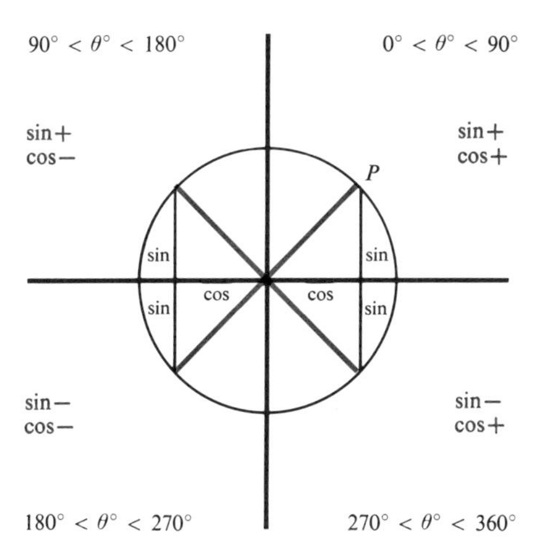

Fig. 9

What are the values of:

(i) $\sin 0^\circ$; (ii) $\cos 0^\circ$; (iii) $\sin 90^\circ$; (iv) $\cos 90^\circ$; (v) $\sin 180^\circ$;
(vi) $\cos 180^\circ$; (vii) $\sin 270^\circ$; (viii) $\cos 270^\circ$; (ix) $\sin 360^\circ$; (x) $\cos 360^\circ$?

Summary

1 In the triangle in Figure 10,

$$BC = r \sin \theta°,$$

$$AC = r \cos \theta°$$

and

$$\sin \theta° = \frac{BC}{AB}\left(\frac{\text{opposite}}{\text{hypotenuse}}\right),$$

$$\cos \theta° = \frac{AC}{AB}\left(\frac{\text{adjacent}}{\text{hypotenuse}}\right).$$

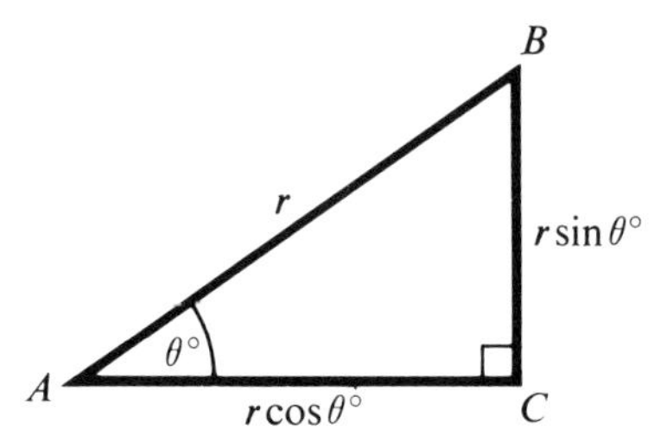

Fig. 10

2 The signs of the sine and cosine of angles between 0° and 360° are represented by Figure 9 above.

3 To calculate the sine or cosine of an angle greater than 90° we can

(i) draw a diagram like Figure 8;
(ii) calculate the acute angle between OP' and the x axis (i.e. $\angle PON$);
(iii) look up the sine or cosine of $\angle P'ON'$ in the tables;
(iv) give the correct sign.

Exercise A

1 Use sines or cosines to calculate x in each of the following triangles:

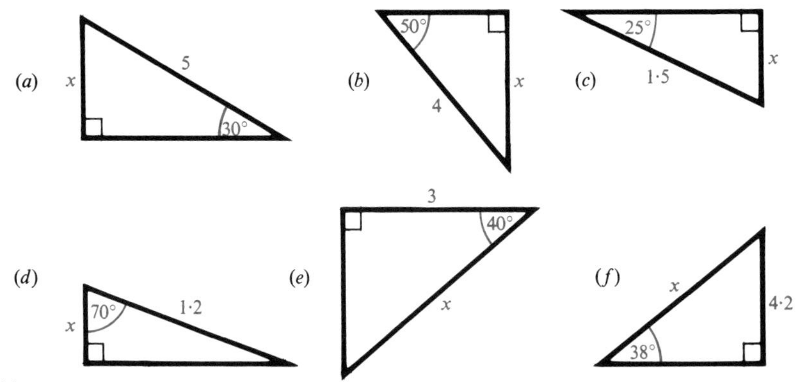

Fig. 11

2 Use your tables to find the value of:

(i) $\sin 30°$; (ii) $\cos 30°$; (iii) $\sin 57{\cdot}3°$;
(iv) $\sin 95°$; (v) $\cos 100°$; (vi) $\sin 170°$;
(vii) $\cos 160°$; (viii) $\sin 280°$; (ix) $\cos 280°$;
(x) $\sin 300°$; (xi) $\cos 330°$.

3 Find two angles for which (i) $\sin \theta° = 0{\cdot}5$; (ii) $\cos \theta° = 0{\cdot}5$; (iii) $\sin \theta° = {}^{-}0{\cdot}5$; (iv) $\cos \theta° = {}^{-}0{\cdot}5$. Are your answers the *only* possibilities?

4 Draw a circle of radius 10 cm, and draw the triangle OPN (see Figure 12). Measure PN and ON. Hence write down an approximate value for (i) $\sin 20°$; (ii) $\cos 20°$. Use your tables to check your answers. Use the same method to calculate $\sin \theta°$ and $\cos \theta°$ for $\theta = 0, 30, 60, 90, \ldots, 360$.

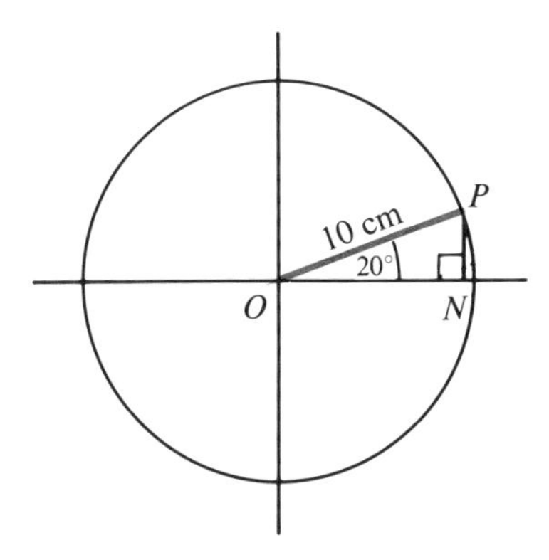

Fig. 12

Use your results to draw the graphs of f: $x \to \sin x°$ and g: $x \to \cos x°$ for $0 \leqslant x \leqslant 360$.

5 Figure 13 shows an equilateral triangle of side 2 units. Use Pythagoras' rule to show that $XA = \sqrt{3}$ units. Hence write down the value of sin 60° leaving square roots in your answer. Write down also the values of (i) sin 30°; (ii) cos 60°; (iii) cos 30°.

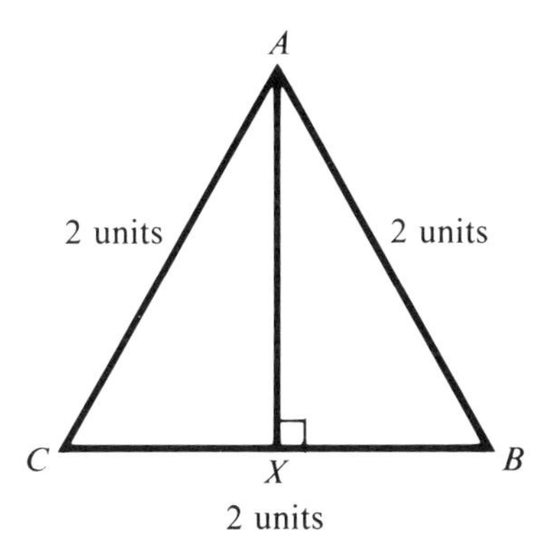

Fig. 13

6 Figure 14 shows an isosceles triangle in which $AB = BC = 1$ unit. Use Pythagoras' rule to calculate AC, giving your answer in the form $AC = \sqrt{x}$ units. Hence write down the value of (i) $\sin 45°$; (ii) $\cos 45°$ leaving square roots in your answer.

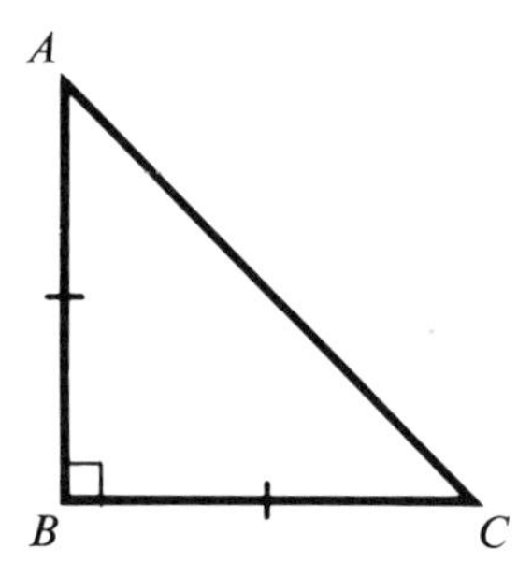

Fig. 14

7 Use Figure 15 to help you explain why $\sin(90° - \theta°) = \cos\theta°$.

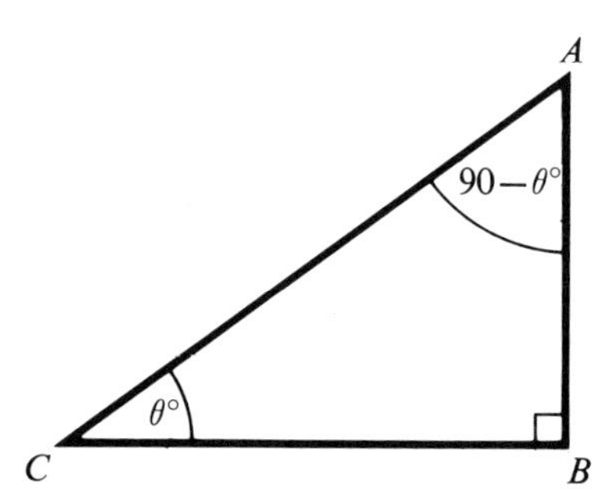

Fig. 15

If you only had sine tables, how would you find the value of cos 20°?

8 If $\sin 2\theta° = 0{\cdot}417$, calculate θ.

9 Figure 16 shows a ladder, AB, of length 6 m leaning against a vertical wall. M is the mid-point of the ladder. The base of the ladder begins to slip away from the wall. Calculate:

(i) the height of M above the ground
and (ii) the distance of M from the vertical wall, when

$$\theta = 0, 10, 20, \ldots, 80, 90.$$

Tabulate your results as follows:

θ (in degrees)	0	10	20	30	. . .	90
Height of M above ground (p)						
Distance of M from wall (q)						

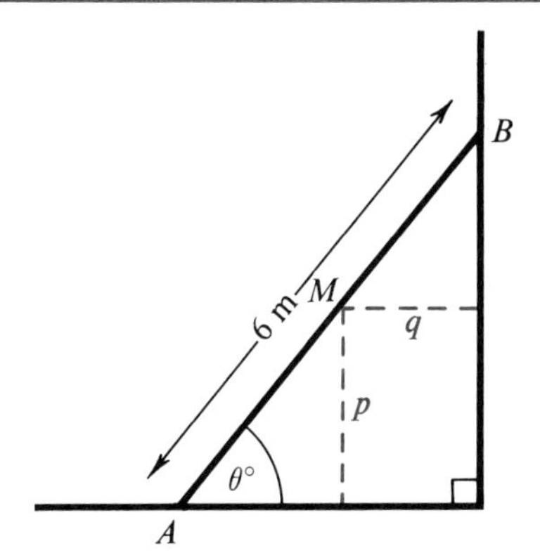

Fig. 16

Draw a graph of p against q using the same scale on both axes. What is the locus of M as the ladder slides down the wall?

2 Tangents of an angle

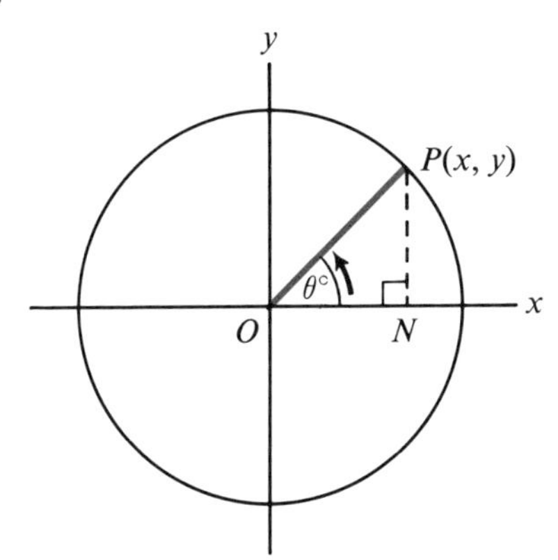

Fig. 17

(*a*) As the line segment OP in Figure 17 rotates in a positive sense from its initial position for which $\theta = 0$, the x and y coordinates of P vary. Thus the ratio $\frac{PN}{ON}$ varies as θ increases from 0 to 90.

At any time $\frac{PN}{ON}$ will have a particular value. For example, when $\theta = 30$,

$$PN = \sin\theta° = 0{\cdot}5$$

and

$$ON = \cos\theta° = 0{\cdot}867,$$

so that

$$\frac{PN}{ON} = 0{\cdot}577.$$

Use your sine and cosine tables to find the value of $\frac{PN}{ON}$ when $\theta = 10, 20, 30, 40, \ldots, 80$.

What is the value of $\frac{PN}{ON}$ when $\theta = 0$?

What happens to the value of $\frac{PN}{ON}$ as θ approaches 90?

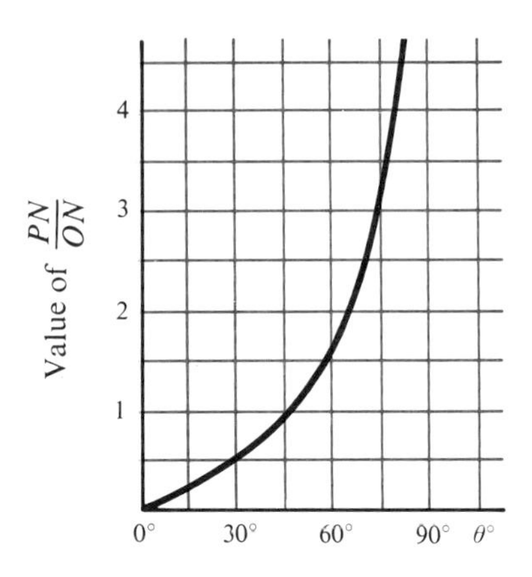

Fig. 18

Figure 18 shows the graph of $\frac{PN}{ON}$ for θ between 0 and 90.

(*b*) Now consider what happens for $90 < \theta < 180$ (see Figure 19).

In this case PN is positive and ON is negative so that $\frac{PN}{ON}$ is negative.

When $\theta = 120$, we have

$$PN = \sin 120° = \sin 60° = 0{\cdot}867$$

and

$$ON = \cos 120° = {}^{-}\cos 60° = {}^{-}0{\cdot}5.$$

Hence

$$\frac{PN}{ON} = -\frac{0{\cdot}867}{0{\cdot}5} = {}^{-}1{\cdot}734.$$

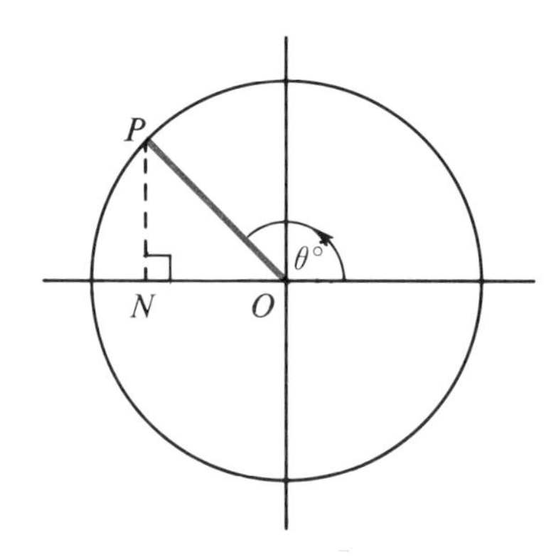

Fig. 19

Work out $\frac{PN}{ON}$ when θ is 100, 110, ..., 170 and draw a graph similar to Figure 18.

What is the value of $\frac{PN}{ON}$ when $\theta = 180$?

(*c*) Work out the values of $\frac{PN}{ON}$ for $\theta = 190, 200, \ldots, 260$. Graph your results.

What happens to the value of $\frac{PN}{ON}$ as θ approaches 270?

Now work out the values of $\frac{PN}{ON}$ for $\theta = 290, 300, \ldots, 350$ and graph your results.

What is the value of $\frac{PN}{ON}$ when $\theta = 360$?

(*d*) If you graph the values of $\frac{PN}{ON}$ for $0 \leqslant \theta \leqslant 360$ (i.e. if you draw Figure 18 and the three graphs for $90 < \theta \leqslant 180$, $180 < \theta \leqslant 270$ and $270 < \theta \leqslant 360$ on the same axis) you will obtain Figure 20.

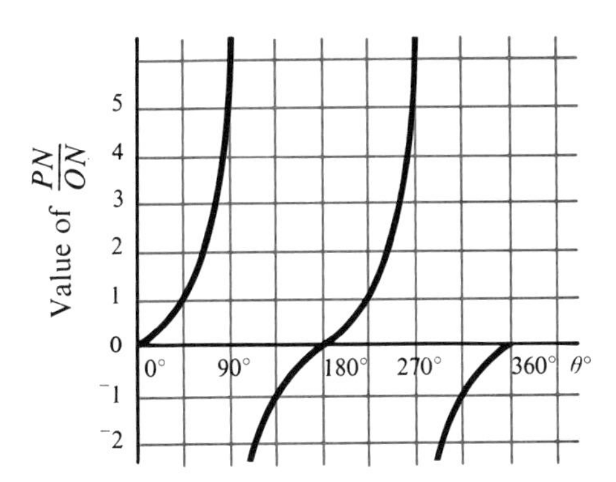

Fig. 20

The ratio $\frac{PN}{ON} = \frac{\sin\theta°}{\cos\theta°}$ is called the *tangent of* $\theta°$ and is written 'tan $\theta°$':

$$\tan\theta° = \frac{\sin\theta°}{\cos\theta°}.$$

(*e*) Figure 21 shows a triangle *OPN* and an enlargement of *OPN* scale factor *r*.

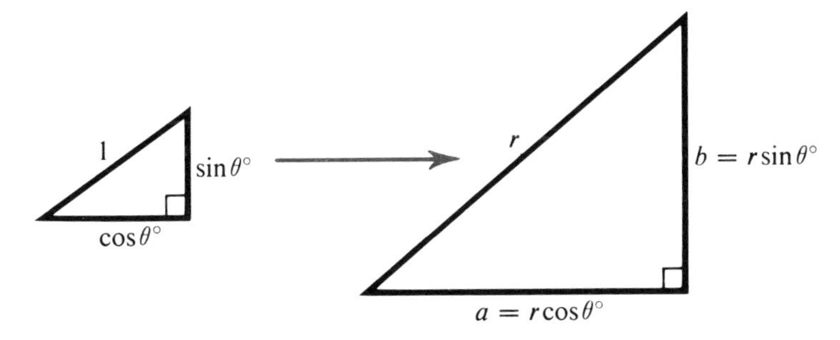

Fig. 21

Do you agree that $\tan\theta^\circ = \dfrac{r\sin\theta^\circ}{r\cos\theta^\circ} = \dfrac{b}{a}$?

[Using the terminology of Section 1(*b*), $\tan\theta^\circ = \dfrac{\text{opposite}}{\text{adjacent}}$.]

Since $\tan\theta^\circ = \dfrac{b}{a}$, then, multiplying both sides of *a*, we have

$$b = a\tan\theta^\circ$$

(see Figure 22).

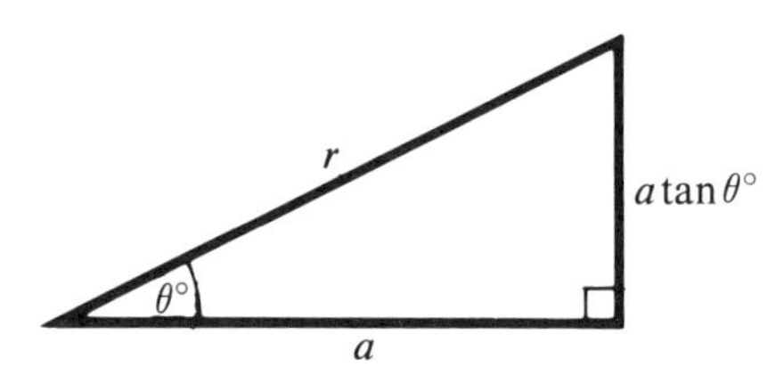

Fig. 22

(*f*) The values of $\tan\theta^\circ$ for $0 \leqslant \theta < 90$ are tabulated in your tangent tables. Use the tables to find the value of (i) tan 30°; (ii) tan 27·4°; (iii) tan 89°; (iv) tan 120°.

(*g*) Consider Figure 23. Since $\tan\theta^\circ = \dfrac{\text{opposite}}{\text{adjacent}}$, then

$$\tan\theta^\circ = \frac{AB}{BC} = \frac{4}{6} = 0{\cdot}667 \text{ (to 3 s.f.)}$$

$$\theta^\circ = 33{\cdot}7^\circ.$$

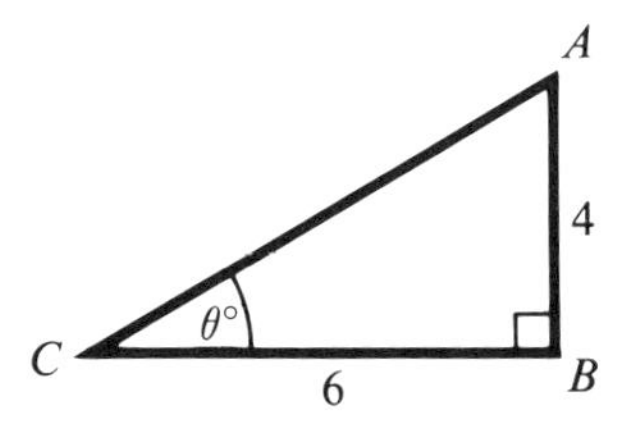

Fig. 23

Use this method to calculate θ in the three triangles in Figure 24.

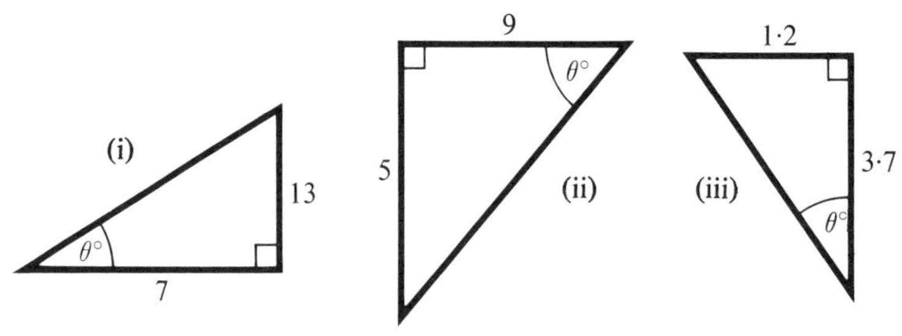

Fig. 24

(h) Use the equation $b = a\tan\theta°$ (see Figure 22) to calculate the length of AB in the triangles in Figure 25.

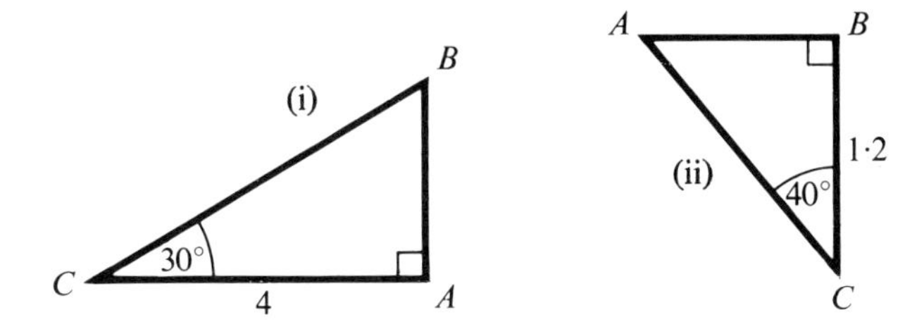

Fig. 25

Summary

1 $\tan\theta° = \dfrac{\sin\theta°}{\cos\theta°}$.

2 In triangle PQR, $\tan\theta° = \dfrac{b}{a}$, and $b = a\tan\theta°$.

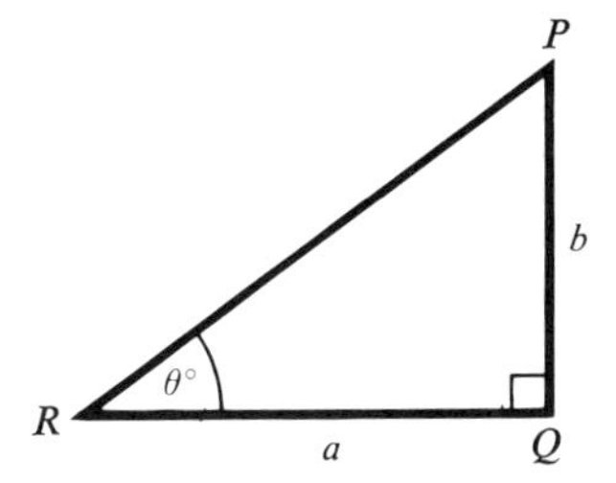

Fig. 26

3 The signs of $\tan\theta°$, for $0 \leqslant \theta \leqslant 360$, are given in Figure 27.

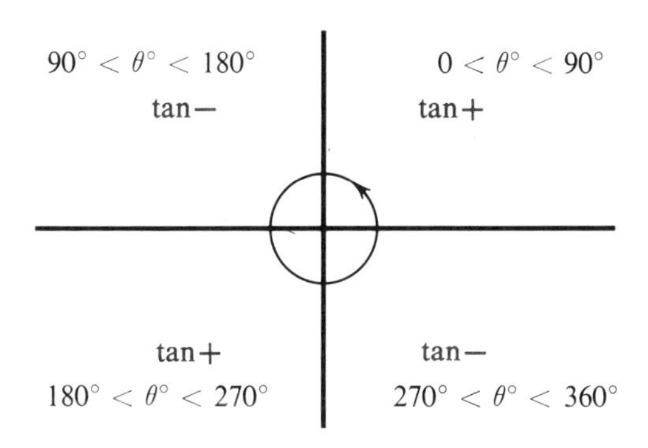

Fig. 27

Hence for $0 \leqslant \theta \leqslant 360$ we have:

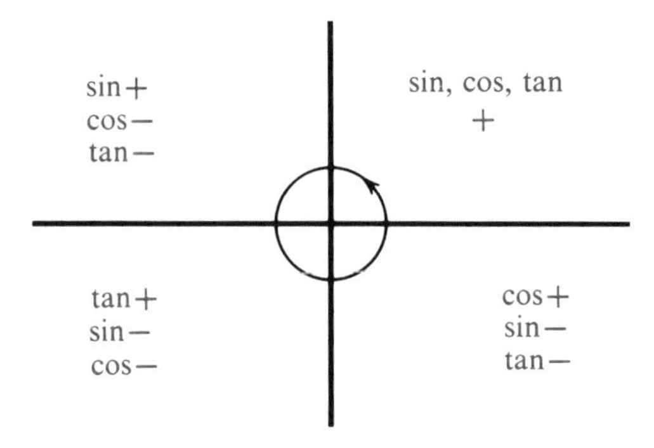

Fig. 28

Exercise B

1 Calculate θ in each of the triangles shown in Figure 29.

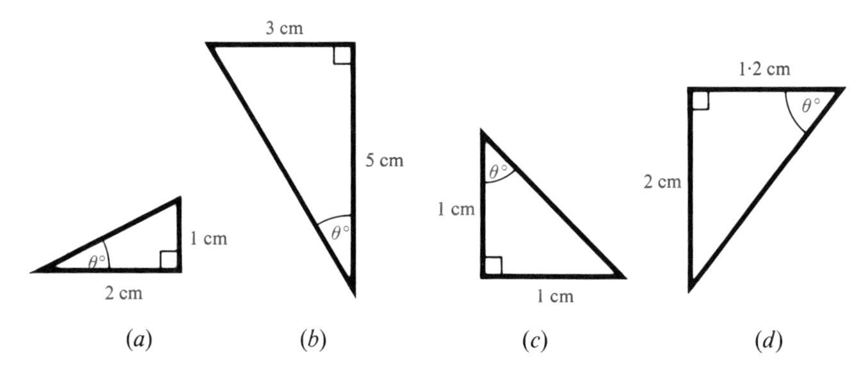

Fig. 29

2 Calculate x in each of the following triangles:

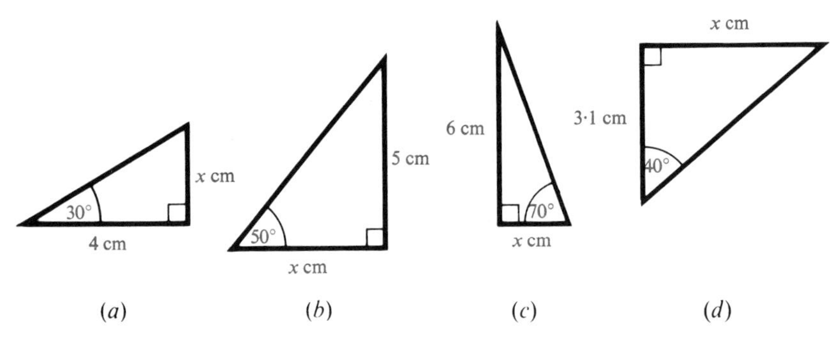

Fig. 30

3 Find two values of θ for which (i) $\tan\theta° = 0{\cdot}5$; (ii) $\tan\theta° = 1$; (iii) $\tan\theta° = 2$; (iv) $\tan\theta° = {}^-1$; (v) $\tan\theta° = {}^-0{\cdot}216$.

4 Find the value of (i) $\tan 110°$; (ii) $\tan 200°$; (iii) $\tan 170°$; (iv) $\tan 230°$.

5 Use Figures 13 and 14 (Exercise A) to write down the values of (i) $\tan 60°$; (ii) $\tan 30°$; (iii) $\tan 45°$. (Leave $\sqrt{3}$ in your answers to (i) and (ii).)

6 Calculate (i) $\tan 30° \times \tan 60°$; (ii) $\tan 20° \times \tan 70°$; (iii) $\tan 55° \times \tan 35°$. Use Figure 31 to help you write down the value of $\tan \theta° \times \tan(90° - \theta°)$. If $\tan \alpha° = x$, what is $\tan(90° - \alpha°)$ in terms of x?

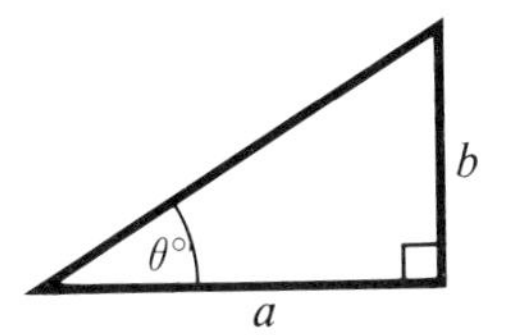

Fig. 31

7 If $\tan \theta° = \frac{1}{2}$, what is (i) $\sin \theta°$; (ii) $\cos \theta°$?

8 You are given that $\tan \theta° = \frac{3}{4}$. *Without using tables*, calculate (i) $\sin \theta°$; (ii) $\cos \theta°$. (Draw a right-angled triangle.)

9 If $\tan \theta° = \dfrac{a}{b}$, find (i) $\sin \theta°$; (ii) $\cos \theta°$ in terms of a and b.

10 Express BD in Figure 32 in terms of r and θ. Hence express DC in terms of r, θ and α. If $\theta = 40$, $\alpha = 35$ and $r = 3$ cm calculate (i) DC and (ii) AC.

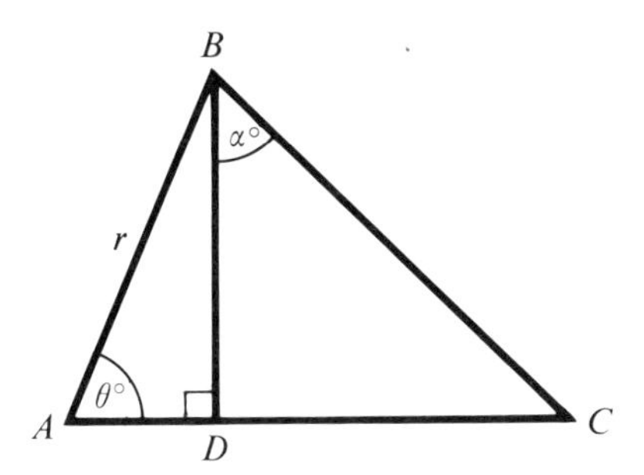

Fig. 32

11 If $0 \leqslant x \leqslant 90$, find a value of x for which

(i) $\sin x° = \tan x°$;
(ii) $\cos x° = \tan x°$;
(iii) $\sin x° = \cos x°$.

If $\sin x° = \cos x°$, what is the value of $\tan x°$?

12 (i) Solve the equation $\tan x° = 1$ for $0 \leqslant x \leqslant 360$. (The solution set contains two members.)
(ii) $f: x \to \tan x°$; $g: x \to 2x$. Find fg and gf in the form $fg: x \to \ldots$; $gf: x \to \ldots$.
(iii) Solve the equations (*a*) $\tan 2x° = 1$; (*b*) $2 \tan x° = 1$, for $0 \leqslant x \leqslant 360$.

3 Using sin, cos and tan

(*a*) Tangents, sines and cosines can be used to solve problems which can be reduced to the study of right-angled triangles. Some examples are given below.

(*b*) A surveyor wishes to find the height of a church tower (see Figure 33). He stands at a distance 100 m from the base of the tower and sets up his measuring instruments. He finds that the angle between the horizontal DB and the line DC is 17°. This angle ($\angle CDB$) is known as *the angle of elevation* of the tower from D.

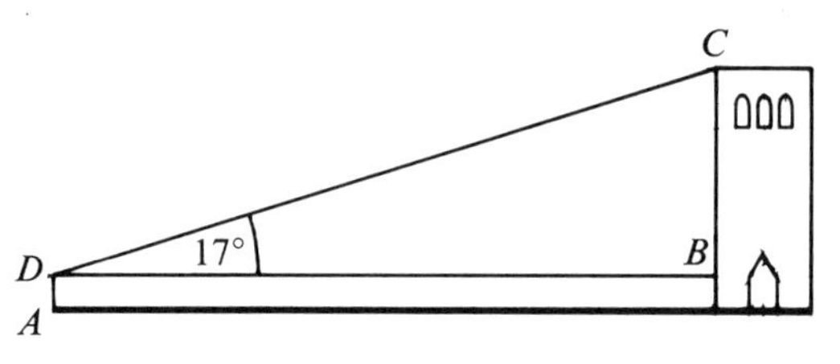

Fig. 33

To find the height of the tower we can use tangents. Since

$$CB = DB \tan 17°$$

then

$$\begin{aligned} CB &= 100 \tan 17° \text{ m} \\ &= 100 \times 0{\cdot}306 \text{ m} \\ &= 30{\cdot}6 \text{ m.} \end{aligned}$$

Hence, if the measurement of the angle of elevation was taken from a height 1 m above the ground (i.e. if $AD = 1$ m), the height of the tower is 31·6 m.

(*c*) *The angle of depression* of the base P of the oil rig in Figure 34 from the point A at the top of the cliff is 24°. What is the angle of elevation of A from P? If the height of the cliff is 50 m (i.e. if $AM = 50$ m), write down an equation involving $\tan 24°$, PM and AM. Hence calculate PM. Do you agree that the oil rig is 112 m from the base of the cliff?

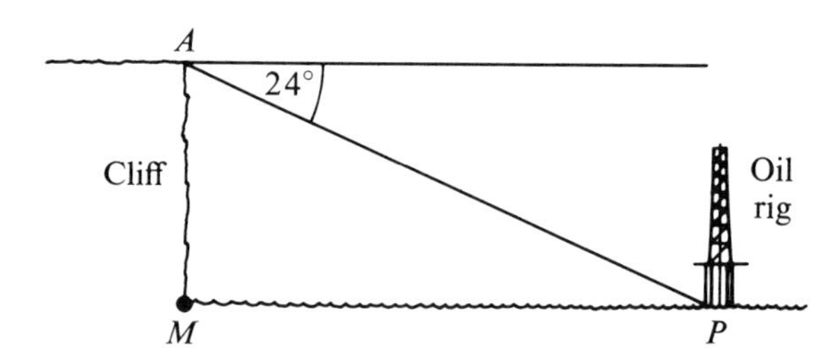

Fig. 34

(*d*) An aircraft flies from base for 600 km on a *bearing* 060° (bearings are measured in a clockwise direction from due North). It then flies 500 km on a bearing 090° (that is, due East). Suppose we wish to find the direction in which the aircraft must fly and the distance it must travel to return directly to base. The route back to base is represented by CA in Figure 35.

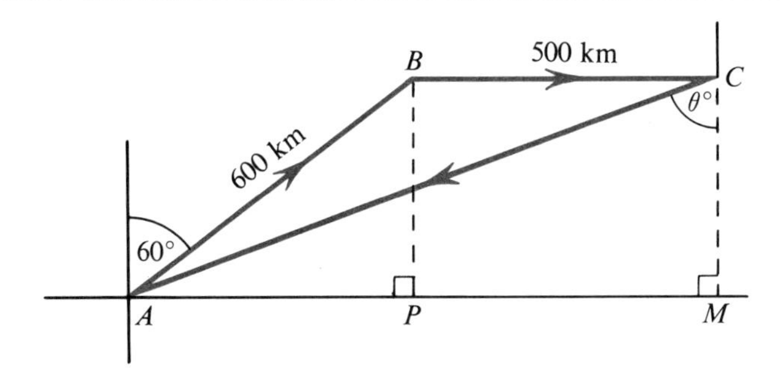

Fig. 35

To find the bearing we calculate CM and AM and then use tangents to calculate $\angle ACM$.

From triangle ABP, we have

$$\begin{aligned} BP &= 600 \sin 30° \text{ km} \\ &= 600 \times 0{\cdot}5 \text{ km} \\ &= 300 \text{ km.} \end{aligned}$$

Hence

$$CM = BP = 300 \text{ km.}$$

To calculate AM:

$$\begin{aligned} AM = AP + PM &= AP + 500 \text{ km} \\ &= (600 \cos 30° + 500) \text{ km} \\ &= (600 \times 0{\cdot}867 + 500) \text{ km} \\ &= 1020 \text{ km (to 3 S.F.).} \end{aligned}$$

Hence

$$\begin{aligned} \tan \theta° &= \frac{AM}{CM} = \frac{1020}{300} \\ &= 3{\cdot}4, \end{aligned}$$

so that $\theta = 73{\cdot}6$.

The aircraft must therefore fly on a bearing of $73{\cdot}6° + 180° = 253{\cdot}6°$.

To calculate CA, the distance the aircraft must fly, we can use

$$\cos 73{\cdot}6° = \frac{CM}{CA} = \frac{300}{CA}$$

so that

$$\begin{aligned} CA &= \frac{300}{\cos 73{\cdot}6°} \text{ km} \\ &= 1060 \text{ km (to 3 S.F.).} \end{aligned}$$

Summary

1 The angle of elevation of a point A from a point P (A is 'higher' than P) is the angle between the horizontal through P and the line through A and P. (Figure 36.)

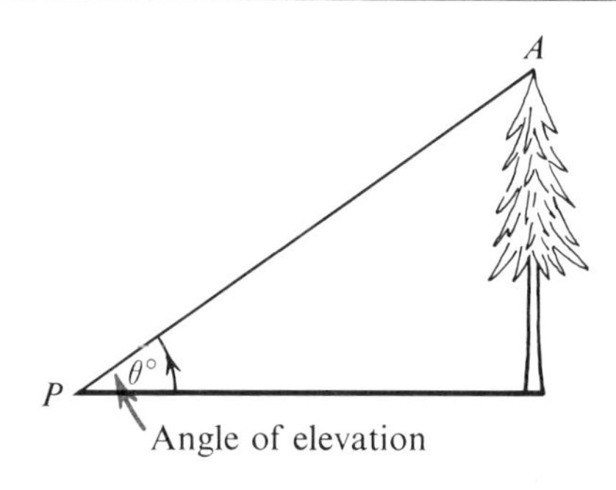

Fig. 36

2 The angle of depression (or the angle of declination) of a point A from a point P (A is 'lower' than P) is the angle between the horizontal through P and the line through A and P. (Figure 37.)

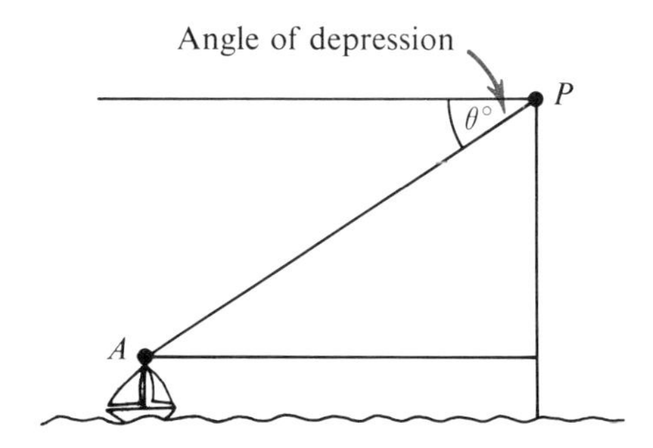

Fig. 37

Exercise C

1 The angle of elevation of the top of the Post Office tower, measured from a point 300 m from its base, is 32·2°. Calculate its height.

2 The angle of depression of a point at ground level 800 m from the Eiffel Tower, measured from the top of the tower, is 20·5°. Find the height of the tower.

3 A certain radar station can only detect aircraft with an angle of elevation, measured from the station, of more than 6°.

What is the nearest that an aircraft, flying at an altitude of 1500 m, can approach without being detected?

4 The angle of depression of the boat in Figure 38 from the point A at the top of the cliff 50 m above sea level is 17°. Calculate the distance of the boat from the base of the cliff. What is the angle of depression of the boat from A when it is a distance 100 m from the base of the cliff?

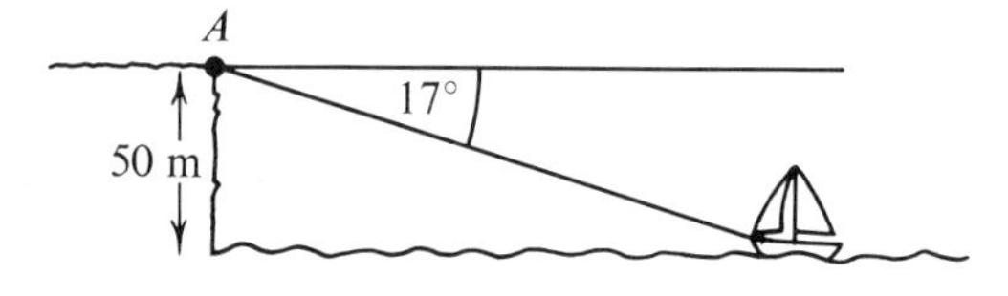

Fig. 38

5 The two towers in Figure 39 are 150 m apart. The angle of elevation of the top of Jodan tower from the top of Gable tower is 10°. If Gable tower is 30 m high, what is the height of Jodan tower?

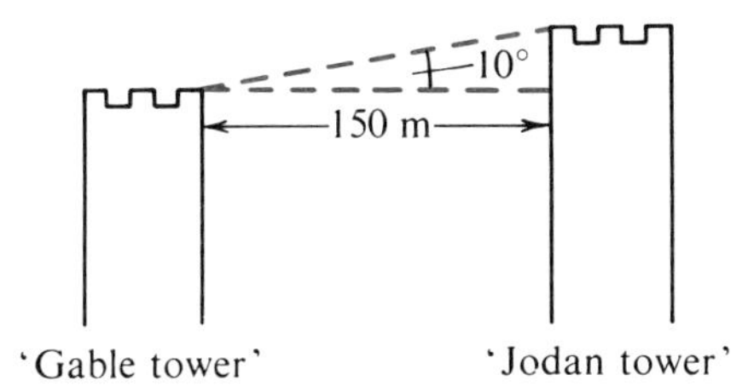

Fig. 39

6 A tree of height 20 m casts a shadow of length 35 m at a certain time of day. What is the angle of elevation of the sun at this time?
What length of shadow would a tree of height 25 m cast at the same time of day?

7 A man wishes to calculate the height of a tree on the opposite bank of a river. He stands at point A on the river bank (see Figure 40) and measures the angle

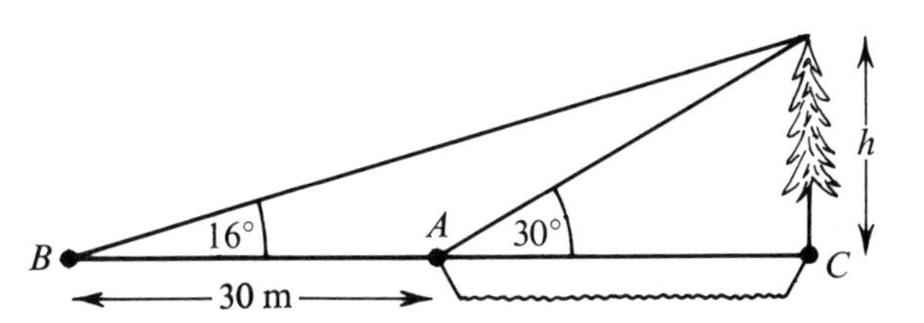

Fig. 40

of elevation of the top of the tree as 30°. He then walks 30 m from point A to point B, B lying on the straight line through A and C and measures the angle of elevation of the top of the tree as 16°. If the height of the tree is h, then $\tan 30° = \dfrac{h}{AC}$.

Write down a similar equation involving h, AC and 16°.

Solve the simultaneous equations and so find h. What is the width of the river?

8 What are the lengths of sides of an equilateral triangle of height 3 cm?

9 In Figure 41, $AB = 4$ cm, $\angle CAB = 30°$, $\angle CDB = 30°$, and $\angle DBE = 40°$. Calculate (i) CB; (ii) BD; (iii) DE.

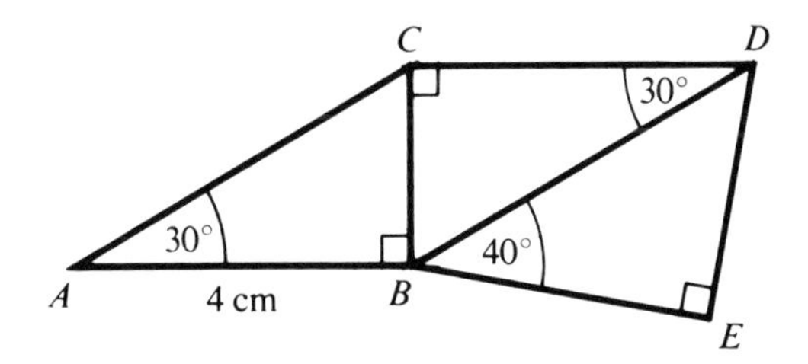

Fig. 41

10 A ship sets out from Port A on a bearing of 050° and travels in a straight line (assuming the earth to be flat!). What is the bearing of the Port from the ship once it has left Port? When the ship has travelled 50 km it changes direction and heads due East. After travelling 30 km it docks at Port B. Figure 42 represents the ship's journey.

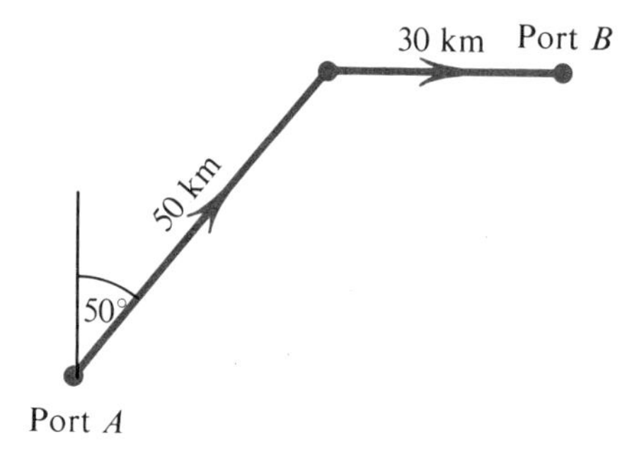

Fig. 42

(i) What is the bearing of Port A from Port B?
(ii) What is the 'straight line' distance from Port A to Port B?

11 An aircraft flies a distance of 300 km on a bearing 060° and then 500 km on a bearing 120°. Calculate its distance

(i) South; (ii) East of its starting point.

12 Two cyclists start from Rawmarsh and travel at a steady speed of 15 km per hour along straight roads which intersect each other at an angle of 30° (see Figure 43). Calculate the distance apart of the cyclists after (i) 2 hours; (ii) 3 hours. If road X runs due North, what is the bearing of the cyclist on road Y from the cyclist on road X at these two times?

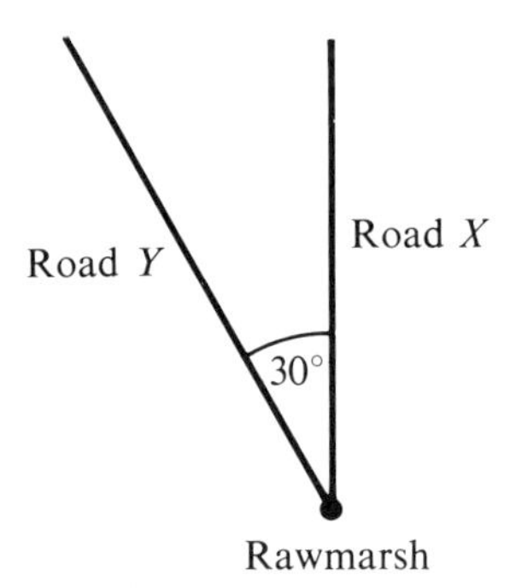

Fig. 43

4 Converting polar coordinates to Cartesian coordinates and vice versa

(a) The point P in Figure 4(a) has polar coordinates $(2, 30°)$.

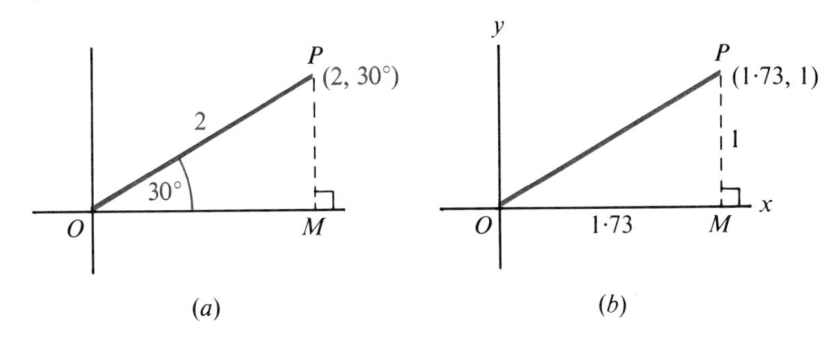

Fig. 44

In triangle PMO,

$$PM = 2\sin 30° = 2 \times \tfrac{1}{2} = 1,$$

and

$$OM = 2\cos 30° = 2 \times 0{\cdot}867 = 1{\cdot}73 \text{ (to 3 s.f.)}.$$

The *Cartesian coordinates* of P are therefore $(1{\cdot}73, 1)$ [see Figure 44(*b*)].

If the polar coordinates of a point are (i) $(2, 60°)$; (ii) $(1, 45°)$, what are the Cartesian coordinates?

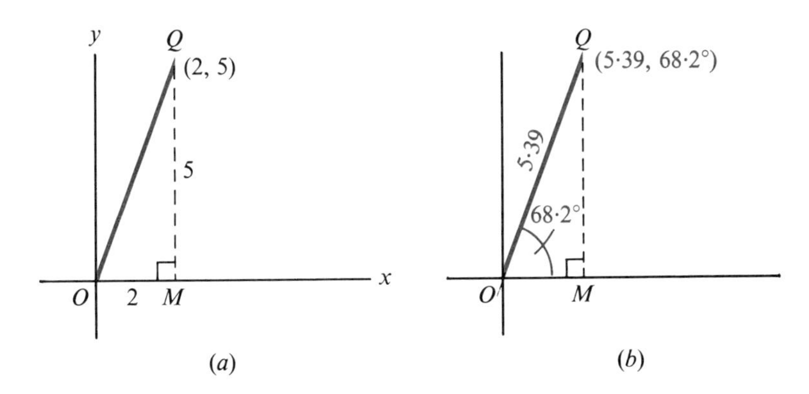

Fig. 45

(*b*) Figure 45(*a*) shows a point Q with Cartesian coordinates $(2, 5)$.

$$\tan \angle QOM = \tfrac{5}{2} = 2{\cdot}5$$

and so

$$\angle QOM = 68{\cdot}2°.$$

Also

$$QO^2 = 5^2 + 2^2 = 29.$$

Hence

$$QO = \sqrt{29} = 5{\cdot}39.$$

The polar coordinates of Q are therefore $(5{\cdot}39, 68{\cdot}2°)$ [see Figure 45(*b*)].

If the Cartesian coordinates of a point are (i) $(4, 4)$; (ii) $(3, 0)$; (iii) $(^-2, 1)$ what are the polar coordinates?

(c) The point P in Figure 46(a) has polar coordinates $(r, \theta°)$.
Do you agree that $PM = r \sin \theta°$?
Write down a similar expression for OM in terms of θ.

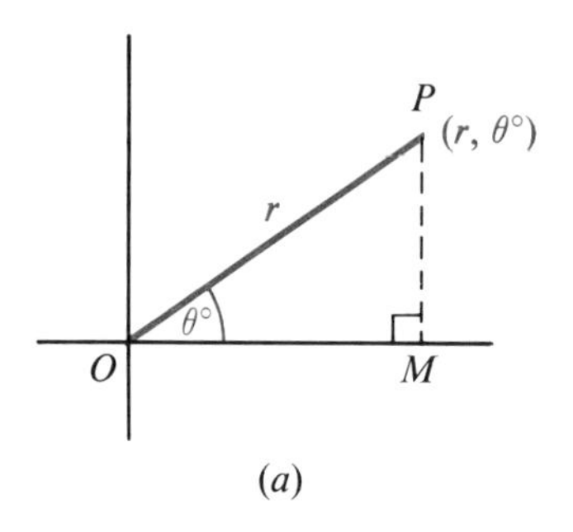

(a)

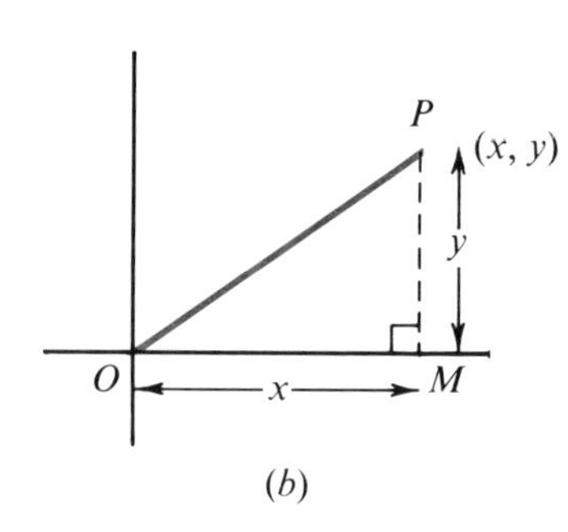

(b)

Fig. 46

Suppose P has Cartesian coordinates (x, y). Compare Figure 46(a) with Figure 46(b). We can see that:

(i) $x = OM = \mathrm{r} \cos \theta°$;
(ii) $y = PM = \mathrm{r} \sin \theta°$;
(iii) $\tan \theta° = \dfrac{PM}{OM} = \dfrac{y}{x}$.

These are, in fact, the equations we used in (c) and (d) to convert Cartesian coordinates to polar coordinates, and vice-versa.

Summary

The relationships between the polar coordinates $(r, \theta°)$ of a point P and its Cartesian coordinates (x, y) are:

(i) $x = r \cos \theta°$;
(ii) $y = r \sin \theta°$;
(iii) $\tan \theta° = \dfrac{y}{x}$.

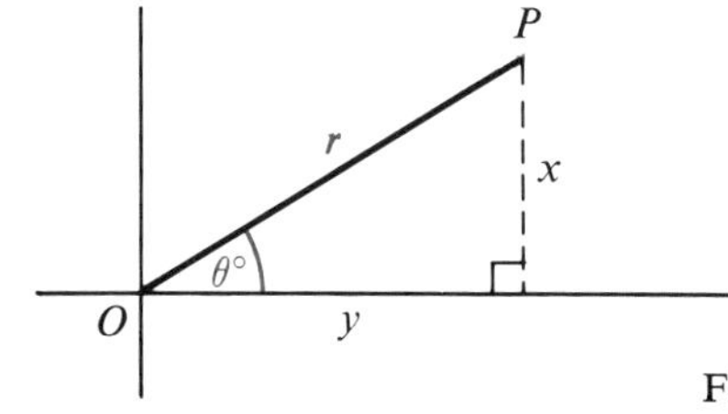

Fig. 47

Exercise D

1 Convert the following Cartesian coordinates to polar coordinates: (i) $(2, 0)$; (ii) $(0, 2)$; (iii) $(2, 2)$; (iv) $(\surd 3, 1)$; (v) $(1, \surd 3)$; (vi) $(4, 2)$; (vii) $(2, 4)$; (viii) $(^-2, 4)$; (ix) $(^-2, ^-4)$; (x) $(4, ^-2)$; (xi) $(3, 7)$; (xii) $(^-2, 9)$; (xiii) $(4, ^-7)$.

2 Convert the following polar coordinates to Cartesian coordinates: (i) $(2, 90°)$; (ii) $(1, 0°)$; (iii) $(3, ^-270°)$; (iv) $(2, 30°)$; (v) $(1, 45°)$; (vi) $(1, 135°)$; (vii) $(5, 60°)$; (viii) $(5, ^-300°)$; (ix) $(3, 170°)$.

3 (*a*) The line l in Figure 48 has Cartesian equation $x = y$. Use the equations $x = r\cos\theta°$, $y = r\sin\theta°$, to show that its polar equation is $\sin\theta° = \cos\theta°$. Hence show that its polar equation can be written as $\tan\theta° = 1$. Would it be true to say that an alternative way of writing its equation is $\theta = 45$? Explain your answer.
(*b*) What is the polar equation of the line with Cartesian equation $y = {}^{-}x$?

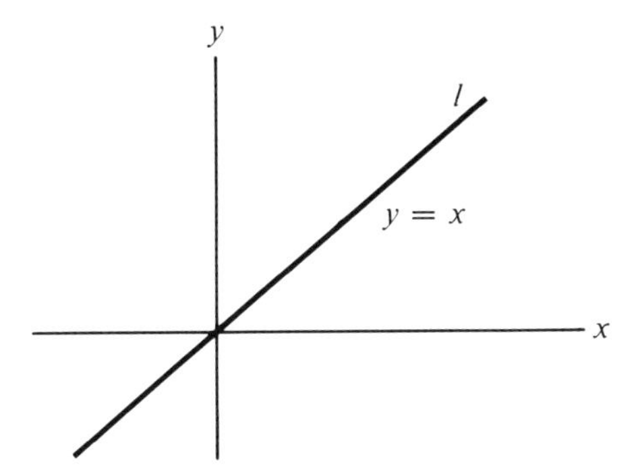

Fig. 48

4 Draw the straight lines with polar equation $\tan\theta° = \frac{1}{2}$. If the points with Cartesian coordinates $(x_1, 2)$, $(2, y_1)$, $(x_2, 4)$, $(4, y_2)$ lie on this line find x_1, y_1, x_2 and y_2. What is the Cartesian equation of the line?

5 (*a*) Graph the following: (i) $\tan\theta° = 1$; (ii) $\tan\theta° = 3$; (iii) $x = y$; (iv) $y = 3x$; (v) $\tan\theta° = {}^{-}2$.
(*b*) What is the angle $\theta°$ between the line $y = 3x$ and the positive x axis? (See Figure 49.) Write down the equation of the line in terms of $\tan\theta°$.

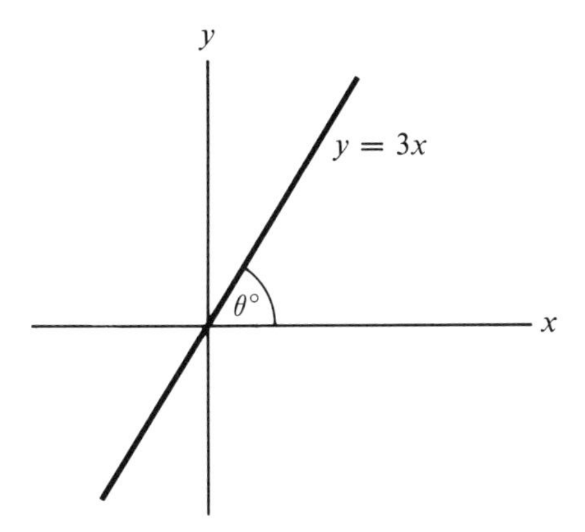

Fig. 49

6 Answer question 5(*b*) for the lines (i) $y = 5x$; (ii) $3y = 2x$.

4 Concerning Pythagoras

(*a*) For the triangle in Figure 50, Pythagoras' rule states that

$$AB^2 + BC^2 = AC^2.$$

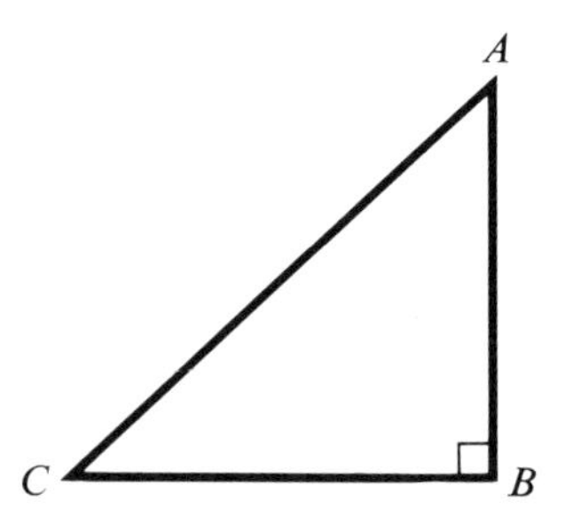

Fig. 50

Use the rule to calculate AC if $AB = 3$ cm and $BC = 6$ cm.

(b) Look at Figure 51. Using Pythagoras' rule we obtain

$$r\sin\alpha^\circ . r\sin\alpha^\circ + r\cos\alpha^\circ . r\cos\alpha^\circ = r . r,$$

that is,

$$r^2\sin^2\alpha^\circ + r^2\cos^2\alpha^\circ = r^2.$$

Dividing both sides by r^2,

$$\sin^2\alpha^\circ + \cos^2\alpha^\circ = 1.$$

[Notice that $(\sin\alpha^\circ)^2$ is written $\sin^2\alpha^\circ$; $\sin\alpha^{\circ 2}$ would mean $\sin(\alpha^\circ)^2$.]

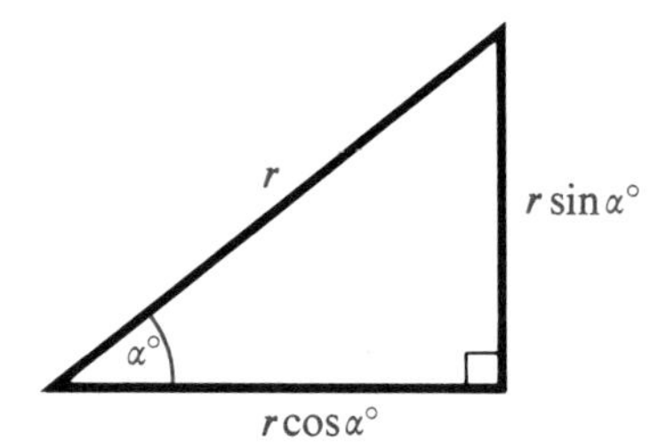

Fig. 51

(c) Figure 52 represents an enlargement of Figure 51 with scale factor $\dfrac{1}{\cos\alpha^\circ}$.

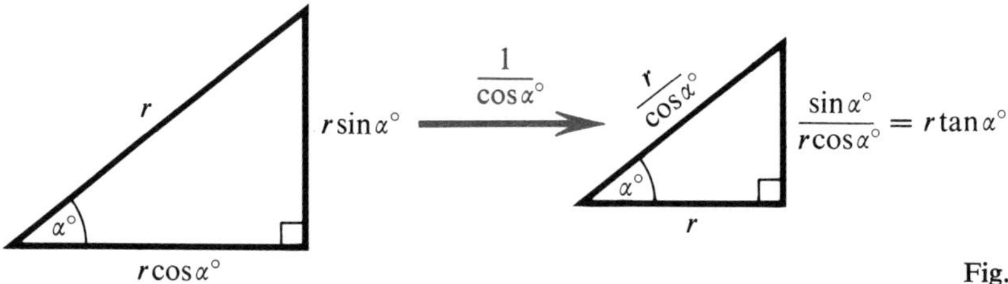

Fig. 52

Using Pythagoras' rule we have:

$$r^2\tan^2\alpha^\circ + r^2 = \frac{r^2}{\cos^2\alpha^\circ}$$

$$\tan^2\alpha^\circ + 1 = \frac{1}{\cos^2\alpha^\circ}.$$

Divide both sides of $\sin^2\alpha^\circ + \cos^2\alpha^\circ = 1$ by $\cos^2\alpha^\circ$. Did you obtain $\tan^2\alpha^\circ + 1 = \dfrac{1}{\cos^2\alpha^\circ}$?

By enlarging Figure 51 with scale factor $\dfrac{1}{\sin\alpha^\circ}$ obtain a similar expression involving $\sin\alpha^\circ$ and $\tan\alpha^\circ$.

Divide both sides of $\sin^2\alpha^\circ + \cos^2\alpha^\circ = 1$ by $\sin^2\alpha^\circ$. What do you notice?

Summary

Pythagoras' rule can be expressed in the forms:

(i) $\sin^2\alpha^\circ + \cos^2\alpha^\circ = 1$;

(ii) $1 + \tan^2\alpha^\circ = \dfrac{1}{\cos^2\alpha^\circ}$;

(iii) $1 + \dfrac{1}{\tan^2\alpha^\circ} = \dfrac{1}{\sin^2\alpha^\circ}$.

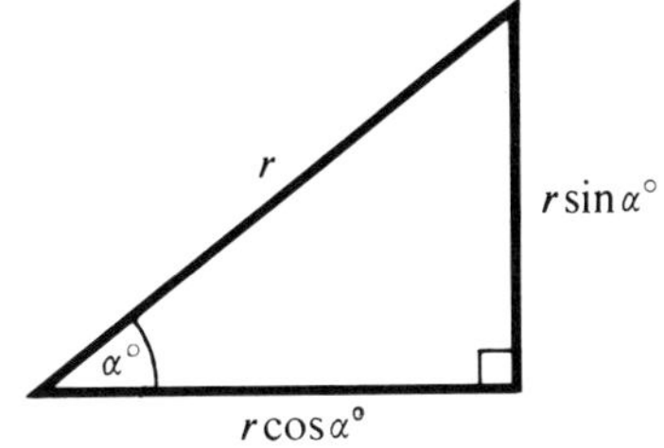

Fig. 53

Exercise E

1 From your tables find (i) $\sin 30^\circ$; (ii) $\cos 30^\circ$; (iii) $\sin 45^\circ$; (iv) $\cos 45^\circ$; (v) $\sin 70^\circ$; (vi) $\cos 70^\circ$. Calculate: (i) $\sin^2 30^\circ$; (ii) $\cos^2 30^\circ$; (iii) $\sin^2 45^\circ$; (iv) $\cos^2 45^\circ$; (v) $\sin^2 70^\circ$; (vi) $\cos^2 70^\circ$. Use your answer to calculate the value of $\sin^2\theta^\circ + \cos^2\theta^\circ$ for $\theta = 30$, 45 and 70. Is $\sin^2\theta^\circ + \cos^2\theta^\circ = 1$ in each case? Why wouldn't you expect to obtain the result $\sin^2\theta^\circ + \cos^2\theta^\circ = 1$ from your tables?

2 If $\sin\theta^\circ = \frac{1}{2}$, use the expression $\sin^2\theta^\circ + \cos^2\theta^\circ = 1$ to calculate $\cos\theta^\circ$ (you should obtain two answers).

3 Use equation (ii) in the summary to calculate the values of $\tan\theta^\circ$ when $\cos\theta^\circ = \frac{1}{2}$.

4 The equation of a circle of radius 2 in Cartesian form is $x^2 + y^2 = 4$ (see Figure 54). Use the equations $x = r\sin\theta^\circ$, $y = r\cos\theta^\circ$ to show that its equation can also be written $r = 2$.

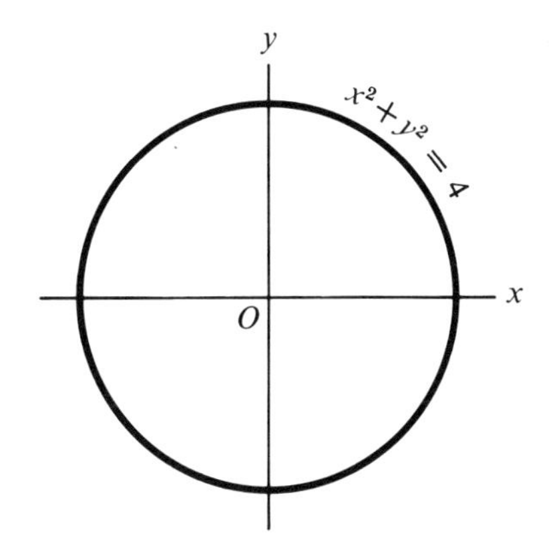

Fig. 54

'It appears that our troops are outnumbered by a good ratio.'

6 Ratio, proportion and application of slide rule

1 Ratio

(*a*) In 1415, Henry V led the English army to victory over the French at Agincourt. The English army consisted of 1000 horsemen, 6000 archers and 3000 men on foot; the French army consisted of 7500 horsemen, 500 archers and 32 000 men on foot.

The English army had a total force of 10 000 men. How many men did the French army have?

Do you agree that there were four times as many Frenchmen as Englishmen, that is, the ratio of the number of Frenchmen to the number of Englishmen was 40 000 to 10 000 or 4 to 1?

What was the ratio of (i) the number of Englishmen on foot to the number of Frenchmen on foot; (ii) the number of French archers to the number of English archers; (iii) the number of English horsemen to the number of French horsemen?

Although the English were outnumbered by 4 to 1, they won a convincing victory. This was mainly due to the torrential rain which caused the French horses to lose their footing and fall in the mud. The English archers, who outnumbered the French archers by 12 to 1, were then able to exercise their advantage to the full.

(b) If we wish to find the ratio of $\frac{1}{2}$ metre to 10 metres we can:

(i) work in metres so that the ratio is $\frac{1}{2}$ to 10, which equals 1 to 20;

(ii) work in centimetres so that the ratio is 50 to 1000, which also equals 1 to 20.

What is the ratio when working in millimetres?

Notice that ratio compares quantities measured in the *same units* and that it has *no units* itself.

Instead of using the word 'to' in stating a ratio we can use the symbol ':' and so write 1 to 20 as 1:20.

Since the ratio is 1:20, the first length is $\frac{1}{20}$ of the second length. This means that with every ratio there is an associated fraction. For example, the fraction associated with the ratio 4:14 is $\frac{4}{14}$ or $\frac{2}{7}$.

What fractions are associated with (i) 2:3, (ii) 3:2, (iii) $\frac{1}{2}$:5, (iv) 5 to $\frac{1}{2}$?

(c) Figure 1 shows a rectangle $ABCD$ and its image under an enlargement centre O and scale factor 3.

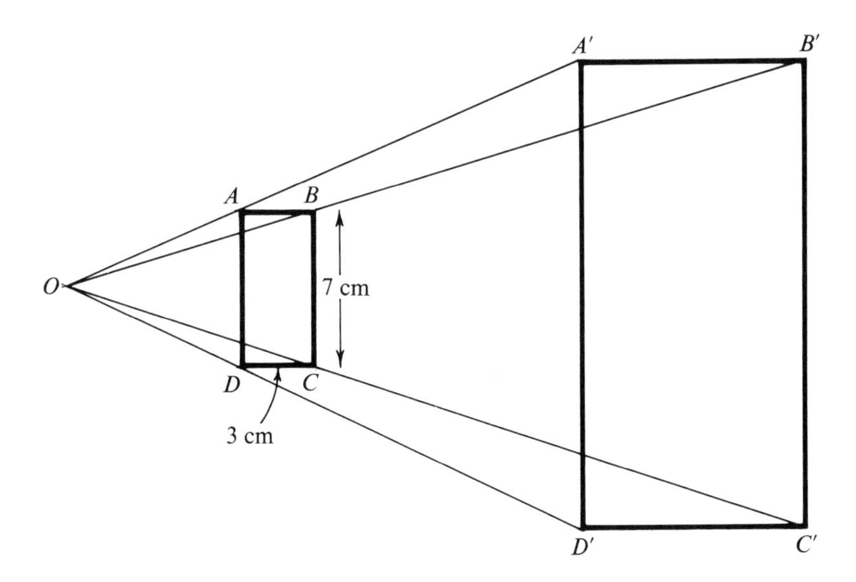

Fig. 1

Write down the associated fractions for the following ratios:

(i) $A'O:AO$;

(ii) $OD:OD'$;

(iii) $BC:B'C'$;

(iv) perimeter of $A'B'C'D'$ to the perimeter of $ABCD$;

(v) area of $ABCD$ to the area of $A'B'C'D'$.

Exercise A

1 Calculate the ratio and the associated fraction of the following quantities:

(*a*) 15 cm^3 to 900 cm^3; (*b*) 17 to 51;
(*c*) 250 g to 2 kg; (*d*) 56 p to £4·48;
(*e*) 15 cm to 200 m.

2 In a sale, prices are reduced in the ratio 3:5. Calculate the sale prices of the articles whose ordinary prices are:

(*a*) £2; (*b*) £1·25; (*c*) 35p.

3 In what ratio must 36 be increased to become 45?

4 In what ratio must 320 g be decreased to become 200 g?

5 Two distances are in the ratio 12:7. If the longer distance is 42 km, what is the shorter distance?

6 If $d = 1\frac{1}{3}L$ and the value of d is to be doubled, state the ratio of the new value of L to the old.

2 Direct proportion

(*a*) Suppose that a shopkeeper buys 20 cases of whisky for £640 and that we wish to find the cost of 30 cases, assuming that no discount is given for large orders.

One way of doing this is to calculate the cost of 1 case (£$\frac{640}{20}$ = £32) and then multiply this by 30 to obtain £960.

Another way is to use the idea of ratio. Since the ratio of the given number of cases to the required number is 20:30 or 2:3, we need to find the cost of $\frac{3}{2}$ times as many cases. Therefore the cost of 30 cases is

$$£640 \times \tfrac{3}{2} = £960.$$

Use the ratio method to find the cost of (i) 50 cases, (ii) 105 cases, (iii) 10 cases.

(*b*) You should now have found the cost of 10, 20, 30, 50 and 105 cases and so you have the following ordered sets of numbers:

number of cases (n) {10, 20, 30, 50, 105}

cost in £ (c) {320, 640, 960, 1600, 3360}.

If the number of cases is multiplied by some number, the cost in £ is multiplied by the *same* number. For example, trebling the number of cases trebles the cost. When two quantities vary in this way they are said to be directly *proportional* to each other. Thus n is directly proportional to c and c is directly proportional to n.

(*c*) If y is directly proportional to x, fill in the blanks in the following table:

x	7	14	21	35	42
y	9			45	

Exercise B

1 If a set of 30 mathematics text books cost £24 how much would a set of (i) 20; (ii) 35; (iii) 12; (iv) 40 cost?

2 Assuming that y is directly proportional to x, fill in the blanks in the following table:

x	8	16	24	48	64
y	14		42		

3 Repeat Question 2 for the following table:

x	6	15	24	36	84
y	15		60		

4 Repeat Question 2 for the following table:

x	3		12		
y	5	15	20	30	45

5 The extension in the length of a spring is directly proportional to the mass applied to the spring. A spring 26 cm long stretches to a length of 29 cm when it supports a mass of 5 kg. What will be its length when it supports (i) 9 kg; (ii) 750 g?

6 1 cm³ of copper has a mass of 8·8 g and 1 cm³ of aluminium a mass of 2·7 g. What should the mass of a copper saucepan be if an aluminium saucepan of the same shape and size has a mass of 0·75 kg?

3 Scale factors

(*a*) Look at the following table:

x	4	2	3	7	5	6
y	10	5	$7\frac{1}{2}$	$17\frac{1}{2}$	$12\frac{1}{2}$	15

Do you think that x and y are directly proportional to each other?

Let us now consider the ratio of corresponding pairs of values.

The ratio for the first pair is 4:10 or 2:5. What is the ratio for each of the other pairs?

When a ratio is written in the form $1:n$, n can be thought of as a scale factor. If we write the ratio for the first pair, 4:10, in the form $1:n$ then we obtain the ratio $1:2\frac{1}{2}$ and so $2\frac{1}{2}$ is the scale factor.

What can you say about the scale factors for all the corresponding pairs of values?

When two quantities are directly proportional *every* value of one quantity is connected to the corresponding value of the other quantity by the *same scale factor*:

x	4	2	3	7	5	6
↓	↓ $\times 2\frac{1}{2}$	↓ $\times 2\frac{1}{2}$	↓ $\times 2\frac{1}{2}$	↓ $\times 2\frac{1}{2}$	↓ $\times 2\frac{1}{2}$	↓ $\times 2\frac{1}{2}$
y	10	5	$7\frac{1}{2}$	$17\frac{1}{2}$	$12\frac{1}{2}$	15

In the example above, there is a constant scale factor of $2\frac{1}{2}$ and we can write

$$y = 2\tfrac{1}{2}x.$$

(*b*) Find the scale factors for the corresponding pairs of values in Table 1 and hence say whether or not d and t are directly proportional to each other.

TABLE 1

d	2	8	24	48	60
t	1	4	12	24	30

Express t in terms of d.

(*c*) Find the scale factors for the corresponding pairs of values in Table 2.

TABLE 2

u	8	2	6	12	4
v	10	2·5	7·5	16	5

Are u and v directly proportional to each other?

Can you express v in terms of u?

(*d*) In general, if two quantities, p and q, are directly proportional to each other then they can be linked by an equation of the form

$$p = kq,$$

where k is the *constant* scale factor.

Exercise C

1 State in which of the following examples the first quantity is directly proportional to the second:

(*a*) the mass of a rope, the length of the rope;
(*b*) the value of a 'silver coin', its mass;
(*c*) the height of a child, the mass of the child;
(*d*) the area of a wall, the cost of painting it.

2 In the following equations which are the quantities that are directly proportional to each other and what is the constant scale factor linking them?

(*a*) $P = 10Q$; (*b*) $C = 2\pi r$; (*c*) $V = 9{\cdot}8t$.

3 In the example of the whisky cases (the table is given below) find the scale factor and so form an equation linking c and n.

Number of cases (n)	10	20	30	50	105
Cost in £ (c)	320	640	960	1600	3360

4 Assuming that y is directly proportional to x, fill in the blanks in the following table:

x	4	8	24	28	32	44
y			42			

Form an equation between x and y.

4 Using the slide rule

(*a*) Look at Table 3. Investigate whether a and b are directly proportional to each other.

TABLE 3

a	1·2	2	2·5	4	4·5
b	2·64	4·4	5·5	8·8	9·9

It is unnecessary to calculate each scale factor individually; we can decide whether or not a and b are directly proportional by using a slide rule.

Place 2·64 on the C scale against 1·2 on the D scale of your slide rule. Keeping the rule fixed in this position, move the cursor so that the cursor line is over the 2 on the D scale as shown in Figure 2.

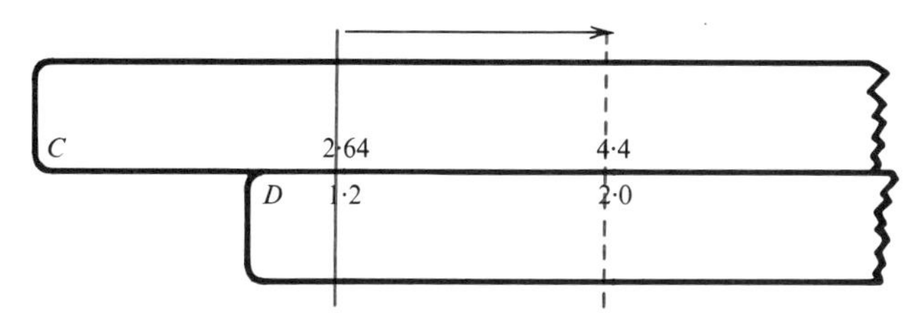

Fig. 2

You should find that 4·4 is the corresponding number on the C scale.

Move the cursor line over 2·5, 4 and 4·5 on the D scale in turn. What do you notice?

The constant scale factor can be obtained by reading the number on the C scale opposite the 1 on the D scale.

(*b*) Now consider the values of c and d given in Table 4.

TABLE 4

c	5	6·5	7·8	9·0	13·0	20·0
d	1·92	2·5	3·0	3·46	5·0	7·7

Use your slide rule to check that c and d are directly proportional to each other. What difficulty arises when you attempt to read the numbers on the C scale corresponding to 13·0 and 20·0 on the D scale?

What is the constant scale factor?

Exercise D

1 Use your slide rule to find whether the following pairs of quantities are directly proportional. If they are, state the scale factor.

(*a*)

p	4·5	6·3	8·1	19·5	24·3
q	3	4·2	5·4	13	16·2

(*b*)

x	1·8	2·7	7·5	9·55	14·6
y	1·32	1·98	5·5	7	10·7

(*c*)

s	1·45	4·2	5·1	6·1	9·0
t	2·38	2·56	8·5	9·4	14·8

(*d*)

u	1.55	4·0	6·2	6·7
v	5·0	12·9	20	21·6

5 Multipliers

(*a*) When discussing the example in Section 2 about the cost of whisky cases, we formed two ordered sets: the set of the numbers of cases, N, and the set of costs, C. So

$$N = \{10, 20, 30, 50, 105\}$$

and

$$C = \{320, 640, 960, 1600, 3360\}.$$

Let us now take pairs of members within the set N and compare them with the corresponding pairs of members within C.

The ratio of the first member of N to the second member is 10:20 or 1:2 and we say that the *multiplier* connecting the first and second members of N is 2.

Check that the multiplier connecting the second and third members is $\frac{3}{2}$, that connecting the third and fourth members is $\frac{5}{3}$ and that connecting the fourth and fifth members is $\frac{21}{10}$.

The red numbers over the arrows in Figure 3 are the multipliers for N:

$$\left\{ 10 \xrightarrow{\times 2} 20 \xrightarrow{\times \frac{3}{2}} 30 \xrightarrow{\times \frac{5}{3}} 50 \xrightarrow{\times \frac{21}{10}} 105 \right\}$$

Fig. 3

These multipliers form a new set

$$M_N = \{2, \tfrac{3}{2}, \tfrac{5}{3}, \tfrac{21}{10}\}.$$

Find the multipliers for C, that is, find the set M_C.

Do you agree that $M_N = M_C$?

(*b*) We know that the numbers of cases of whisky and the costs in £ are directly proportional to each other. We therefore say that N and C are *proportional sets*.

We have seen that $M_N = M_C$ and this suggests that two sets are proportional when the sets of multipliers are equal.

(*c*) Find the multipliers for the ordered sets

$$A = \{4, 2, 3, 7, 5, 6\}$$

and

$$B = \{10, 5, 7\tfrac{1}{2}, 17\tfrac{1}{2}, 12\tfrac{1}{2}, 15\}$$

which we used in Section 3(*a*).

Is $M_A = M_B$?

Does your result support the suggestion in (*b*)?

(*d*) Check that the ordered sets

$$C = \{3, 5, 8, 12, 15\}$$

and

$$D = \{9, 15, 24, 38, 44\}$$

are not proportional sets and that $M_C \neq M_D$.

Example 1

Find the missing members of the following pairs of ordered sets given that the sets are proportional.

$$P = \{8, 4, 12, 9\}, \qquad Q = \{10, *, *, *\}.$$

Method 1 Scale Factors Since the sets are ordered we know that 8 corresponds to 10. The scale factor of the two sets is therefore 8:10 or $1:1\tfrac{1}{4}$.

The sets can be arranged like this:

$$\begin{array}{cccccccccc} \{ & 8 & & 4 & & 12 & & 9 & & \} \\ & \downarrow & \times 1\tfrac{1}{4} & \downarrow & \times 1\tfrac{1}{4} & \downarrow & \times 1\tfrac{1}{4} & \downarrow & \times 1\tfrac{1}{4} & \\ \{ & 10 & & & & & & & & \} \end{array}$$

The next member of the set Q is $1\tfrac{1}{4} \times 4 = 5$. What are the other members? Complete the set $Q = \{10, 5, \quad, \quad\}$.

Method 2 Multipliers In set P, the first member is 8 and the second member is 4 so the multiplier connecting these members is $\frac{1}{2}$. The member in set Q corresponding to 4 in set P must be $10 \times \frac{1}{2}$ which equals 5.

$$8 \xrightarrow{\times\frac{1}{2}} 4 \xrightarrow{\times 3} 12 \xrightarrow{\times\frac{3}{4}} 9$$

$$10 \xrightarrow{\times\frac{1}{2}} 5 \xrightarrow{\times 3} \quad \xrightarrow{\times\frac{3}{4}}$$

Work out the two remaining members of Q.

Do you get the same result as by method 1?

(*e*) The method of multipliers is very useful when comparing sets which are *not* measured in the same units. Consider the following example.

Four copper rods were measured and weighed. The results formed two ordered sets: L, the set of lengths measured in centimetres and W, the set of masses measured in grammes.

$L = \{1{\cdot}5, 2, 5, 6\}$ and $W = \{13{\cdot}5, 18, 45, 54\}$.

The set of multipliers for set L is:

$$M_L = \{\tfrac{4}{3}, \tfrac{5}{2}, \tfrac{6}{5}\}.$$

Form the set M_W.

Are the sets L and W directly proportional?

Find a relation between the lengths and masses of the copper rods.

Exercise E

In all the following examples, the sets are ordered.

1 Set $P = \{6, {}^{-}5\}$. Write down the set Q where the scale factor of the mapping $P \rightarrow Q$ is:

(i) 7; (ii) $\frac{3}{4}$; (iii) $^{-}8$.

2 $K = \{3, 6, 12\}$ and $L = \{5, x, y\}$ are proportional sets. Find x and y. Did you use multipliers in this question rather than the scale factor? If so, why? What is the scale factor?

3 Given the set $\{4, 12, 60, 30, 3000\}$ complete the following sets which are proportional to it:

(*a*) {5, *, *, *, *}, (*b*) {*, *, *, 5, *}, (*c*) {*, 5, *, *, *}.

Do not use your slide rule. Discuss in each case, whether it is better to use the scale factor or multipliers.

4 Use your slide rule to check whether the following table gives values consistent with proportional sets.

x	20	25	45	50
y	36	45	81	90

If the answer is yes, then state the scale factor.

5 Use your slide rule to discover which of the following sets are proportional. If they are proportional, state the scale factor.

(*a*) $\{3\cdot5, 4\cdot6, 6\cdot1, 7\cdot4\}$ and $\{5\cdot25, 6\cdot9, 9\cdot15, 11\cdot1\}$.
(*b*) $\{12\cdot7, 17\cdot4, 30, 63\}$ and $\{29\cdot2, 40, 69, 147\}$.
(*c*) $\{1\cdot6, 3\cdot0, 4\cdot6, 9\cdot5\}$ and $\{1\cdot12, 2\cdot1, 3\cdot22, 6\cdot65\}$.
(*d*) $\{2, 4\cdot8, 6\cdot5, 9\cdot0\}$ and $\{1\cdot5, 3\cdot6, 4\cdot95, 6\cdot75\}$.

6 The sets $\{a,b,c\}$ and $\{3a,q,r\}$ are proportional. Write down the scale factor and find expressions for q and r. If $q=6$, $r=8$, find b and c. Can you find a?

7 In Figures 4(*a*) and 4(*b*), arrows indicate parallel lines. Calculate x and y.

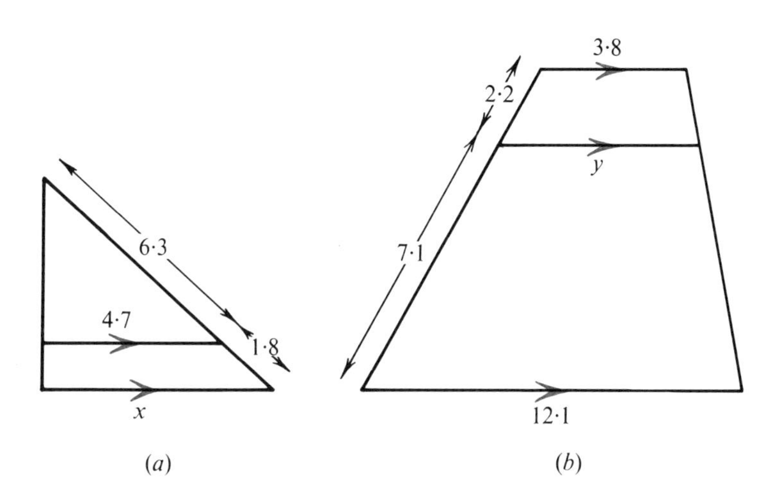

Fig. 4

6 Proportions

(*a*) Consider the two ordered sets:

$$X=\{5,8,9,11\} \quad \text{and} \quad Y=\{75,192,243,363\}.$$

Notice that $M_X=\{\frac{8}{5},\frac{9}{8},\frac{11}{9}\}$.
Find M_Y. Is $M_X=M_Y$?
Are these sets directly proportional?
You should have found that X and Y are not directly proportional.
(*b*) By squaring the elements of set X we form a new set: $\{25,64,81,121\}$.
The notation we shall use is that if in a set P every element is raised to the kth power, the new set formed is denoted by P^k. Hence in this example $X^2=\{25,64,81,121\}$.
List the members of M_{X^2} and compare M_{X^2} with M_Y. What do you notice?
Can you suggest how the members of Y are related to the members of X^2?
(*c*) Since Y is directly proportional to X^2 there is a relation of the form $y=kx^2$ where x^2 denotes any member of X^2, and y denotes the corresponding member of Y. Find k by comparing corresponding members of X^2 and Y.

(*d*) P and Q are two ordered sets:

$$P = \{8, 6, 12, 2\}; \qquad Q = \{3, 4, 2, 12\}.$$

The sets of multipliers associated with these sets are

$$M_P = \{\tfrac{6}{8}, \tfrac{12}{6}, \tfrac{2}{12}\}; \qquad M_Q = \{\tfrac{4}{3}, \tfrac{2}{4}, \tfrac{12}{3}\}.$$

Does $M_P = M_Q$?

Can you see any relation between M_P and M_Q?

(*e*) You should have noticed that if each element of M_Q is inverted (turned upside down) we form the set:

$$M_{Q^{-1}} = \{\tfrac{3}{4}, \tfrac{4}{2}, \tfrac{2}{12}\} \qquad \text{and} \qquad M_{Q^{-1}} = M_P.$$

This suggests that if the members of set Q are inverted then there will be a relation between the members of P and the members of Q^{-1}. Find the reciprocal of each member of set Q and then find the ratio between corresponding members of the two sets P and Q^{-1}.

What do you notice?

The relation between P and Q can be expressed by $p = \dfrac{k}{q}$, where p denotes any member of P and $\dfrac{1}{q}$ the corresponding member of Q^{-1}.

Find the value of k.

(*f*) We have considered relations between two sets which can be expressed in the forms:

$$\text{(i) } y = kx; \qquad \text{(ii) } y = kx^2; \qquad \text{(iii) } y = \frac{k}{x}.$$

The main relations between two sets of values that you are likely to meet are:

(i) Direct function	y proportional to x	which can	$y = kx$
(ii) Square function	y proportional to x^2	be	$y = kx^2$
(iii) Reciprocal function	y proportional to $\dfrac{1}{x}$	expressed in the	$y = \dfrac{k}{x}$
(iv) Cube function	y proportional to x^3	form	$y = kx^3$

Summary

Ratio compares like quantities. For example, 5 minutes and one hour are in the ratio of $5:60 = 1:12$. Ratio has no units.

Proportion. The ordered sets $A = \{2, 3, 5, 8\}$ and $B = \{6, 9, 15, 24\}$ are proportional. The scale factor is the common ratio of corresponding members of the sets. It is used to map the members of A onto the members of B. In this example $A \xrightarrow{\times 3} B$; the scale factor is 3. A *multiplier* is used to map the first member of A onto the second member of A that is $\frac{3}{2} \times 2 = 3$. Since the sets are proportional the same multiplier maps the first member of B onto the second member of B that is $\frac{3}{2} \times 6 = 9$.

A different multiplier maps the second members onto the third, etc.

MULTIPLIERS

$$\begin{array}{llcccccccl}
\text{Set } A & \{ & 2 & \xrightarrow{\times\frac{3}{2}} & 3 & \xrightarrow{\times\frac{5}{3}} & 5 & \xrightarrow{\times\frac{8}{5}} & 8 & \} \\
\text{SCALE FACTOR} & & \downarrow\times 3 & & \downarrow\times 3 & & \downarrow\times 3 & & \downarrow\times 3 & \\
\text{Set } B & \{ & 6 & \xrightarrow{\times\frac{3}{2}} & 9 & \xrightarrow{\times\frac{5}{3}} & 15 & \xrightarrow{\times\frac{8}{5}} & 24 & \}
\end{array}$$

Slide rule exercise

1 How are the numbers on Scale D related to numbers on Scale A? Work out:

(*a*) $(4{\cdot}8)^2$; (*b*) $\sqrt{8{\cdot}4}$; (*c*) $\sqrt{19{\cdot}5}$;
(*d*) $(450)^2$; (*e*) $\sqrt{0{\cdot}071}$; (*f*) $(0{\cdot}034)^2$.

2 How are the numbers on Scale D related to the numbers on Scale K? Work out:

(*a*) $(1{\cdot}26)^3$; (*b*) $(58{\cdot}5)^3$; (*c*) $\sqrt[3]{61}$;
(*d*) $\sqrt[3]{350}$; (*e*) $(0{\cdot}36)^3$; (*f*) $\sqrt[3]{1{\cdot}7}$.

3 How are the numbers on the middle scale related to the numbers on Scale D? Work out:

(*a*) $1/4$; (*b*) $1/1{\cdot}5$; (*c*) $1/92$;
(*d*) $1/270$; (*e*) $1/1/8{\cdot}5$; (*f*) $1/0{\cdot}42$.

4 Work out:

(*a*) $3{\cdot}6/\sqrt{5{\cdot}7}$; (*b*) $(4{\cdot}5)^2/(2{\cdot}8)^3$; (*c*) $4{\cdot}6^3 \times \sqrt{5{\cdot}3}$;
(*d*) $\dfrac{35 \times 0{\cdot}08 \times 4{\cdot}8}{25}$; (*e*) $\sqrt{(15{\cdot}8)^3}$; (*f*) $\sqrt{45 \times 0{\cdot}045}$.

Exercise F

1 If y is proportional to x^2, complete the following table:

x	8	12	15		24
y		252		700	1008

2 The radius of the 'outer' circle of a shooting target is 1·5 times the radius of the 'bull'. If the area of the bull is 12 cm^2, find the area of the inner ring (shaded in Figure 5).

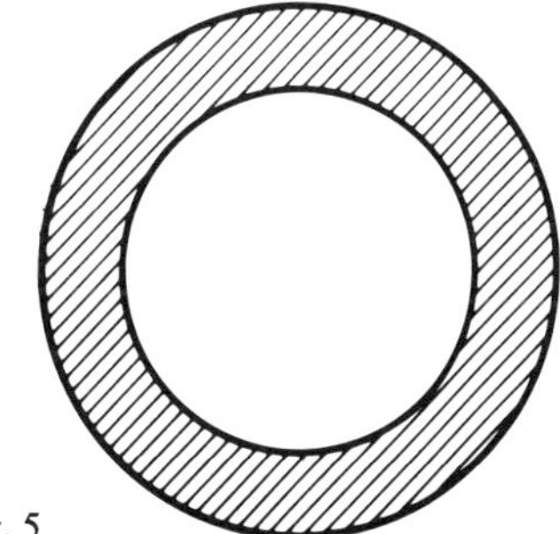

Fig. 5

3 Complete the following table of values on the assumption that:

(*a*) y is directly proportional to x;

(*b*) y is proportional to $\frac{1}{x}$.

x	6	24	54	150
y		100		

4 If y is proportional to x^3, complete the following table:

x	2	4	8	12	16
y			128		1024

5 Complete the following table of values on the assumption that:

(*a*) y is proportional to $\frac{1}{x}$;

(*b*) y is proportional to x^2;

(*c*) y is proportional to x^3.

x	0·7	2·1	2·8	3·5	4·9
y		10			

7 Testing relationships between sets of values

(*a*) Here are two ordered sets:

$$X = \{16, 54, 128, 250, 432\},$$
$$Y = \{2, 3, 4, 5, 6\}.$$

Can you spot a relation between the members of the sets X and Y?

The following sections show how to SEARCH for other relations using your slide rule.

(*b*) Consider set X. The multiplier between the first two members can be found by setting 54 on the D scale against 16 on the C scale. By moving the cursor to the appropriate end of the slide rule the multiplying factor 3·38 is obtained on scale D (see Figure 6).

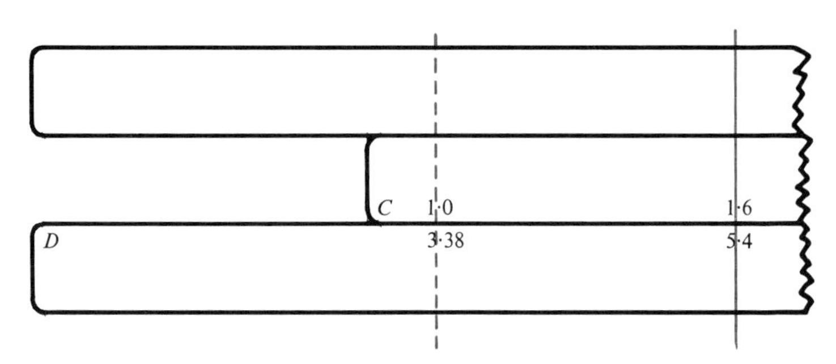

Fig. 6

If we now keep the *cursor fixed* and close the rule so that the 1 on the *C* scale is directly above the 1 on the *D* scale, the value under the cursor line on scale *A* gives the square of the first multiplying factor (see Figure 7).

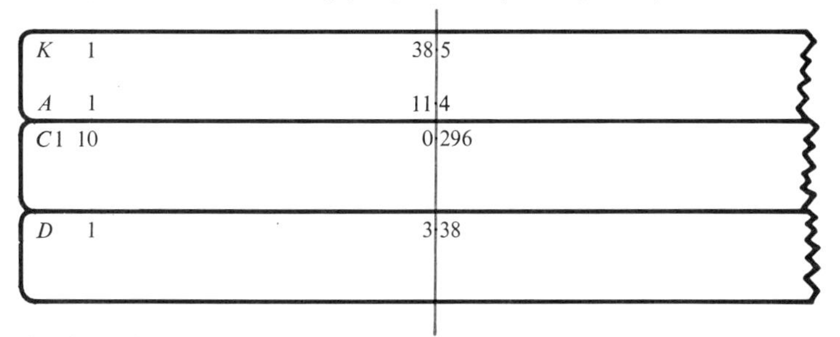

Fig. 7

What do the values 38·5 and 0·296 under the cursor lines on scales *K* (cube) and *C*1 (reciprocal) represent?

(*c*)

Members of *X*	Multipliers for *X*	Squares of multipliers for *X*	Cubes of multipliers for *X*	Reciprocals of multipliers for *X*
16				
	3·38	11·4	38·5	0·296
54				
128				
250				
432				

Fig. 8

Use the method of Section (*b*) to complete the table of multipliers in Figure 8 by considering in turn the pairs (54, 128), (128, 250) and (250, 432).

Repeat the process for the set of values for *Y*.

Members of *Y*	Multipliers for *Y*	Squares of multipliers for *Y*	Cubes of multipliers for *Y*	Reciprocals of multipliers for *Y*
2				
	1·5	2·25	3·38	0·667
3				
4				
5				
6				

Fig. 9

Look at the two tables. Are any two of the ten columns of values identical? If two of the columns are identical then this suggests a relation between the two sets. In this example the columns headed 'Multipliers for X' and 'Cubes of multipliers for Y' are identical. This suggests a relation between the members of the sets X and Y^3 which can be expressed in the form $x = ky^3$ where x denotes any member of X and y^3 the corresponding member of Y^3.

Consider the table of values for x and y^3:

y^3	8	27	64	125	216
x	16	54	128	250	432

We can see that $2y^3 = x$.

8 The symbol '$\propto$'

(*a*) We use the symbol '$\propto$' to represent the words 'is proportional to'. A statement like: 'velocity, v, is proportional to the time, t' is written $v \propto t$. In the same way 'the stopping distance, d, of a car is proportional to the square of its speed, s' is written $d \propto s^2$, and 'the pressure, p, is inversely proportional to the volume, v' is written $p \propto \frac{1}{v}$.

Express as statements:

(i) $m \propto \frac{1}{n^2}$;

(ii) $q^2 \propto p^3$.

Write in symbols (using $\propto$):

(iii) 'The volume, v, is proportional to the cube of the length, l.'

(iv) 'A quantity x is inversely proportional to the square of a quantity y.'

(*b*) We have seen in previous sections that when two quantities are proportional to each other the relationship can be expressed in terms of a formula. For example:

$y \propto x$ can be written $y = kx$;

$y \propto x^2$ can be written $y = kx^2$;

$y \propto \frac{1}{x}$ can be written $y = \frac{k}{x}$.

Sometimes k is referred to as 'the constant of proportionality'.

Express each of the following as a formula:

(i) $p^2 \propto \frac{1}{q}$; (ii) $d^2 \propto b^3$; (iii) $m \propto \frac{1}{n^2}$.

(*c*) The heating power in watts of an electrical fire is proportional to the square of the current flowing through it.

Letting the power be p watts and the current be i amps, we can write

$$p \propto i^2.$$

This can be replaced by $p = ki^2$ where k is some constant.

If the power is 1000 watts when the current is 5 amps then substituting these values we obtain:

$$1000 = k \times 5 \times 5; \qquad k = 40.$$

The formula connecting p and i is therefore

$$p = 40i^2.$$

If the power is 2000 watts when the current is 4 amps and $p = ki^2$ what is the value of k?

Exercise G

1 Express the following statements by (i) using the $\propto$ notation; (ii) using a constant of proportionality k.

(*a*) The increase in length, d, of a rod is proportional to the increase in temperature, t.

(*b*) The circumference, c, of a circle is proportional to its radius, r.

(*c*) The mechanical energy of motion, e, of a motor-car is proportional to the square of its velocity, v.

(*d*) The volume, v, of a sphere is proportional to the cube of its radius.

(*e*) The distance to the horizon is proportional to the square root of the observer's height above the surface of the sea.

2 If $y \propto x$ and $y = 12$ when $x = 2$ find y when $x = 5$.

3 $x \propto \dfrac{1}{y^2}$ and $x = 3$ when $y = 4$. Find x when $y = 8$.

4 If $y \propto x^3$ complete this table of values

x	2	6	8	
y	0.1			12·8

If $y = ax^3$ what is the value of a?

5 Some corresponding values of x and y are shown in the table:

x	1	5	10	20
y	5	125	500	2000

Which one or more of the following could be true?

(*a*) $y \propto x^2$;
(*b*) $y = 5x$;
(*c*) $y = 5x^2$;
(*d*) $y = 30x - 25$.

6 Some corresponding values of F and W are shown in the table:

F	100	200	300	500
W	30	15	10	6

Which one or more of the following is a possible relation between F and W?

(*a*) W is directly proportional to F;
(*b*) W is inversely proportional to F;
(*c*) $W = \frac{3}{10}F$;
(*d*) $FW = 3000$.

7 Use your slide rule to find the relations between the variables x and y in the following tables.

(*a*)

x	2	3	4	5
y	10	22·5	40	62·5

(*b*)

x	18	36	54	72
y	2	16	54	128

(*c*)

x	1·6	2·6	3·6	4·6
y	2·4	3·9	5·4	6·9

(*d*)

x	33·3	20·9	8·62	1·98
y	7·0	5·55	3·56	1·71

(*e*)

x	5	10	16	20	24
y	80	40	25	20	16·67

8 Given that $y \propto \dfrac{1}{x^2}$ complete the following table:

x	20	17	14		8
y		240		600	

9 Find the function for which the following are corresponding pairs:

$$(20, 35), (24, 42), (48, 84), (50, 87{\cdot}5).$$

10 The speed of sound, s, in a gas is found to be proportional to the square root of the pressure, p, and inversely proportional to the square root of the density, d. If the speed is 33 000 cm per second for air when the pressure is 1030 g per cm^2 and the density 0·0013 g per cm^3, find the formula connecting s, p and d. Find the speed of sound in hydrogen (which is 0·07 times as dense as air) at the same pressure and temperature.

7 Looking for an inverse

We have seen how some transformations can be described algebraically using matrices. The mapping

$$\mathbf{T}:\begin{pmatrix}x\\y\end{pmatrix}\to\begin{pmatrix}2&4\\3&5\end{pmatrix}\begin{pmatrix}x\\y\end{pmatrix}$$

is an example of such a transformation.

If **T** maps $P\ (^-3,4)$ onto P', find the coordinates of P'.

When we know the coordinates of an object point, we can find the image. In this chapter we shall consider the reverse problem, that is, whether, knowing the image, we can find the object point(s).

For example, if **T** maps Q onto $Q'\ (^-5,3)$, can you find the coordinates of Q?

1 Thinking geometrically

(*a*) Figure 1 shows a flag F and its image F' after a positive (anticlockwise) rotation of 90° about the origin.

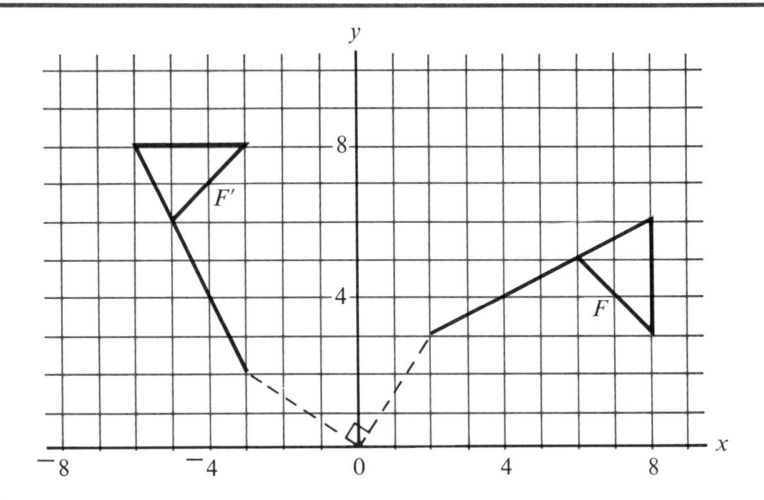

Fig. 1

By considering what happens to the base vectors $\begin{pmatrix}1\\0\end{pmatrix}$ and $\begin{pmatrix}0\\1\end{pmatrix}$, find the matrix **R** which represents this transformation.

Did you obtain the matrix $\begin{pmatrix}0 & ^-1\\1 & 0\end{pmatrix}$?

Describe the inverse transformation which maps F' onto F. By considering what happens to the base vectors, find the matrix **S** which represents this inverse transformation.

Work out **SR**. What can you say about the matrix **SR**? What transformation does it represent?

What can you say about the matrices **R** and **S**?

The matrix $\mathbf{I} = \begin{pmatrix}1 & 0\\0 & 1\end{pmatrix}$ is the identity for the set of 2 by 2 matrices under matrix multiplication.

Since

$$\mathbf{RS} = \mathbf{I} = \mathbf{SR},$$

the matrices **R** and **S** are multiplicative inverses, that is, **R** is the inverse of **S** and **S** is the inverse of **R**.

We often denote the multiplicative inverse of the matrix **R** by $\mathbf{R}^{-1}$. In this case $\mathbf{R}^{-1} = \mathbf{S} = \begin{pmatrix}0 & 1\\^-1 & 0\end{pmatrix}$.

(*b*) Describe the transformation **T** which is represented by the matrix $\mathbf{E} = \begin{pmatrix}2 & 0\\0 & 2\end{pmatrix}$.

Now describe $\mathbf{T}^{-1}$ and, by considering what happens to the base vectors, find the matrix $\mathbf{E}^{-1}$ which represents $\mathbf{T}^{-1}$.

Work out $\mathbf{E}\begin{pmatrix}^-1\\3\end{pmatrix}$. What is the image of the point $(^-1, 3)$ under **T**?

Work out $\mathbf{E}^{-1}\begin{pmatrix}-2\\6\end{pmatrix}$. What point is mapped by $\mathbf{T}$ onto the point $(^-2, 6)$?

What point is mapped by $\mathbf{T}$ onto the point $(^-5, 7)$?

(*c*) We shall now try to find the inverse of the mapping

$$\mathbf{M}:\begin{pmatrix}x\\y\end{pmatrix} \rightarrow \begin{pmatrix}0 & 3\\ -1 & 0\end{pmatrix}\begin{pmatrix}x\\y\end{pmatrix}$$

by considering its geometrical description.

Since $\begin{pmatrix}1\\0\end{pmatrix} \xrightarrow{\mathbf{M}} \begin{pmatrix}0\\-1\end{pmatrix}$ and $\begin{pmatrix}0\\1\end{pmatrix} \xrightarrow{\mathbf{M}} \begin{pmatrix}3\\0\end{pmatrix}$, the effect of $\mathbf{M}$ on the unit square is as shown in Figure 2.

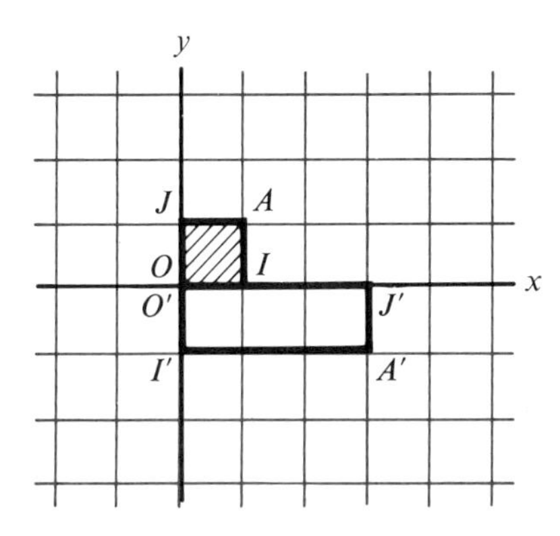

Fig. 2

We can see from this diagram that $\mathbf{M}$ is equivalent to a rotation about the origin followed by a one-way stretch with points on the line $x = 0$ invariant. What is (i) the angle of the rotation; (ii) the scale factor of the stretch?

The inverse transformation $\mathbf{M}^{-1}$ is equivalent to a one-way stretch with points on the line $x = 0$ invariant followed by a rotation about the origin. State the scale factor of this stretch and the angle of this rotation. By considering what happens to the base vectors, write down the matrices which represent these two transformations.

Do you agree that

$$\mathbf{M}^{-1}:\begin{pmatrix}x\\y\end{pmatrix} \rightarrow \begin{pmatrix}0 & -1\\ 1 & 0\end{pmatrix}\begin{pmatrix}\frac{1}{3} & 0\\ 0 & 1\end{pmatrix}\begin{pmatrix}x\\y\end{pmatrix},$$

and therefore

$$\mathbf{M}^{-1}:\begin{pmatrix}x\\y\end{pmatrix} \rightarrow \begin{pmatrix}0 & -1\\ \frac{1}{3} & 0\end{pmatrix}\begin{pmatrix}x\\y\end{pmatrix}?$$

Check that

$$\begin{pmatrix}0 & -1\\ \frac{1}{3} & 0\end{pmatrix}\begin{pmatrix}0 & 3\\ -1 & 0\end{pmatrix} = \begin{pmatrix}1 & 0\\ 0 & 1\end{pmatrix} = \begin{pmatrix}0 & 3\\ -1 & 0\end{pmatrix}\begin{pmatrix}0 & -1\\ \frac{1}{3} & 0\end{pmatrix}.$$

Find the coordinates of the point mapped by $\mathbf{M}$ onto $(^-3, ^-4)$.

(*d*) So far we have considered only transformations of the form

$$\begin{pmatrix} x \\ y \end{pmatrix} \to \begin{pmatrix} a & b \\ c & d \end{pmatrix} \begin{pmatrix} x \\ y \end{pmatrix},$$

that is, transformations which map the origin onto itself.

The following example shows you how to proceed when the origin is mapped onto some other point.

Example 1

Describe a sequence of transformations which maps the square $PQRS$ (see Figure 3) onto the square $P'Q'R'S'$. Hence find a matrix description of the single transformation **U** which does this.

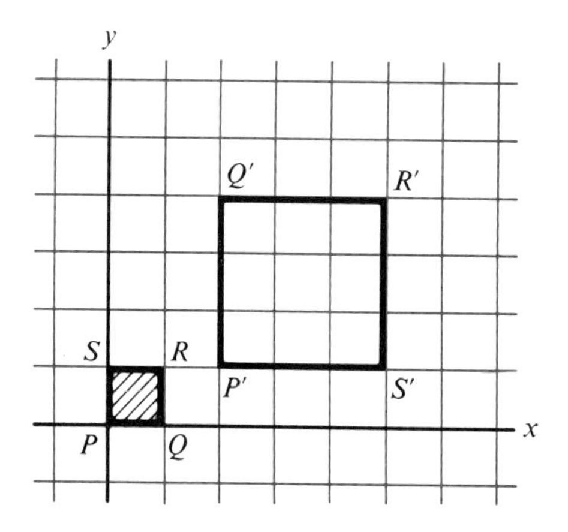

Fig. 3

A sequence of three transformations which maps $PQRS$ onto $P'Q'R'S'$ is the enlargement, **E**, centre the origin and scale factor 3 followed by the reflection, **M**, in the line $y = x$ followed by the translation, **T**, described by the vector $\begin{pmatrix} 2 \\ 1 \end{pmatrix}$. See Figure 4.

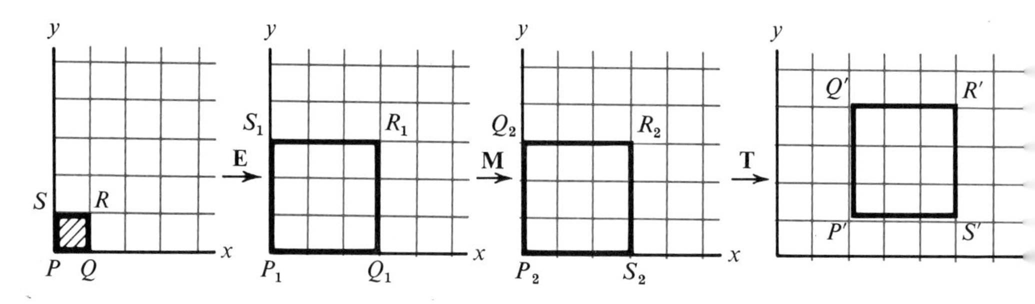

Fig. 4

These transformations are defined by the mappings:

$$\mathbf{E}:\begin{pmatrix}x\\y\end{pmatrix}\to\begin{pmatrix}3&0\\0&3\end{pmatrix}\begin{pmatrix}x\\y\end{pmatrix},$$

$$\mathbf{M}:\begin{pmatrix}x\\y\end{pmatrix}\to\begin{pmatrix}0&1\\1&0\end{pmatrix}\begin{pmatrix}x\\y\end{pmatrix},$$

$$\mathbf{T}:\begin{pmatrix}x\\y\end{pmatrix}\to\begin{pmatrix}x\\y\end{pmatrix}+\begin{pmatrix}2\\1\end{pmatrix}.$$

Therefore we can write:

$$\mathbf{E}:\begin{pmatrix}x\\y\end{pmatrix}\to\begin{pmatrix}3&0\\0&3\end{pmatrix}\begin{pmatrix}x\\y\end{pmatrix},$$

$$\mathbf{ME}:\begin{pmatrix}x\\y\end{pmatrix}\to\begin{pmatrix}0&1\\1&0\end{pmatrix}\begin{pmatrix}3&0\\0&3\end{pmatrix}\begin{pmatrix}x\\y\end{pmatrix},$$

$$\mathbf{TME}:\begin{pmatrix}x\\y\end{pmatrix}\to\begin{pmatrix}0&1\\1&0\end{pmatrix}\begin{pmatrix}3&0\\0&3\end{pmatrix}\begin{pmatrix}x\\y\end{pmatrix}+\begin{pmatrix}2\\1\end{pmatrix}.$$

Since $\mathbf{U}=\mathbf{TME}$,

$$\mathbf{U}:\begin{pmatrix}x\\y\end{pmatrix}\to\begin{pmatrix}0&3\\3&0\end{pmatrix}\begin{pmatrix}x\\y\end{pmatrix}+\begin{pmatrix}2\\1\end{pmatrix},$$

which can be written more simply as

$$\mathbf{U}:\begin{pmatrix}x\\y\end{pmatrix}\to\begin{pmatrix}3y+2\\3x+1\end{pmatrix}.$$

Describe geometrically the sequence of transformations which will map $P'Q'R'S'$ back onto $PQRS$ via $P_2Q_2R_2S_2$ and $P_1Q_1R_1S_1$.

Write down the mappings which define the transformations $\mathbf{E}^{-1}$, $\mathbf{M}^{-1}$ and $\mathbf{T}^{-1}$. Use the fact that $\mathbf{U}^{-1}=\mathbf{E}^{-1}\mathbf{M}^{-1}\mathbf{T}^{-1}$ to show that

$$\mathbf{U}^{-1}:\begin{pmatrix}x\\y\end{pmatrix}\to\begin{pmatrix}\frac{1}{3}&0\\0&\frac{1}{3}\end{pmatrix}\begin{pmatrix}0&1\\1&0\end{pmatrix}\left[\begin{pmatrix}x\\y\end{pmatrix}+\begin{pmatrix}^-2\\^-1\end{pmatrix}\right],$$

and express this in a simpler form.

Use your last answer to find the images of $P'(2,1)$, $Q'(2,4)$, $R'(5,4)$ and $S'(5,1)$ under $\mathbf{U}^{-1}$. Do you obtain $P(0,0)$, $Q(1,0)$, $R(1,1)$ and $S(0,1)$ respectively? If not, try again.

(*e*) Draw a diagram to show the image of the unit square under the mapping

$$\mathbf{M}:\begin{pmatrix}x\\y\end{pmatrix}\to\begin{pmatrix}1&0\\0&0\end{pmatrix}\begin{pmatrix}x\\y\end{pmatrix}.$$

Describe the transformation in your own words.

Find the images under **M** of (i) (3, 0), (ii) (3, 5), (iii) (3, $^-2$).

If the domain of **M** is the set of all points in the plane, what is the range?

Is **M** a one–one mapping or a many–one mapping?

Does **M** have an inverse? Give a reason for your answer.

If $\begin{pmatrix} x \\ y \end{pmatrix} \xrightarrow{\mathbf{M}} \begin{pmatrix} 3 \\ 0 \end{pmatrix}$, what can you say about x and y?

Exercise A

1 Describe, in words, the inverse of each of the following transformations:

(*a*) enlargement, centre the origin and scale factor $\frac{1}{2}$;
(*b*) positive rotation of 120° about the origin;
(*c*) reflection in the line $2x + 3y = 0$;
(*d*) one-way stretch with points on the line $y = 0$ invariant and scale factor 4.

2 Describe the effect on the unit square of each of the following mappings:

(i) $\mathbf{A}: \begin{pmatrix} x \\ y \end{pmatrix} \to \begin{pmatrix} 0 & 1 \\ 1 & 0 \end{pmatrix} \begin{pmatrix} x \\ y \end{pmatrix}$; (ii) $\mathbf{B}: \begin{pmatrix} x \\ y \end{pmatrix} \to \begin{pmatrix} ^-2 & 0 \\ 0 & ^-2 \end{pmatrix} \begin{pmatrix} x \\ y \end{pmatrix}$;

(iii) $\mathbf{C}: \begin{pmatrix} x \\ y \end{pmatrix} \to \begin{pmatrix} 2 & 0 \\ 0 & 1 \end{pmatrix} \begin{pmatrix} x \\ y \end{pmatrix}$; (iv) $\mathbf{D}: \begin{pmatrix} x \\ y \end{pmatrix} \to \begin{pmatrix} 1 & 3 \\ 0 & 1 \end{pmatrix} \begin{pmatrix} x \\ y \end{pmatrix}$.

Hence find $\mathbf{A}^{-1}$, $\mathbf{B}^{-1}$, $\mathbf{C}^{-1}$ and $\mathbf{D}^{-1}$.

3 The matrix which represents reflection in $x = 0$ is

$$\begin{pmatrix} ^-1 & 0 \\ 0 & 1 \end{pmatrix}.$$

Explain (i) the geometrical meaning, (ii) the algebraic meaning of

$$\begin{pmatrix} ^-1 & 0 \\ 0 & 1 \end{pmatrix} \begin{pmatrix} ^-1 & 0 \\ 0 & 1 \end{pmatrix} = \begin{pmatrix} 1 & 0 \\ 0 & 1 \end{pmatrix}.$$

By considering other geometrical transformations which are self-inverse, find four more self-inverse matrices.

4 A transformation **T** is equivalent to enlargement centre the origin and scale factor 3 followed by reflection in $y = x$.

(*a*) What matrix represents **T**?
(*b*) Describe $\mathbf{T}^{-1}$ and find the matrix which represents this transformation.
(*c*) **T** maps the point A onto A' $(5, {}^-2)$. What are the coordinates of A?

5 A translation **T** is defined by the mapping

$$\begin{pmatrix} x \\ y \end{pmatrix} \to \begin{pmatrix} x \\ y \end{pmatrix} + \begin{pmatrix} ^-2 \\ 3 \end{pmatrix}.$$

(*a*) What mapping defines the inverse translation $\mathbf{T}^{-1}$?
(*b*) If **T** maps P, Q and R onto P' $(3, 5)$, Q' $({}^-6, 2)$ and R' $({}^-3, 0)$, what are the coordinates of P, Q and R?

6 Figure 5 shows the unit square $OIAJ$ and its image $O'I'A'J'$ under six different transformations. Break down each transformation into a sequence of simpler transformations and hence describe it in the form

$$\begin{pmatrix} x \\ y \end{pmatrix} \to \begin{pmatrix} a & b \\ c & d \end{pmatrix}\begin{pmatrix} x \\ y \end{pmatrix} + \begin{pmatrix} e \\ f \end{pmatrix}.$$

(*Hint*: make the translation the last transformation of the sequence.)

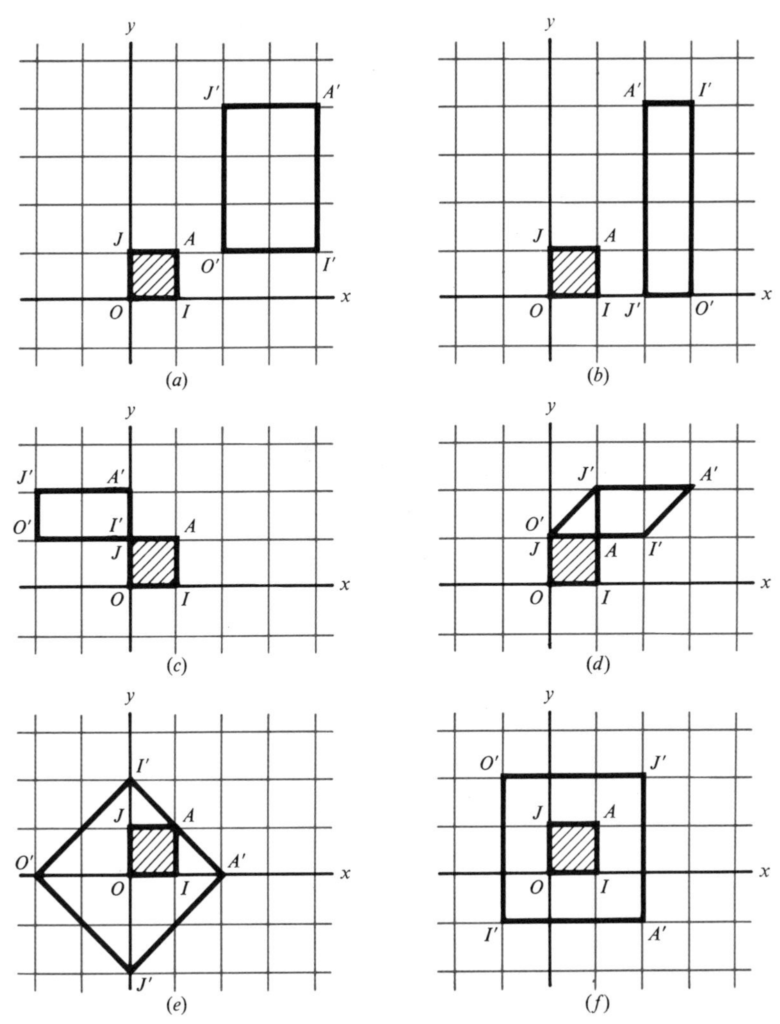

Fig. 5

7 Use the method of Section 1(d) to describe in the form

$$\begin{pmatrix} x \\ y \end{pmatrix} \to \begin{pmatrix} a & b \\ c & d \end{pmatrix}\begin{pmatrix} x \\ y \end{pmatrix} + \begin{pmatrix} e \\ f \end{pmatrix}$$

the inverse of the transformation shown in Figure 5(a).

8 A transformation $\mathbf{V}$ is defined by the mapping

$$\mathbf{V}:\begin{pmatrix}x\\y\end{pmatrix}\to\begin{pmatrix}1&1\\0&1\end{pmatrix}\begin{pmatrix}x\\y\end{pmatrix}+\begin{pmatrix}2\\-1\end{pmatrix}.$$

(*a*) Find the image under $\mathbf{V}$ of the rectangle with vertices $P(^-1,0)$, $Q(^-1,1)$, $R(1,1)$, $S(1,0)$ and hence describe $\mathbf{V}$ as a combination of two simple transformations.

(*b*) Explain why

$$\mathbf{W}:\begin{pmatrix}x\\y\end{pmatrix}\to\begin{pmatrix}1&^-1\\0&1\end{pmatrix}\begin{pmatrix}x\\y\end{pmatrix}+\begin{pmatrix}^-3\\1\end{pmatrix}$$

defines the inverse transformation.

2 Thinking algebraically

We have found the inverses of some transformations by considering their geometrical description. However, some transformations are not easy to describe geometrically, so we shall now investigate whether algebra can help us.

(*a*) Suppose, for example, that we wish to find the inverse of the one–one mapping

$$\mathbf{M}:\begin{pmatrix}x\\y\end{pmatrix}\to\begin{pmatrix}2&5\\1&3\end{pmatrix}\begin{pmatrix}x\\y\end{pmatrix}.$$

We must find a, b, c, d such that

$$\begin{pmatrix}a&b\\c&d\end{pmatrix}\begin{pmatrix}2&5\\1&3\end{pmatrix}=\begin{pmatrix}1&0\\0&1\end{pmatrix},$$

that is

$$\begin{pmatrix}2a+b&5a+3b\\2c+d&5c+3d\end{pmatrix}=\begin{pmatrix}1&0\\0&1\end{pmatrix}.$$

To make $5a+3b=0$, we could choose $a={}^-3$ and $b=5$ or $a=3$ and $b={}^-5$ or $a=6$ and $b={}^-10$, etc. Do any of these values for a and b make $2a+b=1$? If so, which ones?

Now choose values for c and d to make

$$2c+d=0 \qquad \text{and} \qquad 5c+3d=1.$$

Write down the matrix $\begin{pmatrix}a&b\\c&d\end{pmatrix}$ with the values of a, b, c and d which you have chosen and check that

$$\begin{pmatrix}a&b\\c&d\end{pmatrix}\begin{pmatrix}2&5\\1&3\end{pmatrix}=\begin{pmatrix}1&0\\0&1\end{pmatrix}=\begin{pmatrix}2&5\\1&3\end{pmatrix}\begin{pmatrix}a&b\\c&d\end{pmatrix}.$$

Write down the mapping which defines $\mathbf{M}^{-1}$.

(*b*) Compare the matrix you produced with the original matrix $\begin{pmatrix} 2 & 5 \\ 1 & 3 \end{pmatrix}$. What has happened to:

(i) the numbers in the leading diagonal;
(ii) the numbers in the other diagonal?

(*c*) Use the patterns which you noticed in (*b*) to write down the multiplicative inverses of:

(i) $\mathbf{P} = \begin{pmatrix} 7 & 5 \\ 4 & 3 \end{pmatrix}$; (ii) $\mathbf{Q} = \begin{pmatrix} 9 & 11 \\ 4 & 5 \end{pmatrix}$;

(iii) $\mathbf{R} = \begin{pmatrix} 3 & 2 \\ 7 & 5 \end{pmatrix}$; (iv) $\mathbf{S} = \begin{pmatrix} 2 & 5 \\ 3 & 8 \end{pmatrix}$.

Check, by multiplication, whether your answers are correct.

Now do the same with $\mathbf{T} = \begin{pmatrix} 4 & 5 \\ 1 & 3 \end{pmatrix}$. Have you found the inverse of **T**?

How can you adjust your matrix to give $\mathbf{T}^{-1}$?

(*d*) Figure 6 shows the effect on the unit square of the transformation represented by **T**.

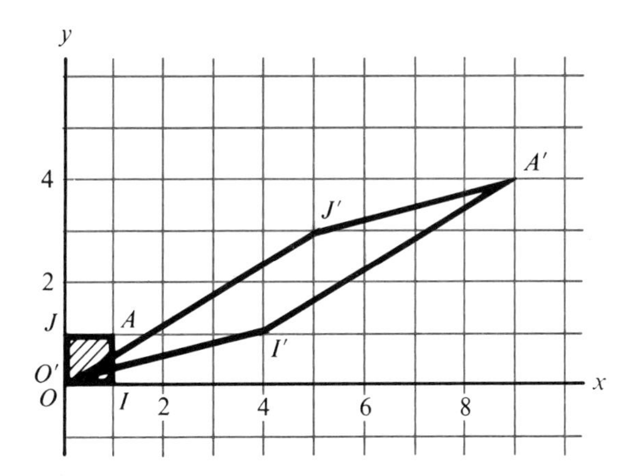

Fig. 6

What is the area factor of the transformation? You may remember that this factor can be found from the matrix by finding the difference between the products of the numbers in each diagonal:

$$(4 \times 3) - (1 \times 5) = 7.$$

We call 7 the *determinant* of **T** and write

$$|\mathbf{T}| = 7.$$

What are the determinants of **P**, **Q**, **R** and **S**?

(*e*) To find the multiplicative inverse of **T** we interchange the numbers in the leading diagonal and change the signs of the numbers in the other diagonal. This gives

$$\begin{pmatrix} 3 & ^-5 \\ ^-1 & 4 \end{pmatrix}.$$

We then divide each element by $|\mathbf{T}|$ and obtain

$$\mathbf{T}^{-1} = \begin{pmatrix} \frac{3}{7} & -\frac{5}{7} \\ -\frac{1}{7} & \frac{4}{7} \end{pmatrix}.$$

Find the multiplicative inverses of:

(i) $\begin{pmatrix} 4 & 2 \\ 5 & 3 \end{pmatrix}$; (ii) $\begin{pmatrix} 3 & 2 \\ 6 & 5 \end{pmatrix}$;

(iii) $\begin{pmatrix} 4 & 2 \\ 3 & 1 \end{pmatrix}$; (iv) $\begin{pmatrix} ^-1 & ^-2 \\ 1 & 3 \end{pmatrix}$.

Check, by multiplication, whether your answers are correct.

(*f*) What happens when you try to find the multiplicative inverse of

$$\begin{pmatrix} 4 & 2 \\ 6 & 3 \end{pmatrix}?$$

Draw a diagram to show the effect on the unit square of the transformation described by this matrix.

Do you think that this transformation is a one–one or a many–one mapping?

(*g*) Find the multiplicative inverse of the matrix

$$\begin{pmatrix} 2 & 4 \\ 3 & 5 \end{pmatrix}$$

and hence write down the inverse of the mapping

$$\mathbf{T}: \begin{pmatrix} x \\ y \end{pmatrix} \rightarrow \begin{pmatrix} 2 & 4 \\ 3 & 5 \end{pmatrix} \begin{pmatrix} x \\ y \end{pmatrix}.$$

Now solve the problem posed at the beginning of this chapter, that is, find the coordinates of Q if **T** maps Q onto Q' $(^-5, 3)$.

Exercise B

1 Find the multiplicative inverses of the following matrices. In each case check your result by multiplication.

(*a*) $\begin{pmatrix} 1 & 2 \\ 2 & 5 \end{pmatrix}$; (*b*) $\begin{pmatrix} 3 & 2 \\ 4 & 3 \end{pmatrix}$; (*c*) $\begin{pmatrix} 8 & 3 \\ 4 & 2 \end{pmatrix}$;

(*d*) $\begin{pmatrix} 7 & 3 \\ 5 & 2 \end{pmatrix}$; (*e*) $\begin{pmatrix} ^-2 & 2 \\ 2 & 3 \end{pmatrix}$; (*f*) $\begin{pmatrix} ^-4 & ^-3 \\ 5 & 3 \end{pmatrix}$;

(*g*) $\begin{pmatrix} 5 & 7 \\ ^-2 & 3 \end{pmatrix}$; (*h*) $\begin{pmatrix} ^-6 & 4 \\ 4 & ^-2 \end{pmatrix}$; (*i*) $\begin{pmatrix} ^-2 & ^-3 \\ ^-4 & ^-5 \end{pmatrix}$.

2 The transformation $\mathbf{W}$ defined by

$$\mathbf{W}: \begin{pmatrix} x \\ y \end{pmatrix} \rightarrow \begin{pmatrix} 3 & 4 \\ 1 & 2 \end{pmatrix} \begin{pmatrix} x \\ y \end{pmatrix}$$

maps the rectangle $ABCD$ onto the parallelogram $A'B'C'D'$ with vertices $A'(4,2)$, $B'(19,7)$, $C'(27,11)$, $D'(12,6)$.

(*a*) Find the multiplicative inverse of $\begin{pmatrix} 3 & 4 \\ 1 & 2 \end{pmatrix}$.

(*b*) Use the inverse mapping $\mathbf{W}^{-1}$ to find the coordinates of A, B, C, and D.

(*c*) Find the areas of $ABCD$ and $A'B'C'D'$ and explain the connection between these areas and (i) the determinant of $\begin{pmatrix} 3 & 4 \\ 1 & 2 \end{pmatrix}$; (ii) the determinant of the inverse of $\begin{pmatrix} 3 & 4 \\ 1 & 2 \end{pmatrix}$.

3 A matrix $\mathbf{M}$ is such that

$$|\mathbf{M}| = |\mathbf{M}^{-1}|.$$

What is the value of $|\mathbf{M}|$? Is there more than one possible value?

4 What point is mapped onto $(^-3, 7)$ by the transformation

$$\begin{pmatrix} x \\ y \end{pmatrix} \rightarrow \begin{pmatrix} 3 & 1 \\ 5 & 2 \end{pmatrix} \begin{pmatrix} x \\ y \end{pmatrix}?$$

5 A transformation $\mathbf{D}$ is defined by

$$\begin{pmatrix} x \\ y \end{pmatrix} \rightarrow \begin{pmatrix} 7 & 5 \\ 4 & 3 \end{pmatrix} \begin{pmatrix} x \\ y \end{pmatrix} + \begin{pmatrix} 2 \\ ^-5 \end{pmatrix}.$$

Use an algebraic method to find the inverse transformation and hence find the coordinates of the point mapped by $\mathbf{D}$ onto $(4, ^-4)$.

6 (*a*) Investigate some transformations represented by matrices whose determinant is 0 by finding their effect on the unit square or any other figures of your choice.

(*b*) Matrices whose determinant is zero have no multiplicative inverse. How does this link up with the geometrical properties which you found in (*a*)?

7 For what values of x does

$$\begin{pmatrix} x^2 & x \\ 1 & 1 \end{pmatrix}$$

have no inverse?

8 (*a*) Find the determinant of each of the following matrices:

(i) $\begin{pmatrix} 1 & 1 \\ 0 & 1 \end{pmatrix}$; (ii) $\begin{pmatrix} 0 & 1 \\ 1 & 0 \end{pmatrix}$; (iii) $\begin{pmatrix} 0 & 0 \\ 0 & 1 \end{pmatrix}$;

(iv) $\begin{pmatrix} 0 & 0 \\ 0 & 0 \end{pmatrix}$; (v) $\begin{pmatrix} 1 & 1 \\ 1 & 0 \end{pmatrix}$.

(*b*) Draw diagrams to show the effect on the unit square of the transformations represented by each of these matrices and describe the transformations as accurately as you can.
(*c*) Investigate the range of each of these transformations if the domain is the set of all points in the plane.
(*d*) In each case find all the points which are mapped onto (0,4).

9 The numerical value of the determinant of a matrix gives the area factor of the associated transformation. Investigate whether the sign of a determinant has any geometrical significance.

Summary

For the 2 by 2 matrix

$$\mathbf{A} = \begin{pmatrix} a & b \\ c & d \end{pmatrix},$$

the number $ad - bc$ is called the determinant of $\mathbf{A}$ and is denoted by $|\mathbf{A}|$.

When $|\mathbf{A}| \neq 0$, $\mathbf{A}$ has a multiplicative inverse. This inverse is

$$\mathbf{A}^{-1} = \begin{pmatrix} \frac{d}{|\mathbf{A}|} & \frac{-b}{|\mathbf{A}|} \\ \frac{-c}{|\mathbf{A}|} & \frac{a}{|\mathbf{A}|} \end{pmatrix}.$$

When $|\mathbf{A}| = 0$, $\mathbf{A}$ has no multiplicative inverse.

If a one–one transformation is represented by $\mathbf{A}$, then the inverse transformation is represented by $\mathbf{A}^{-1}$.

If the transformations $\mathbf{S}$ and $\mathbf{T}$ have inverses $\mathbf{S}^{-1}$ and $\mathbf{T}^{-1}$ then $(\mathbf{TS})^{-1} = \mathbf{S}^{-1}\mathbf{T}^{-1}$.

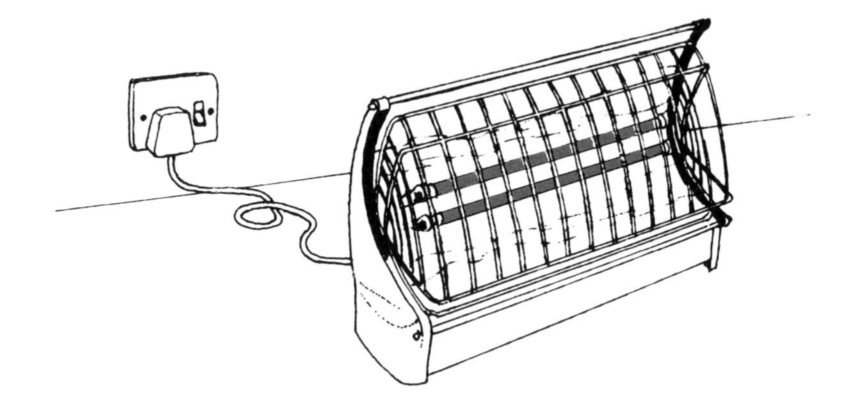

8 Quadratic functions

1 A reminder

(*a*) Since multiplication is distributive over addition for real numbers we know that:

(i) $a(b+c) = ab + ac$; for example $2(3+\frac{1}{2}) = (2 \times 3) + (2 \times \frac{1}{2})$;
(ii) $(b+c)a = ba + ca$; for example $(\frac{1}{3}+7)4 = (\frac{1}{3} \times 4) + (7 \times 4)$.

Explain why we can say that $p(q+r) = (q+r)p$. Multiply out, i.e. write without bracket (i) $2(3+x)$; (ii) $(3x+1)x$.

(*b*) Notice that

$$\begin{aligned} a(b-c) &= a(b + {}^{-}c) \\ &= a.b + a.{}^{-}c \\ &= ab + {}^{-}ac \\ &= ab - ac. \end{aligned}$$

Multiply out (i) $(b-c)a$; (ii) $3(2-x)$; (iii) ${}^{-}3(2-\frac{1}{2}x)$.

(*c*) We can use the distributive law in the 'opposite direction' to insert brackets (i.e. to *factorize* expressions). For example,

$$2ab + a^2 b = ab(2+a).$$

Factorize (i) $a^2 + ab$; (ii) $3x - x^2$; (iii) $\frac{1}{2}x^2 - ax$.

2 Double brackets

(*a*) The area of the red rectangle in Figure 1 is $(4+\frac{1}{2})(1\frac{1}{2}+5)$. The entry $\frac{1}{2}.5$ ($\frac{1}{2}.5$ means $\frac{1}{2}\times 5$) in the combination table in Figure 2 is the area of the shaded rectangle. What do the other entries in the table represent?

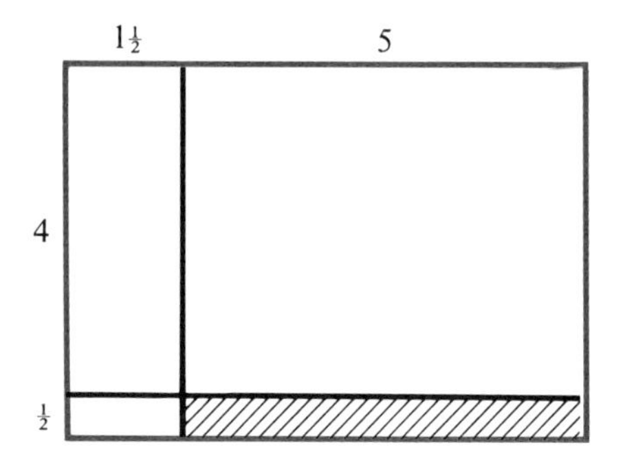

Fig. 1

$\bullet$	$1\frac{1}{2}$	5
4	$4.1\frac{1}{2}$	4.5
$\frac{1}{2}$	$\frac{1}{2}.1\frac{1}{2}$	$\frac{1}{2}.5$

Fig. 2

Complete the statement $(4+\frac{1}{2})(1\frac{1}{2}+5) = 4.1\frac{1}{2} + \quad + \quad + \frac{1}{2}.5$ and check that your statement is correct by calculating both sides of the equation.

(*b*) Use Figures 3 and 4 to help you explain why

$$(a+b)(c+d) = ac+ad+bc+bd.$$

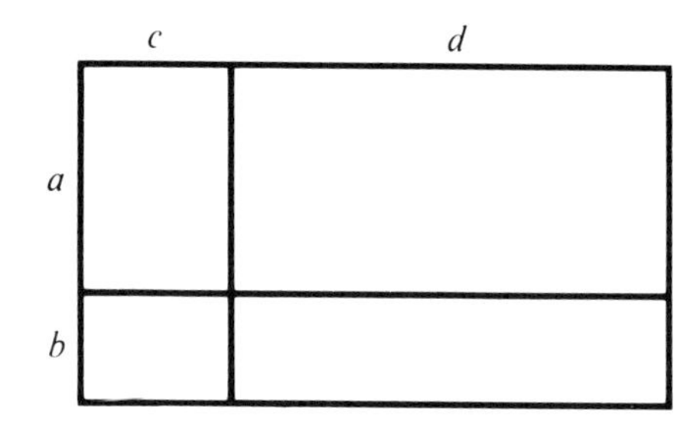

Fig. 3

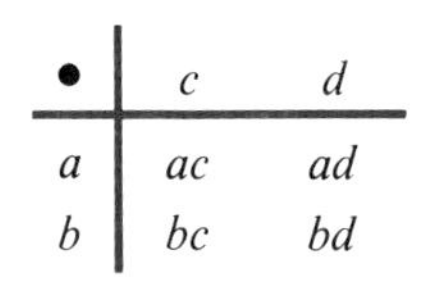

$\bullet$	c	d
a	ac	ad
b	bc	bd

Fig. 4

Multiply out (i) $(x+2)(x+1)$; (ii) $(2+x)(3+x)$; (iii) $(x+1)(x+1)$; (iv) $(2x+1)(x+1)$.

(*c*) We can obtain the result in (*b*) by using the distributive law in two stages:

$$(a+b)(c+d) = a(c+d)+b(c+d)$$

[compare this with $\qquad (a+b)z = az+bz$]

$$= ac+ad+bc+bd.$$

(*d*) Copy and complete

$$(2-x)(1+x) = 2(1+x) - x(1+x)$$

Explain how the combination table in Figure 5 helps you with this problem.

$\bullet$	1	x
2	2	$2x$
$-x$	$-x$	$-x^2$

Fig. 5

Multiply out (i) $(x-1)(x-2)$; (ii) $(x-1)(x+1)$; (iii) $(2x-1)(x+1)$.

(*e*) Your answers in (*b*) and (*d*) may begin to suggest to you that expressions of the form x^2+bx+c can be expressed as the product of two *factors* $(x+p)$ and $(x+q)$.

For example, $(x-1)$ and $(x-2)$ are the factors of x^2-3x+2.

Which of the following are the factors of $x^2+7x+12$:

(i) $(x+6)(x+2)$; (ii) $(x+12)(x+1)$; (iii) $(x+3)(x+4)$?

If $x^2+7x+12=(x+a)(x+b)$, what can you say about (i) $a+b$ and (ii) $a\times b$?

(*f*) Which of the following are the factors of x^2-x-12:

(i) $x+2)(x-6)$; (ii) $(x-12)(x+1)$; (iii) $(x-3)(x+4)$;
(iv) $(x-4)(x+3)$; (v) $(x-2)(x+6)$?

If $x^2-x-12=(x+a)(x+b)$, what can you say about (i) $a+b$ and (ii) $a\times b$?

Summary

1 $(a+b)(c+d)=(a+b)c+(a+b)d$
$\qquad\qquad\qquad\;\; = ac+bc+ad+bd,$

and

$(a+b)(c+d)=a(c+d)+b(c+d)$
$\qquad\qquad\qquad\;\; = ac+ad+bc+bd = ac+bc+ad+bd.$

2 If $x^2+bx+c=(x+p)(x+q)$, then $(x+p)$, $(x+q)$ are the factors of x^2+bx+c. Similarly if $ax^2+bx+c=(mx+p)(nx+q)$ then $(mx+p)$, $(nx+q)$ are the factors of ax^2+bx+c. For example, $2x^2+x-1=(2x-1)(x+1)$.

Exercise A

1 Copy Figure 3 and shade in the areas (i) $a(c+d)$; (ii) $b(c+d)$. Explain why $(a+b)(c+d)=a(c+d)+b(c+d)$ with reference to your diagram.

2 Copy Figure 3 and shade in the areas (i) $(a+b)c$; (ii) $(a+b)d$. Explain why $(a+b)(c+d)=(a+b)c+(a+b)d$ with reference to your diagram.

3 Copy Figure 6 twice. On your first copy, shade in the area $d(b-c)$. On the second copy, shade in the area $db - dc$. What do you conclude?

4 Explain carefully how you could use Figure 7 to show that

$$(x-2)(x-1) = x^2 - 3x + 2.$$

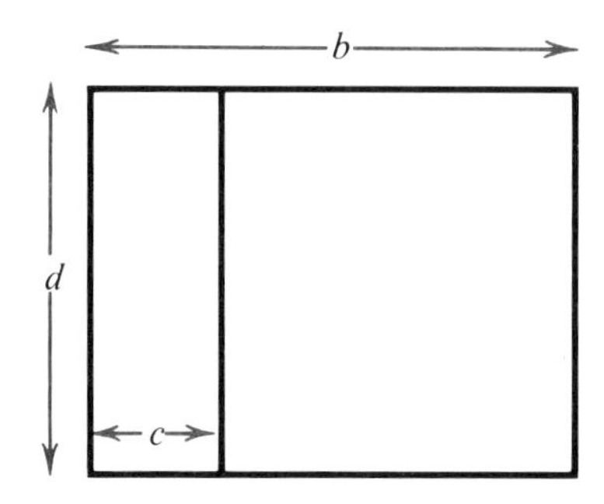

Fig. 6

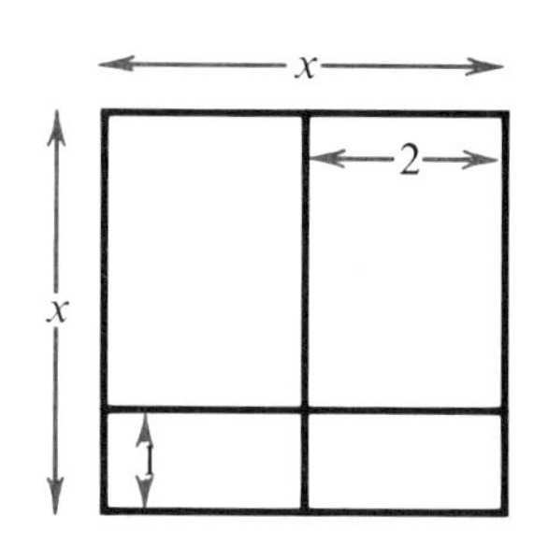

Fig. 7

5 Multiply out:

(i) $(x+2)(x+4)$; (ii) $(x+1)(x+6)$;
(iii) $(x-1)(x-1)$; (iv) $(6-x)(x+1)$;
(v) $(2x+1)(x+2)$; (vi) $\left(\frac{x}{2}+1\right)(x-1)$;
(vii) $(1-2x)(1-x)$; (viii) $(x+1)^2$;
(ix) $(x+4)^2$; (x) $(2x-1)^2$.

6 You are given one factor of each of the following expressions. Find the other factor.

(i) $x^2+7x+12$; $(x+3)$; (ii) x^2+4x+4; $(x+2)$;
(iii) x^2-x-6; $(x-3)$; (iv) $x^2+6x-16$; $(x+8)$;
(v) x^2-3x+2; $(x-1)$; (vi) $2x^2+5x+2$; $(2x+1)$;
(vii) $2x^2+x-1$; $(x+1)$; (viii) $3x^2+5x-2$; $(x+2)$;
(ix) $20x^2-19x+3$; $(5x-1)$; (x) $4x^2-25$; $(2x-5)$;
(xi) x^2-x; x; (xii) $2x^2-3x$; $(2x-3)$.

7 If $P(x) = x^2 + x + 2$, find (i) $P(1)$; (ii) $P(^-1)$; (iii) $P(0)$; (iv) $P(10)$; (v) $P(^-10)$.

3 The quadratic function

(*a*) In previous books we have discussed functions of the form $f: x \to ax + b$ (i.e. linear functions). We learned that their graphs are straight lines with gradient a and intercept on the y axis, b.

In this chapter we will discuss functions of the form $f: x \to ax^2 + bx + c$ $(a \neq 0)$, which are known as *quadratic functions*.

(b) Copy and complete this table of values for the function $f: x \to x^2 + 2x - 8$:

x	$^-5$	$^-4$	$^-3$	$^-2$	$^-1$	0	1	2	3
x^2	25	16		4	1		1		
$2x$	$^-10$	$^-8$		$^-4$	$^-2$		2		
$x^2 + 2x - 8$	7	0		$^-8$	$^-9$		$^-5$		

(c) The arrow diagram in Figure 8 represents f. Is f one to one or many to one?

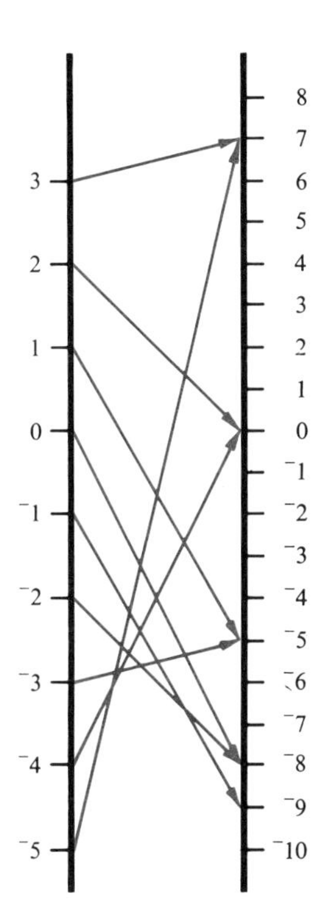

Fig. 8

Which member of the range of f is the image of one, and only one, member of the domain?

Notice that members of the domain of f, other than $^-1$, are mapped in pairs onto members of the range. For example, $^-4 \to 0$ and $2 \to 0$, i.e. if $f(x) = 0$, then $x = {}^-4$ or 2.

Notice also that $^-4$ and 2 are 'equidistant' from $^-1$ on the number line.

Are $^-5$ and 3 equidistant from $^-1$ on the number line? If x is (i) $^-5$; (ii) 3, what is $f(x)$?

What can you say about (i) $f(10)$ and $f(^-12)$; (ii) $f(^-1 + a)$ and $f(^-1 - a)$, where a is any real number?

What do your answers suggest to you about the graph of f?

(*d*) Figure 9 shows the graph of f for the domain $^{-}5 \leqslant x \leqslant 3$. The graph is symmetrical about the line $x = {}^{-}1$. The curve is called a parabola.

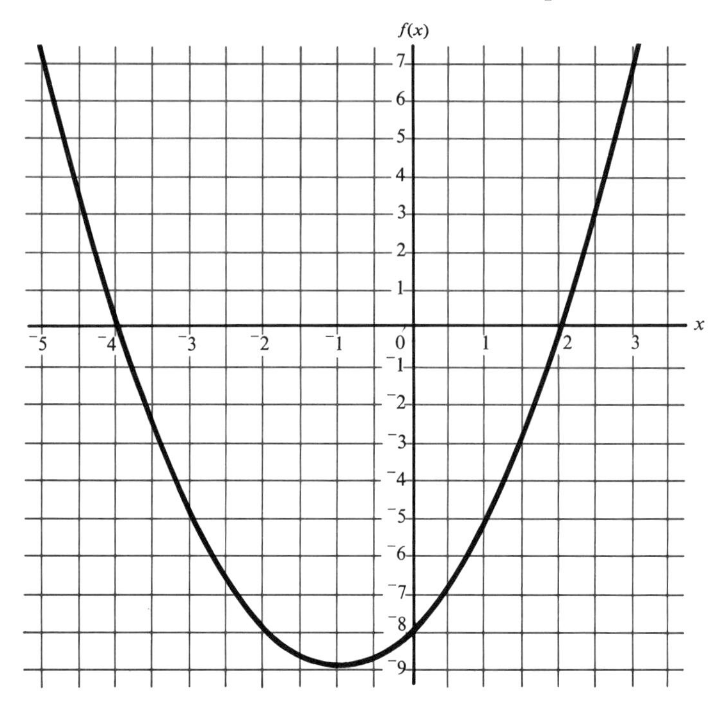

Fig. 9

Use the graph to solve the equations (i) $x^2 + 2x - 8 = 0$; (ii) $x^2 + 2x - 8 = 7$; (iii) $x^2 + 2x - 8 = \frac{1}{2}$.

(*e*) The solution set of each of the equations in (*d*) contains two members. How many members are there of the solution set of the equation $x^2 + 2x - 8 = k$ if k is (i) $^{-}9$; (ii) $^{-}4$; (iii) $^{-}12$?

What is the *least* value of $x^2 + 2x - 8$?

(*f*) Figure 10 shows the graphs of the quadratic functions (*a*) $f\colon x \to x^2 + 4x + 4$; (*b*) $g\colon x \to x^2 + 1$.

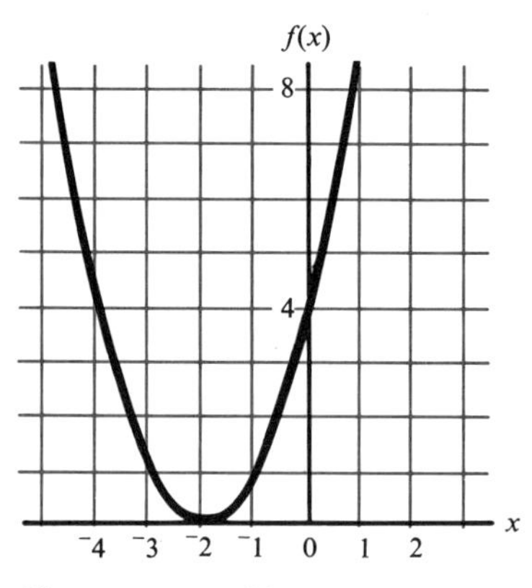

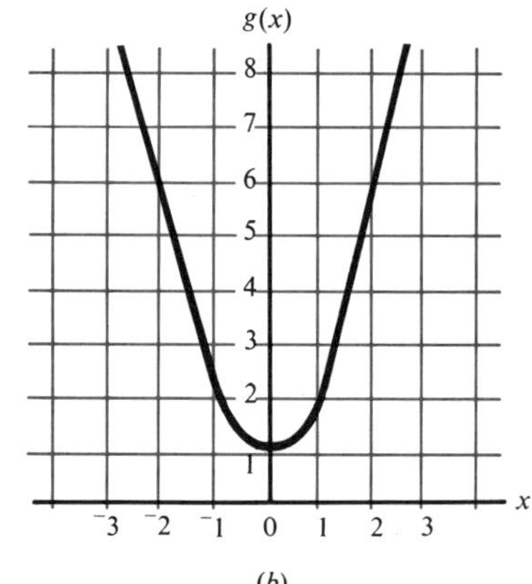

Fig. 10

(*a*) (*b*)

What is the equation of the line of symmetry of each graph?
How many members are there in the solution sets of the following equations:

(i) $x^2 + 4x + 4 = 0$; (ii) $x^2 + 1 = 0$?

Summary

1 A quadratic function f is of the form f: $x \rightarrow ax^2 + bx + c$. Its graph is a parabola, and it has a line of symmetry.

2 $f: x \rightarrow ax^2 + bx + c$ is a many to one function. Only one member of the range is the image of exactly one member of the domain. All other members of the domain are mapped in pairs onto their images.

3 The solution set of the equation $ax^2 + bx + c = 0$ may contain (i) 2 members; (ii) 1 member; (iii) 0 members. These cases are illustrated by graphs (*a*), (*b*) and (*c*) in Figure 11.

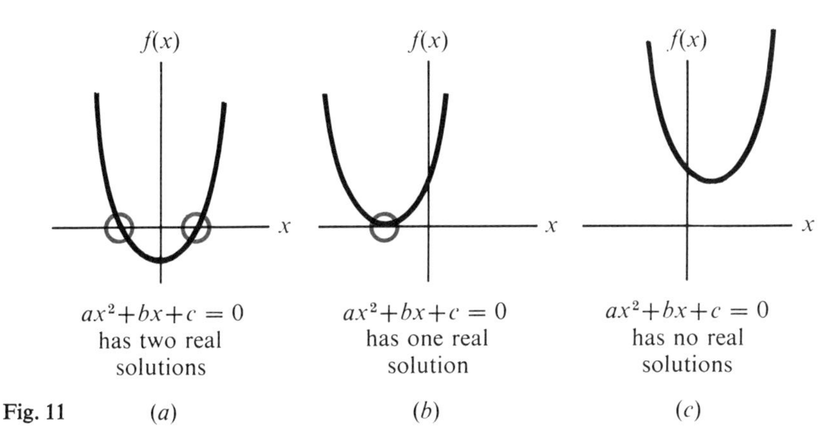

Fig. 11 (*a*) (*b*) (*c*)

Exercise B

1 Draw the graph of each of the following functions for the domain $^-4 \leqslant x \leqslant 4$. (Use the same scale for each graph.)

(i) $f: x \rightarrow x^2$; (ii) $g: x \rightarrow x^2 - 1$; (iii) $h: x \rightarrow (x-1)^2$.

What is the equation of the line of symmetry of each graph? Which geometrical transformation will map the graph of (i) f onto g; (ii) g onto h; (iii) f onto h?

2 On the same axes draw the graphs of (i) $f: x \rightarrow x^2 + 2x + 1$; (ii) $f: x \rightarrow 2x + 5$. Use your graphs to solve the equations:

(*a*) $x^2 + 2x + 1 = 2x + 5$; (*b*) $x^2 - 4 = 0$.

3 If $f: x \rightarrow x^2 - 1$, show that $f(a) = f(^-a)$. What does your answer suggest about the graph of f?

4 $f: x \rightarrow x^2 - 2x + 1$. Show that $f(1+a) = f(1-a)$. [*Hint*: $f(1+a) = (1+a)^2 - 2(1+a) + 1$]. Interpret your answer geometrically.

5 A stone is thrown over a cliff and the distance in metres it has fallen in t seconds is approximately

$$5t^2 + 20t.$$

Draw a graph showing the distance fallen as a function of time. Estimate the time when the stone has fallen 200 m.

6 (*a*) By drawing graphs find the least values of the expressions:

(i) $x^2 + 7x + 4$; (ii) $x^2 + 2x$.

(*b*) By drawing graphs find the greatest values of the expressions:

(i) $^-x^2$; (ii) $^-x^2 + 2x + 6$.

7 By drawing graphs find the number of elements in the solution sets of the equations:

(i) $x^2 - 2x - 3 = 0$; (ii) $x^2 + 2x + 1 = 0$; (iii) $x^2 + 7 = 0$;
(iv) $x^2 - 7 = 0$; (v) $x^2 + 4x + 3 = 0$; (vi) $x^2 + x + 4 = 0$.

Use your graphs to solve each equation.

4 Inverses of quadratic functions

(*a*) Compare Figure 12 with Figure 8. Do you agree that Figure 12 represents the inverse of $f: x \to x^2 + 2x - 8$? Is the inverse of f a function?

Use Figure 12 to help you draw the graph of the inverse of f taking 1 cm to represent 2 units on both axes. (Notice, for example, that 7 is mapped onto both 3 and $^-5$). On the same axes draw also the graph of f. Which geometrical transformation will map the graph of f onto the graph of its inverse?

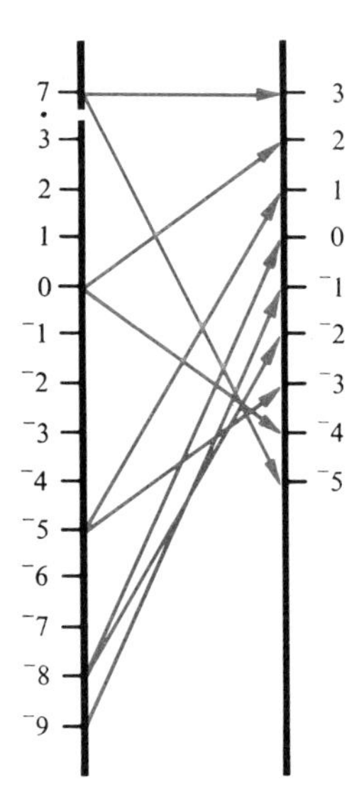

Fig. 12

(*b*) You will remember that we can use the flow diagram method to help us express the inverse of a function in the form $x \to \ldots$.

For example, consider the function $f\colon x \to x^2 - 4$:

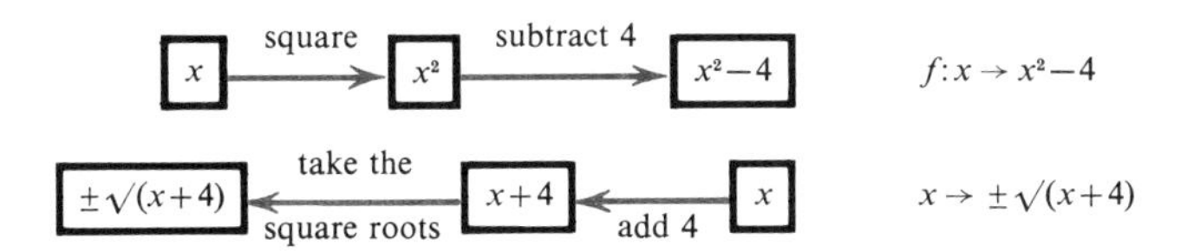

Fig. 13

The inverse relation is $x \to \pm\sqrt{(x+4)}$.

Use Figure 13 to help you solve the equations

(i) $x^2 - 4 = 0$;

(ii) $x^2 - 4 = 12$.

(*c*) Use the method above to try to express the inverse of $f\colon x \to x^2 + 2x - 8$ in the form $x \to \ldots$. If you think you have succeeded, use your mapping to find the images of (i) 0; (ii) $^-8$. Check your answers using Figure 12 and then read on.

(*d*) Unless you first expressed $x^2 + 2x - 8$ in a different form you will have found it impossible to construct f by a flow diagram.

Now check that $x^2 + 2x - 8 = (x+1)^2 - 9$, and study Figure 14.

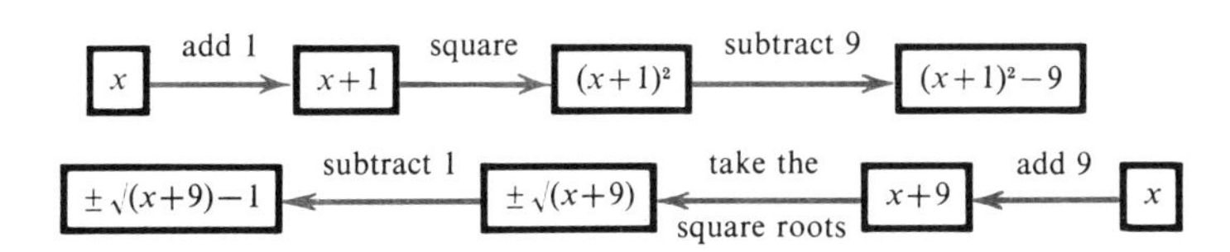

Fig. 14

The inverse of f is $x \to \pm\sqrt{(x+9)} - 1$. Use the mapping to find the images of (i) 0; (ii) $^-8$ and check your answers using Figure 12.

Use the flow diagram to solve the equations:

(i) $x^2 + 2x - 8 = 0$; (ii) $x^2 + 2x - 8 = 7$.

(*e*) Section (*d*) suggests that if we can express a quadratic function in the form $f\colon x \to (x+p)^2 + q$, then we can find its inverse. Notice that if

$$x^2 + 4x - 6 = (x+p)^2 + q, \text{ then } p = 2.$$

$$\text{So} \quad x^2 + 4x - 6 = (x+2)^2 + q.$$

What is the value of q?

Express the inverse of $f\colon x \to x^2 + 4x - 6$ in the form $x \to \ldots$.

(*f*) If $x^2 + bx + c = (x+p)^2 + q$, what is p in terms of b? Find q in terms of b and c.

Summary

1 The inverse of a quadratic function is a one to many relation.

2 The inverse relation can be expressed in the form $x \to \ldots$ by first expressing $x^2 + bx + c$ in the form $(x + p)^2 + q$ and using a flow diagram.

3 $x^2 + bx + c = \left(x + \frac{b}{2}\right)^2 + c - \frac{b^2}{4}$. [See ($f$) above.]

Exercise C

1 Complete each of the following:

(i) $x^2 + 8x + 6 = (x + 4)^2 + \cdots$; (ii) $x^2 - 6x - 3 = (x - 3)^2 + \cdots$;
(iii) $x^2 + x - 1 = (x + \frac{1}{2})^2 + \cdots$.

2 (a) Draw flow diagrams to form the functions:

(i) $f\colon x \to x^2 + 3x + 2$; (ii) $f\colon x \to x^2 - 3$; (iii) $f\colon x \to x^2 + 2x$;
(iv) $f\colon x \to (x - 3)^2$; (v) $f\colon x \to x^2 + 4x + 4$.

Hence find the inverse relation of each and write it in the form $x \to \ldots$.
(b) Solve the equations:

(i) $x^2 + 3x + 2 = 0$; (ii) $x^2 - 3 = 0$; (iii) $x^2 + 2x = 0$;
(iv) $(x - 3)^2 = 0$; (v) $x^2 + 4x + 4 = 0$.

3 Write the function $x \to x^2 + 4x + 6$ in the form $x \to (x + 2)^2 + \cdots$. What difficulty arises when you try to solve the equation

$$x^2 + 4x + 6 = 0?$$

4 Graph the function $f\colon x \to x^2 + 9$. Use a flow diagram to express the inverse of f in the form $x \to \ldots$. Try to solve the equation $x^2 + 9 = 0$. Comment with reference to your graph.

5 Express $x^2 + bx + c$ in the form $(x + p)^2 + q$. Hence express the inverse of $f\colon x \to x^2 + bx + c$ in the form $x \to \ldots$. Solve the equation $x^2 + bx + c = 0$.

5 Factors and solutions of quadratic equations

(a) Calculate (i) 2×0; (ii) $\frac{1}{2} \times 0$; (iii) $0 \times 1{\cdot}7$; (iv) 0×2; (v) 0×0; (vi) 1×0; (vii) 0×1.

(b) (i) If a and b are numbers and $a \times b = 0$, what can you say about a and b?
(ii) If $(x + 1)(x - 2) = 0$, what can you say about $(x + 1)$ and $(x - 2)$?
(iii) If $(x + 1) = 0$, what is x? If $(x - 2) = 0$ what is x?
(iv) What values of x make the expression $(x + 1)(x - 2)$ zero?
(v) Multiply out $(x + 1)(x - 2)$.
(vi) What values of x make the expression $x^2 - x - 2$ zero?
(vii) Solve the equation $x^2 - x - 2 = 0$.
(viii) Where does the graph of $f\colon x \to x^2 - x - 2$ cut the x axis?

(*c*) You should have discovered in (*b*) that if we can express $x^2 + bx + c$ in the form $(x + p)(x + q)$ then we can solve the equation $x^2 + bx + c = 0$ and the solutions are $x = {}^-p$ and $x = {}^-q$. For example, consider the equation

$$x^2 - 3x - 4 = 0.$$

Check that

$$(x - 4)(x + 1) = x^2 - 3x - 4.$$

Hence

$$(x - 4)(x + 1) = 0.$$

This is true if (i) $(x - 4) = 0$ or if (ii) $(x + 1) = 0$, that is, if $x = 4$ or ${}^-1$.
Where does the graph of $f\colon x \to x^2 - 3x - 4$ cut the x axis?

Example 1

Solve the equation

$$2x^2 + 5x - 3 = 0.$$

$$2x^2 + 5x - 3 = (2x - 1)(x + 3),$$

so

$$(2x - 1)(x + 3) = 0$$

and hence

$$x = \tfrac{1}{2} \text{ or } {}^-3.$$

Example 2

Solve the equation

$$(x - 1)^2 = x + 1.$$

Multiplying out the brackets,

$$x^2 - 2x + 1 = x + 1.$$

Subtracting x from both sides,

$$x^2 - 3x + 1 = 1.$$

Subtracting 1 from each side

$$x^2 - 3x = 0.$$

Factorizing:

$$x(x - 3) = 0,$$

and hence

$$x = 0 \text{ or } 3.$$

(*d*) It is often difficult to spot the factors of a quadratic expression. In such cases, quadratic equations can be solved by writing expressions like $x^2 + bx + c$ in the form $(x + p)^2 + q$ and proceeding as below:
Consider the equation $x^2 - 4x + 1 = 0$.
Can you spot the factors of $x^2 - 4x + 1$?
Check that $x^2 - 4x + 1 = (x - 2)^2 - 3$.
Hence $(x - 2)^2 - 3 = 0$.

Adding 3 to each side, we have

$$(x-2)^2 = 3$$

and taking the square root of each side,

$$x - 2 = \pm\sqrt{3}.$$

Hence

$$x = 2 \pm \sqrt{3}$$

$$x = 2 + 1{\cdot}732 \text{ or } 2 - 1{\cdot}732$$

that is

$$x = 3{\cdot}732 \text{ or } 0{\cdot}268.$$

[Notice that the factors of $x^2 - 4x + 1$ are $(x - 3{\cdot}732)$ and $(x - 0{\cdot}268)$.]

Now solve the equation $2x^2 - 12x + 10 = 0$ by first dividing both sides by 2. Did you get $x = 5$ or 1?

Notice that if we were to write the factors of $2x^2 - 12x + 10$, we must re-introduce the 2 which was 'lost' from the expression when we divided by 2:

$$2x^2 - 12x + 10 = 2(x-1)(x-5).$$

Exercise D

1 Solve the following equations by first of all expressing the left-hand side in terms of its factors:

(i) $x^2 - 7x + 12 = 0$; (ii) $x^2 + 6x + 9 = 0$;
(iii) $x^2 - 4x - 12 = 0$; (iv) $x^2 - 4 = 0$;
(v) $x^2 - 4x = 0$; (vi) $2x^2 + x - 1 = 0$;
(vii) $2x^2 + 5x + 3 = 0$; (viii) $3x^2 + 4x + 1 = 0$;
(ix) $2x^2 - 7x + 3 = 0$; (x) $x^2 - 25 = 0$;
(xi) $2x^2 + 3x = 0$.

2 Solve the equations in Question 1 by first expressing the left-hand side in the form $(x+p)^2 + q$, and continuing as in section (*d*) above.

3 The solutions of a quadratic equation $x^2 + bx + c = 0$ are $x = 2$ and $x = 3$. (i) Write down the factors of the expression $x^2 + bx + c$; (ii) multiply the factors and rearrange the terms in the form $x^2 + bx + c = 0$.

Answer the same question if the solutions are (i) $x = 1$, $x = {}^{-}1$; (ii) $x = 3$, $x = {}^{-}1$; (iii) $x = \frac{1}{2}$, $x = 10$; (iv) $x = 0$, $x = 1$; (v) $x = 0$, $x = {}^{-}1$.

4 Solve the equations:

(i) $x^2 + x - 1 = x$;
(ii) $x^2 + 3x - 1 = {}^{-}1$;
(iii) $(x+1)^2 = 1$;
(iv) $x^2 + 7x - 4 = 7x$.

5 Where do the graphs of f: $x \to 2x^2 + 2x + 1$; g: $x \to 2x^2 + 2x$ intersect? Solve algebraically the equation $2x^2 + 2x + 1 = 2x^2 + 2x$.

Some properties of the circle

1 Introduction

In this interlude we are going to look at some of the properties of a circle. Before we do this, however, let us remind ourselves of the angle properties of a triangle.

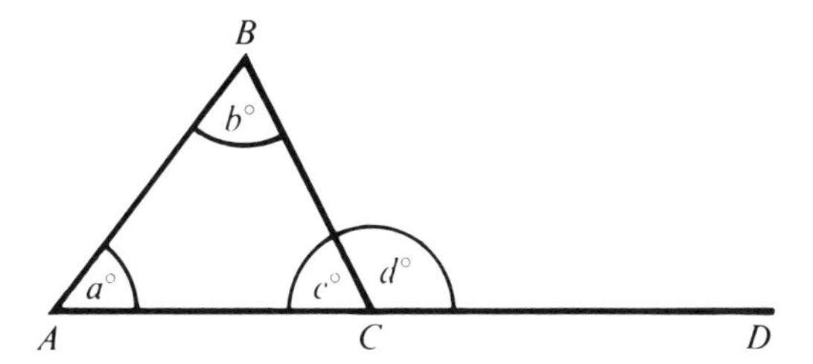

Fig. 1

In Figure 1 the interior angles of the triangle ABC are $a°$, $b°$ and $c°$. Figure 2 will help remind you that the angle sum of a triangle is 180°, i.e. $a° + b° + c° = 180°$

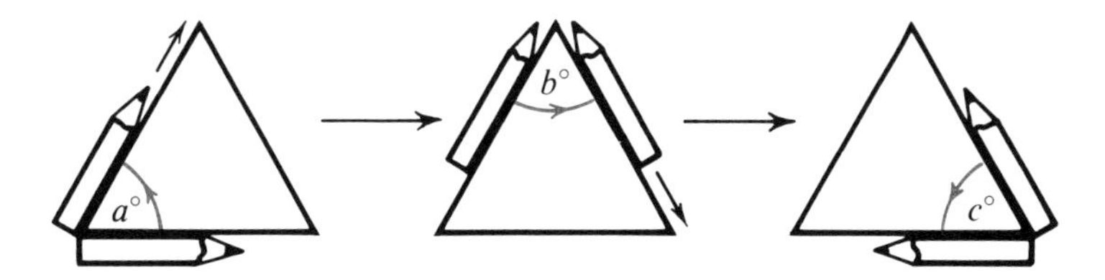

Fig. 2

(in turning through the three angles of the triangle the pencil has been given a half-turn).

However, $d° + c° = 180°$, because the two angles lie on a straight line.

Hence $d° = a° + b°$.

That is, the exterior angle ($d°$) of a triangle equals the sum of the two opposite interior angles ($a° + b°$). What does Figure 3 suggest to you about the angles marked $p°$, $q°$ and $r°$?

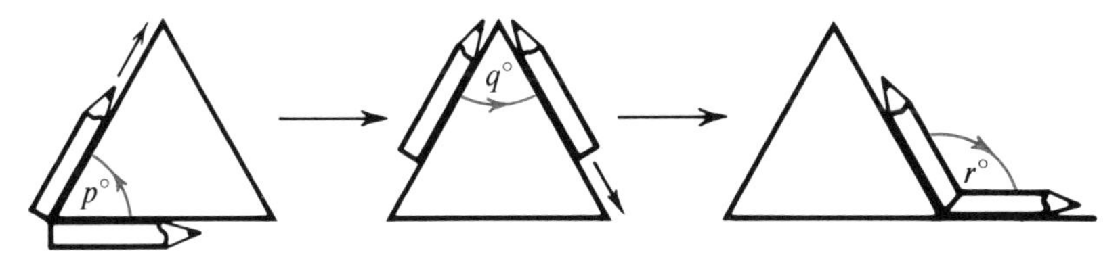

Fig. 3

2 Some descriptive terms about the circle

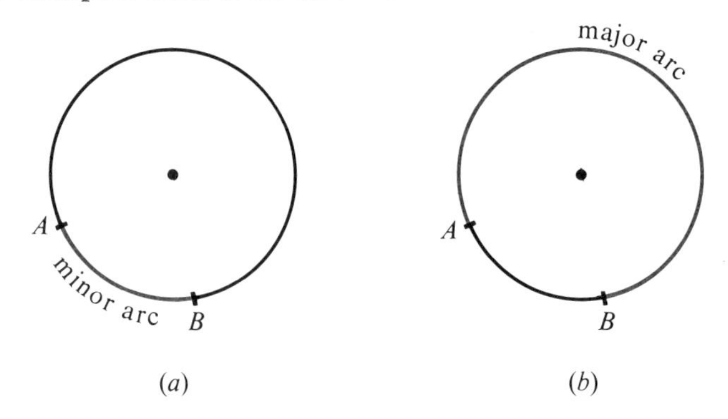

Fig. 4

(*a*) The red arc in Figure 4(*a*) is called a *minor* arc of the circle, and the red arc in Figure 4(*b*), a *major* arc. How do you think we distinguish between minor and major arcs?

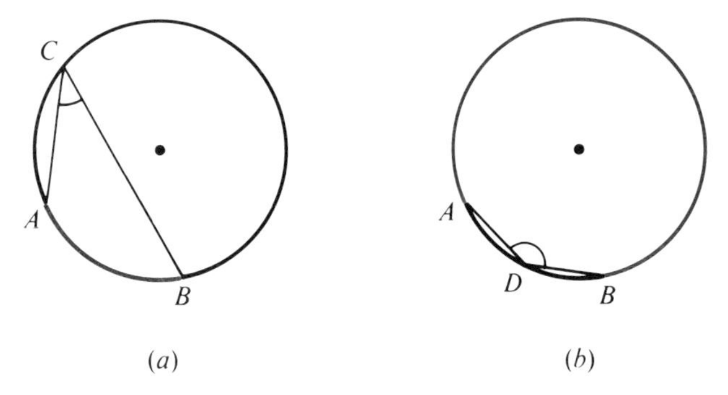

Fig. 5

(*b*) Figure 5(*a*) shows an angle *ACB* 'standing on' the (minor) arc *AB*. Notice that *C* lies on the circumference of the circle. We say that angle *ACB* is an angle 'subtended at the circumference of the circle by the (minor) arc *AB*'. How would you describe angle *ADB* in Figure 5(*b*)? Which arcs subtend the angles marked $a°$, $b°$, $c°$, $d°$, $e°$, $f°$ and $g°$ in Figure 6?

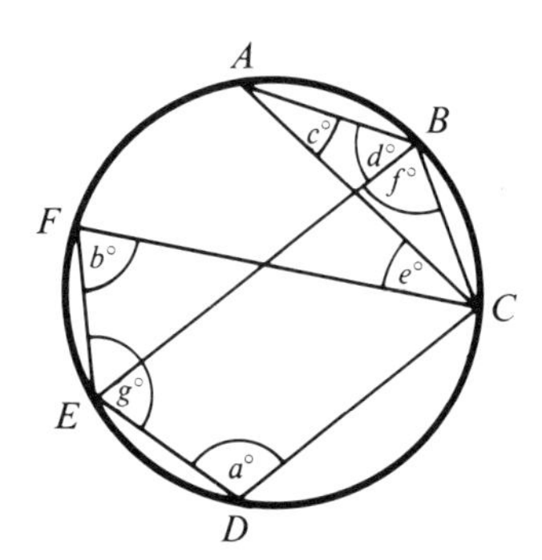

Fig. 6

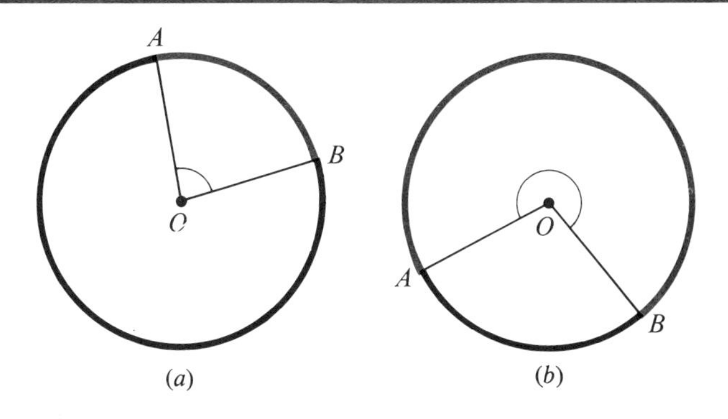

Fig. 7

(*c*) O is the centre of the circles in Figure 7. In Figure 7(*a*) angle AOB is the angle 'subtended at the centre by the (minor) arc AB'. Would you describe the reflex angle AOB in Figure 7(*b*) in exactly the same way?

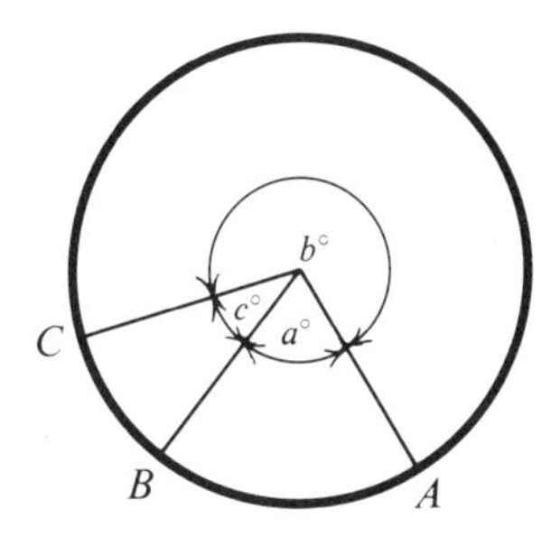

Fig. 8

Describe the angles marked $a°$, $b°$ and $c°$ in Figure 8.

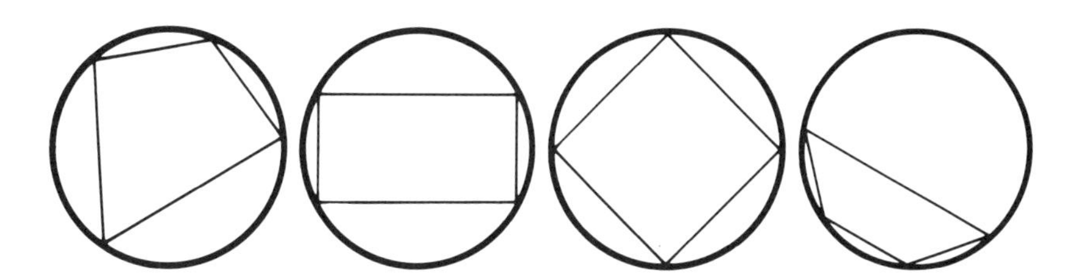

Fig. 9

(*d*) Quadrilaterals whose vertices all lie on the circumference of a circle are called *cyclic quadrilaterals*. Figure 9 shows some examples of cyclic quadrilaterals.

Are all rectangles cyclic quadrilaterals? Give reasons for your answer. Which of the following are always cyclic quadrilaterals: (i) squares; (ii) parallelograms; (iii) rhombuses; (iv) kites?

3 Some properties of the circle

(a) Look at Figures 10(a), (b) and (c).

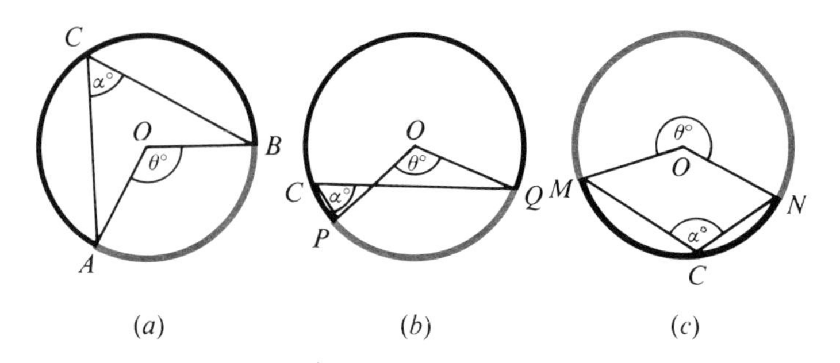

Fig. 10

Describe the angles $\theta°$ and $\alpha°$ in each case by referring to the red arcs.

Draw some diagrams like those in Figure 10 and use your protractor to measure $\theta°$ and $\alpha°$. What do you notice? Draw some more diagrams showing angles at the centre,($\theta°$), and angles on the circumference, ($\alpha°$), subtended by the same arc. Measure $\theta°$ and $\alpha°$ in each case. Is the relationship between θ and α always the same?

Property 1: concerning angles at the centre and angles at the circumference

Study Figure 11. Explain why (i) $\angle CBO = \angle BCO$; (ii) $\angle OCA = \angle CAO$. (Notice that $CO = OA = OB$.)

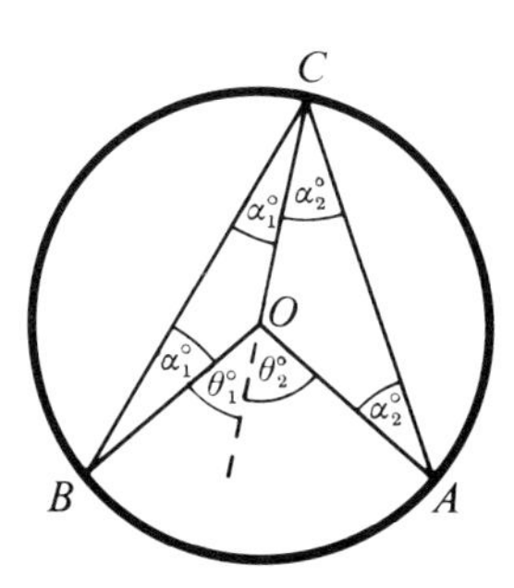

Fig. 11

Since the exterior angle of a triangle is equal to the sum of the two opposite interior angles, we have in $\triangle BOC$,

$$\theta_1^\circ = \alpha_1^\circ + \alpha_1^\circ = 2\alpha_1^\circ,$$

and in $\triangle COA$,

$$\theta_2^\circ = \alpha_2^\circ + \alpha_2^\circ = 2\alpha_2^\circ.$$

Hence

$$\theta_1^\circ + \theta_2^\circ = 2(\alpha_1^\circ + \alpha_2^\circ)$$

i.e.

$$\theta^\circ = 2\alpha^\circ, \text{ where } \angle BOA = \theta^\circ \text{ and } \angle BCA = \alpha^\circ.$$

It can be shown by similar arguments that $\theta^\circ = 2\alpha^\circ$ in the other cases represented by Figures 10(*b*) and (*c*). You might like to do this yourself. We can conclude that 'the angle subtended at the centre of a circle by an arc is twice the angle subtended at the circumference by the same arc'. We will call this Property 1.

There are several properties of the circle, and of cyclic quadrilaterals which can be derived using this result. Use the suggestions that follow to derive the properties for yourself.

Property 2: concerning angles at the circumference subtended by the same arc

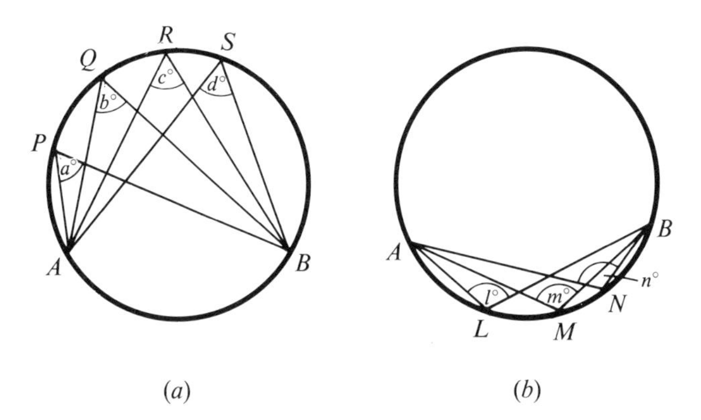

Fig. 12

Copy Figures 12(*a*) and 12(*b*) and measure the angles marked a°, b°, c°, d° and l°, m°, n° (the exact positions of *A, B, P, Q, R, S, L, M, N* are not important). What do you notice?

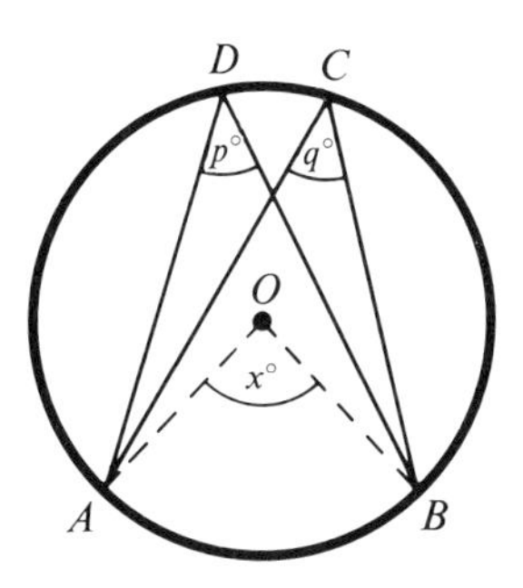

Fig. 13

In Figure 13, $x^\circ = 2p^\circ$ (by Property 1). Write a similar equation involving x° and q°. What can you say about p° and q°?

Does this confirm your findings about the angles marked a°, b°, c° and d° in Figure 12(*a*), and l°, m° and n° in Figure 12(*b*)?

What do your results tell you about angles at the circumference subtended by the same arc?

Property 3: concerning angles in a semi-circle

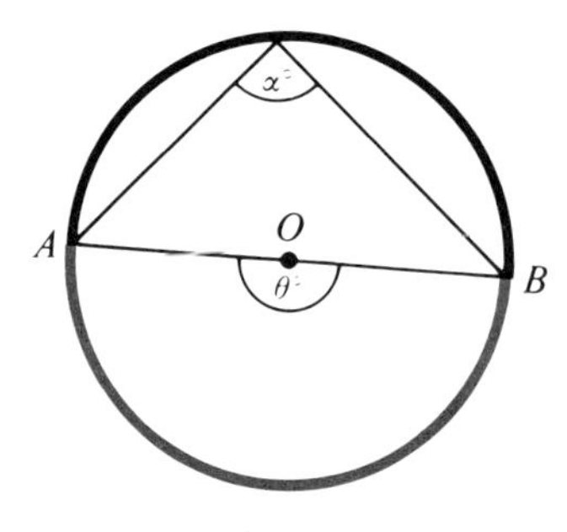

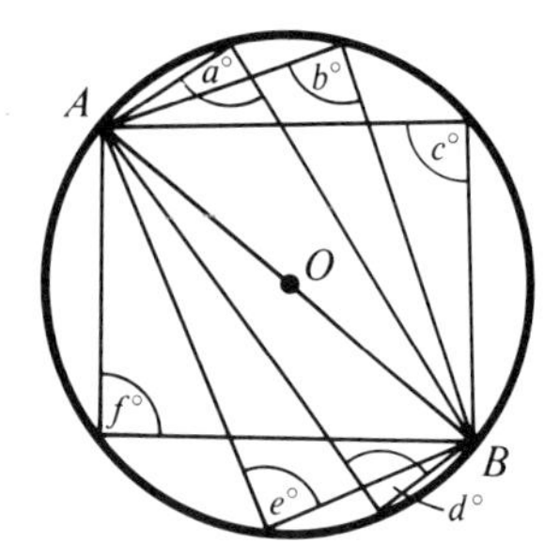

Fig. 14

Fig. 15

What does Property 1 tell you about the relationship between $\theta°$ and $\alpha°$ in Figure 14?

If AOB is a diameter what is the angle θ in degrees?

What is the angle α in degrees?

In Figure 15 AOB is a diameter. What can you say about the angles marked $a°$, $b°$, $c°$, $d°$, $e°$ and $f°$?

Property 4: concerning opposite angles of a cyclic quadrilateral

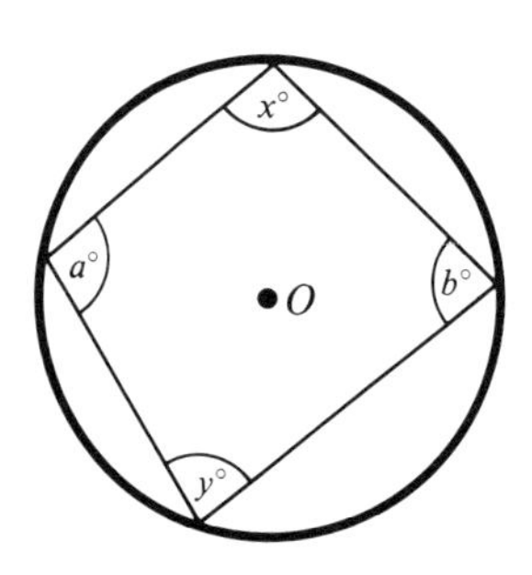

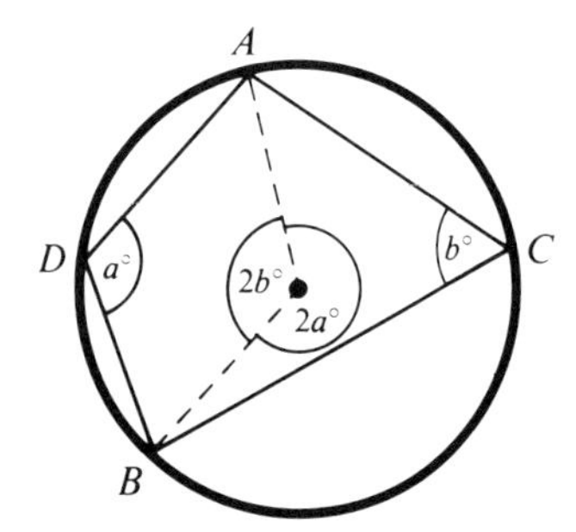

Fig. 16

Fig. 17

Draw some diagrams of cyclic quadrilaterals. Measure the interior angles (the angles marked $a°$, $b°$, $x°$, $y°$ in Figure 16). What do your results suggest about the values of $x° + y°$ and $a° + b°$?

Explain why the labelling of the angles in Figure 17 as $a°$, $b°$, $2a°$ and $2b°$ is correct. What is the value of $2a° + 2b°$? Can you deduce the value of $a° + b°$?

What is the sum in degrees of the opposite angles of any cyclic quadrilateral?

Property 5: concerning the exterior angle of a cyclic quadrilateral

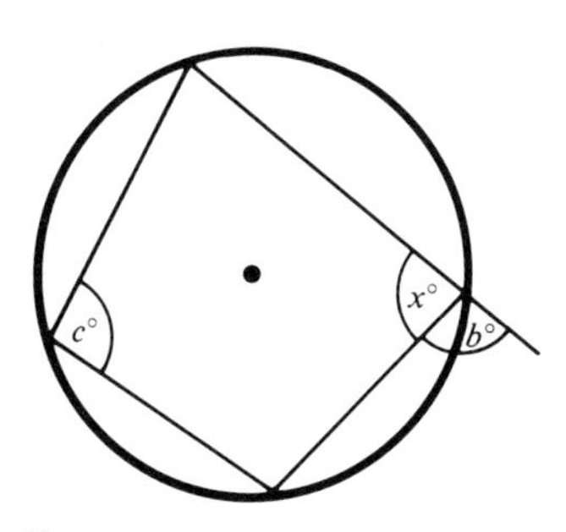

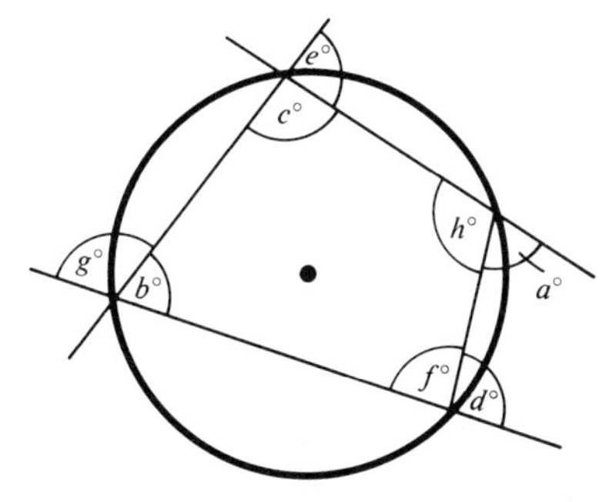

Fig. 18

Fig. 19

In Figure 18,

$$x^\circ + c^\circ = 180^\circ \text{ (why?)}$$

and

$$x^\circ + b^\circ = 180^\circ \text{ (why?)}$$

What do these equations tell you about the exterior angle of a cyclic quadrilateral (b°) and the opposite interior angle (c°)?

Write some equations connecting pairs of angles marked in Figure 19. (For example $a^\circ = b^\circ$.)

Property 6

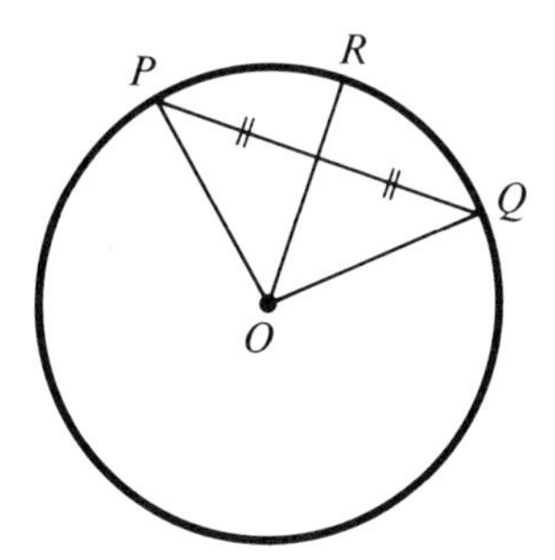

Fig. 20

Explain why triangle POQ in Figure 20 is isosceles.

By the symmetry of an isosceles triangle we know that PQ is perpendicular to OR. Now consider the sequence of diagrams in Figure 21. Angle BOA is decreasing at each stage until OA and OB are coincident. What does this sequence suggest about the angle in which a radius meets a tangent to a circle (i.e. about the angle marked θ°)?

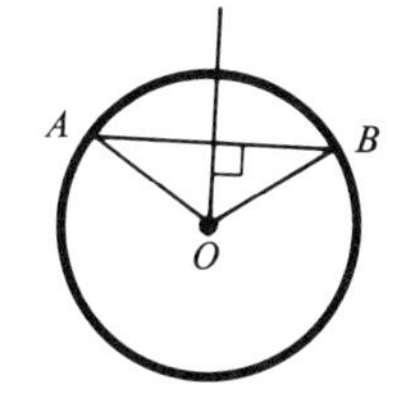

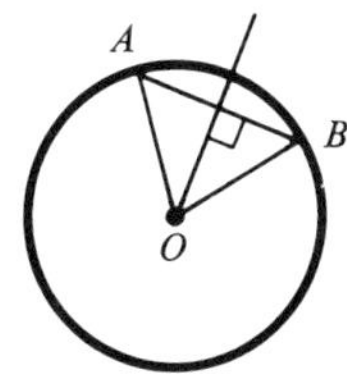

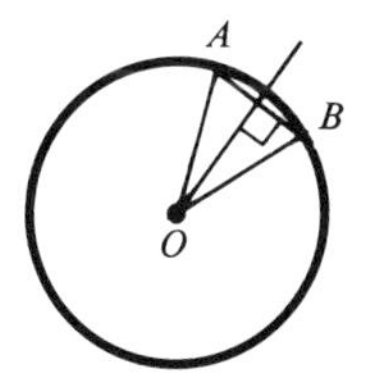

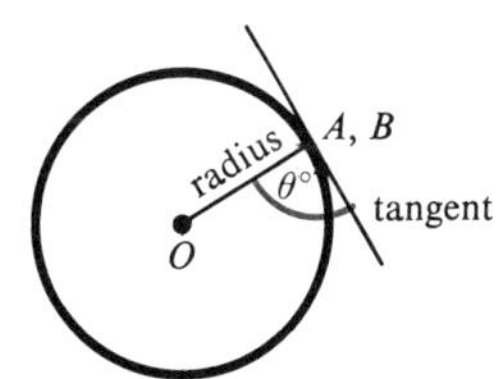

Fig. 21

Property 7

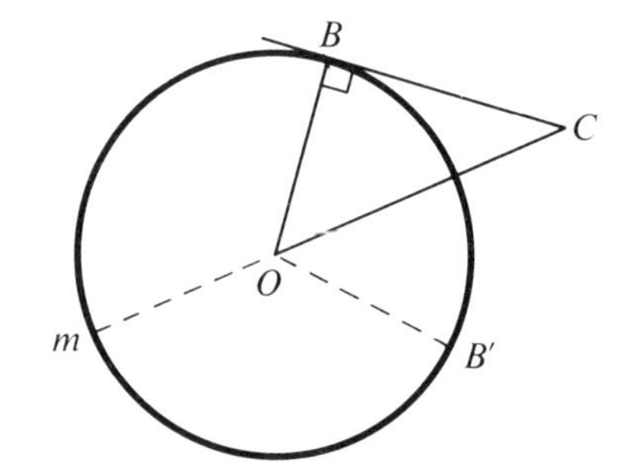

Fig. 22

Since the line m in Figure 22 is a line of symmetry of the circle, B', the image of B after a reflection in m, will be on the circumference of the circle. Where is C', the image of C, under this reflection? How many degrees is the angle $OB'C$? Is the line through $B'C'$ (i.e. through $B'C$) a tangent to the circle? What can you say about the lengths of the line segments CB and CB'? If you draw two tangents from a point to a circle what can you say about the tangents?

Summary

You should have discovered the following about circles:

(i) the angle subtended at the centre by an arc is twice the angle subtended at the circumference by that arc;

(ii) angles at the circumference subtended by the same arc are equal;

(iii) angles in a semi-circle are right angles;

(iv) the opposite angles of a cyclic quadrilateral sum to 180°;

(v) the exterior angle of a cyclic quadrilateral is equal to the opposite interior angle;

(vi) a tangent and radius meet on the circumference of the circle in a right angle;

(vii) if two tangents are drawn to a circle from a point P, to touch the circle at A and B, then $PA = PB$.

Investigation 1

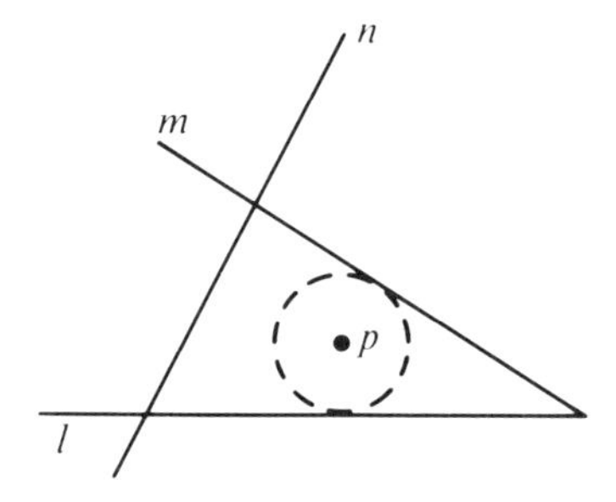

Fig. 23

Copy Figure 23 and draw several more circles which have the lines l and m as tangents. What is the locus of the centres of all the circles which have the lines l and m as tangents?

What is the locus of the centres of the circles which have (i) m and n; (ii) l and n as tangents?

Draw a triangle and construct its in-circle (that is, the circle which touches the three sides of the triangle).

Investigation 2

Find the radius in cm of the largest metal disc that can be cut from a triangular metal plate with sides 12 cm, 8 cm and 10 cm.

Investigation 3

Use any circular object (such as a 2p piece) to draw a circle. Use a pair of compasses and a ruler to find the centre of the circle.

Investigation 4

Figure 24 shows a plan of a circular art-gallery. P is a hidden camera which scans 60°. You have been asked to install cameras as an anti-theft device. How many cameras would you use and exactly where would you fix them (they must be fixed to the walls)?

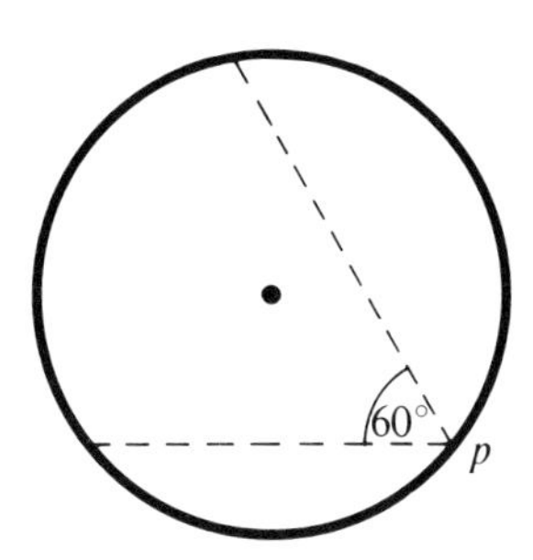

Fig. 24

How many cameras would you need if each scanned (*a*) 40°; (*b*) 90°?

Investigation 5

A circle has radius a cm. What is the maximum area of any quadrilateral inscribed in this circle?

Revision exercises

Computation 2

1 It takes me between 12 and 17 minutes to drive from Abingdon to Oxford station. I must allow at least 5 minutes for parking and buying my ticket. The train I want to catch departs at 16.33 hours. What is the latest time (given in the ordinary way, not on the '24 hour' system) that I can safely leave Abingdon?

2 Calculate in your head 999×23.

3 Calculate in your head $(64 \times 29) - (32 \times 58)$.

4 Calculate in your head $28\,640\,082 \times 50$.

5 Calculate in your head $0{\cdot}125 \times 684$.

6 A mathematics teacher wins £382·75 in a game of roulette. He generously shares it out equally amongst 25 pupils, keeping nothing for himself. How much does each pupil receive?

7 What is the smallest number which must bc added to 3370 to make it a square number?

8 What is the smallest number which must be added to 1700 to make it a cube number?

9 A certain number may be added to both the top and bottom of the fraction $\frac{101}{245}$ to make it equivalent to $\frac{1}{2}$. What is it?

10 Is it true that $123\,456 \times 654\,321 = 80\,779\,853\,376$?

Computation 3

1 Evaluate the following. (Look for easy methods.)

(*a*) $15 + 66 + 92 + 34 + 8 + 85$;
(*b*) $1 + 2 + 3 + \cdots + 97 + 98 + 99$;
(*c*) $1{\cdot}21 + 4{\cdot}89 + 6{\cdot}11 + 8{\cdot}79 + 7{\cdot}84 - 2{\cdot}3 - 7{\cdot}7$.

2 Check the following additions:

(*a*) (in binary);
$$\begin{array}{r} 1110 \\ +111 \\ \hline 10101 \\ \hline \end{array}$$

(*b*) (in base three);
$$\begin{array}{r} 1010 \\ 101 \\ 211 \\ \hline 1322 \\ \hline \end{array}$$

(*c*) $99 + 38 + 88 + 14 = 230$ (in base twelve).

3 A cricketer scores 320 runs in 15 innings, and takes 24 wickets for 371 runs. What are his batting and bowling averages?

4 Boulogne is 243 km from Paris? How long will it take to drive from Boulogne to Paris at an average speed of 35 km/h?

5 Is the record of 10·1 seconds for 100 m faster or slower than the record 9·2 seconds for 100 yards? (A 'yard' is an old unit of length, 1 yard = 0·914 m.)

6 A cube has a volume of 1·679 cm³. What is the length of each of its edges?

7 Is it true that $342 - 89 = 342 + 11 - 100$? Compute by easy methods:

(*a*) $534 - 89$; (*b*) $6345 - 89$; (*c*) $652 - 96$;
(*d*) $796 - 99$; (*e*) $1462 - 989$; (*f*) $7231 - 994$.

Exercise F

1 Give the inverse of the function $x \to 2x - 1$.

2 Simplify $\frac{1}{2} - \frac{1}{3} + \frac{1}{4}$.

3 Give the equation of the straight line passing through $(3, 4)$ and $(6, 7)$.

4 How many square centimetres are there in 1 m²?

5 Find t if $t(t + 7) = 0$.

6 Find the number base of the correct subtraction $234 - 45 = 167$.

7 Find $12\frac{1}{2}\%$ of £2.

8 Give the value of $\sin 90° + \sin 30°$.

9 Solve $x^2 + 2x + 1 = 0$.

10 Give the value of $(^-2)^3 + 2^3$.

Exercise G

1 Find y if $y = \dfrac{1}{x}$ and $x = \frac{3}{4} \div \frac{1}{2}$.

2 Give the value of $(^-3)^2 + 3^2$.

3 Sphere A has three times the diameter of sphere B. How many times greater is its volume?

4 Find p if $\frac{1}{2}(2p - 1) = 7$.

5 A is the point $(1, 2)$. Find the coordinates of point C if

$$\mathbf{AB} = \begin{pmatrix} ^-2 \\ 1 \end{pmatrix} \quad \text{and} \quad \mathbf{BC} = \begin{pmatrix} 3 \\ ^-4 \end{pmatrix}.$$

6 Perform the matrix multiplication

$$\begin{pmatrix} 2 & ^-1 \\ ^-1 & 0 \end{pmatrix}\begin{pmatrix} 1 & 2 \\ 3 & 4 \end{pmatrix}.$$

7 Calculate the gradient of the line joining (2, 5) and (7, 4).

8 What can you say about the sets A and B if $A \cap B = B$?

9 Find $f(^-3)$ if $f(x) = x^3 - x - 3$.

10 What is the probability of obtaining two heads when three coins are tossed?

Exercise H

1 (*a*) What geometrical transformation is associated with the matrix $\begin{pmatrix} 0 & 1 \\ 1 & 0 \end{pmatrix}$?

(*b*) What is the multiplicative inverse of $\begin{pmatrix} 0 & 1 \\ 1 & 0 \end{pmatrix}$?

2 If **R** denotes an anticlockwise rotation of 240° about the origin, describe (i) $\mathbf{R}^2$; (ii) $\mathbf{R}^3$; (iii) $\mathbf{R}^{-1}$.

3 What point is mapped onto $(0, ^-5)$ by the transformation

$$\begin{pmatrix} x \\ y \end{pmatrix} \to \begin{pmatrix} 2 & 4 \\ ^-1 & 3 \end{pmatrix}\begin{pmatrix} x \\ y \end{pmatrix}?$$

4 (*a*) Write down an equation involving x which has the two possible solutions $x = 0$ or $x = 2$.
(*b*) If $p + q = 7$ and $p^2 + q^2 = 25$, find the value of pq.
(*c*) If $r + s = 7$ and $r^2 - s^2 = 28$, find the value of $r - s$.

5 Ludlow is 35 kilometres due north of Hereford, and 32 kilometres due west of Kidderminster. Find the bearing of Kidderminster from Hereford.

6 The sizes of two acute angles in a right-angled triangle are in the ratio 7 to 11. How big are they?

7 The two cylinders in Figure 1 are similar.
(*a*) If the diameter of the circular base of the smaller cylinder is 9 cm what is the diameter of the base of the larger one?
(*b*) What is the ratio of their diameters?
(*c*) What is the ratio of (i) their surface areas; (ii) their volumes?

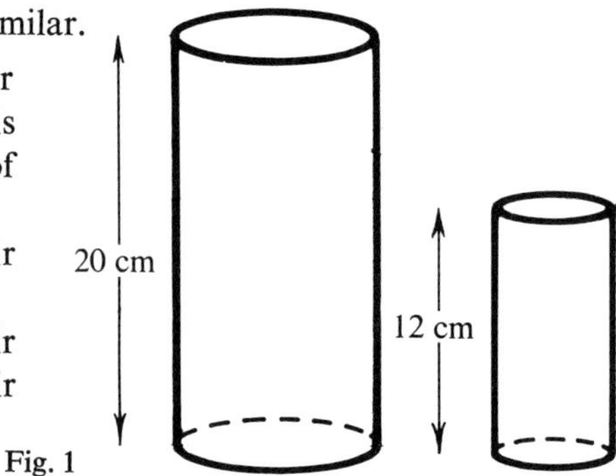

Fig. 1

8 The square $OABC$ is enlarged and then sheared to $OA'B'C'$ as shown in Figure 2. Find the matrix which represents this transformation.

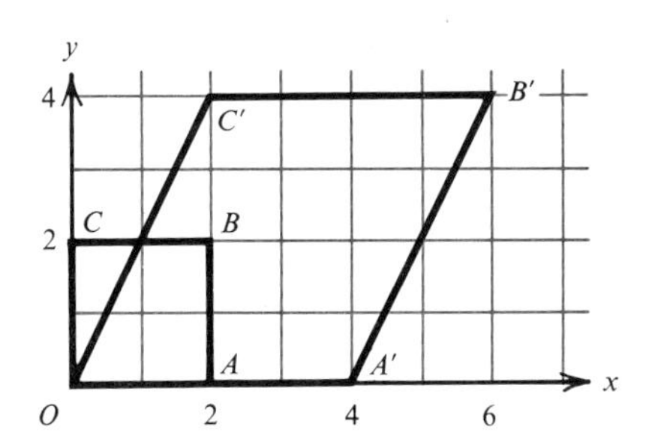

Fig. 2

Exercise I

1 Write down the inverse, $\mathbf{B}$, of the matrix

$$\mathbf{A} = \begin{pmatrix} 5 & 3 \\ 2 & 1 \end{pmatrix}.$$

Simplify $\mathbf{A}^2\mathbf{B}^2$.

2 (*a*) Find the determinants of the matrices:

(i) $\begin{pmatrix} ^-2 & 3 \\ 1 & 5 \end{pmatrix}$; (ii) $\begin{pmatrix} ^-2 & ^-3 \\ ^-4 & ^-6 \end{pmatrix}$.

(*b*) Write down, if possible, the multiplicative inverses of the above matrices.

3 Each of the following matrices represents a transformation. In each case illustrate the transformation by a sketch showing the image of the unit square and describe the transformation geometrically.

(*a*) $\begin{pmatrix} 3 & 0 \\ 0 & 1 \end{pmatrix}$; (*b*) $\begin{pmatrix} 0 & 0 \\ 0 & 1 \end{pmatrix}$; (*c*) $\begin{pmatrix} ^-1 & 0 \\ 0 & 1 \end{pmatrix}$;

(*d*) $\begin{pmatrix} 0 & ^-1 \\ ^-1 & 0 \end{pmatrix}$; (*e*) $\begin{pmatrix} 1 & 0 \\ 0 & 2 \end{pmatrix}$; (*f*) $\begin{pmatrix} 1 & 0 \\ 0 & 0 \end{pmatrix}$.

4 Calculate the areas of the shapes in Figure 3.

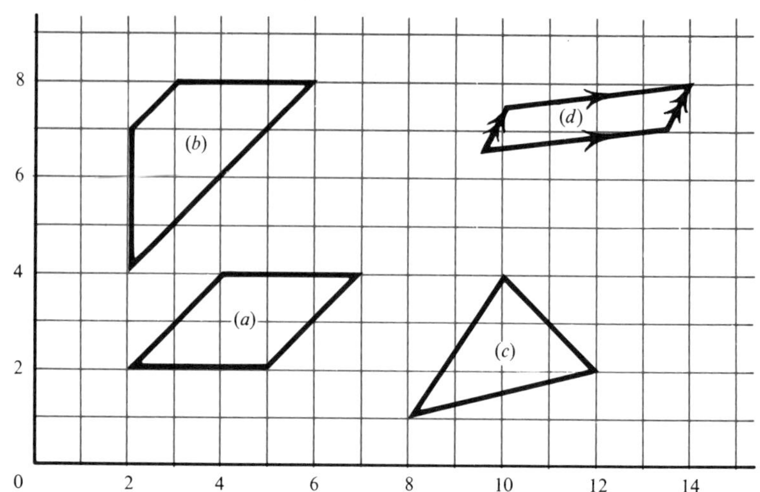

Fig. 3

5 Calculate the volume and surface area of a cube with an edge of 7 cm.

6 Draw a right-angled triangle ABC in which $\tan A = \frac{3}{4}$. Without using tables find $\sin A$ and $\cos A$.

7 A ship sets out from Port Barnacle and sails along a straight course. After a time its position is recorded as 60 km north and 80 km east of the port. How far has it then sailed, and what angle does its course make with a northerly direction?

8 A certain fly is sitting at a point A on the lower rim of an upright cylinder. It climbs on a path of constant slope round the outside of the cylinder, and reaches a point B on the upper rim vertically above A after one rotation. If the circumference of the cylinder is 36 cm and its height is 15 cm, find the length of the fly's journey from A to B.

Exercise J

1 Multiply:

(*a*) $(x+2)(x+7)$; (*b*) $(x-2)(x-7)$;
(*c*) $(x+2)(x-7)$; (*d*) $(x-2)(x+7)$;
(*e*) $(2x+1)(x-4)$; (*f*) $(2x+1)(2x-1)$;
(*g*) $\left(\frac{x}{2}+1\right)(x+1)$; (*h*) $\left(\frac{x}{2}-1\right)(2x+1)$.

2 Solve the following equations:

(*a*) $x^2+2x+2=1$; (*b*) $x^2+5x+8=2$;
(*c*) $x^2+x-6=0$; (*d*) $x^2-x={}^{-}6$;
(*e*) $x^2-9=0$; (*f*) $x^2+9={}^{-}6x$;
(*g*) $x^2+4={}^{-}4x$; (*h*) $x^2=1$.

3 Solve the following equations:

(*a*) $x^2 - 9x = 0$; (*b*) $2x^2 - 5x + 3 = 0$;
(*c*) $3x^2 + 8x + 5 = 0$; (*d*) $4x^2 - 64 = 0$;
(*e*) $2x^2 + 5x = 0$; (*f*) $7x^2 + 6x - 1 = 0$;
(*g*) $9x^2 - 81 = 0$; (*h*) $2x^2 + 6x + 18 = 0$.

4 A transformation maps the unit square $OIAJ$ onto the rhombus with vertices at $O(0,0)$, $I'(2,4)$, $A'(^-2,2)$ and $J'(^-4,^-2)$. Write down the matrix which represents this transformation and hence find the area of $OI'A'J'$.

5 If $\mathbf{A} = \begin{pmatrix} 3 & ^-1 \\ 2 & 1 \end{pmatrix}$, calculate $\mathbf{A}^{-1}$.

6 A transformation $\mathbf{T}$ is defined by

$$\mathbf{T}: \begin{pmatrix} x \\ y \end{pmatrix} \to \begin{pmatrix} 2 & 1 \\ 3 & 2 \end{pmatrix}\begin{pmatrix} x \\ y \end{pmatrix} + \begin{pmatrix} ^-1 \\ 3 \end{pmatrix}.$$

Find the inverse transformation and hence find the coordinates of the point mapped by $\mathbf{T}$ onto $(2, 5)$.

7 If

$$\mathbf{A} = \begin{pmatrix} 1 & 2 & 1 \\ 3 & 0 & ^-2 \\ 2 & 1 & 0 \end{pmatrix} \quad \text{and} \quad \mathbf{B} = \begin{pmatrix} ^-2 & ^-1 & 4 \\ 4 & 2 & ^-5 \\ ^-3 & ^-3 & 6 \end{pmatrix}$$

find $\mathbf{AB}$ and hence give the multiplicative inverses of $\mathbf{A}$ and $\mathbf{B}$.

8 Show that the mapping

$$\begin{pmatrix} x \\ y \\ 1 \end{pmatrix} \to \begin{pmatrix} 3 & ^-2 & 4 \\ 1 & 0 & 6 \\ 0 & 0 & 1 \end{pmatrix}\begin{pmatrix} x \\ y \\ 1 \end{pmatrix}$$

has the same effect as the mapping

$$\begin{pmatrix} x \\ y \end{pmatrix} \to \begin{pmatrix} 3 & ^-2 \\ 1 & 0 \end{pmatrix}\begin{pmatrix} x \\ y \end{pmatrix} + \begin{pmatrix} 4 \\ 6 \end{pmatrix}.$$

9 Simultaneous equations and inequalities

1 Equations with two variables

Consider the equation

$$2x + y = 12.$$

If $x = 2$, what is the value of y?

One solution of the equation $2x + y = 12$ is $x = 2$, $y = 8$. Write down some other solutions of this equation. How many solutions are there?

Now write down some solutions of the equation

$$x - y = 3.$$

How many solutions does this equation have?

Can you find a solution of the equations

$$\begin{cases} 2x + y = 12 \\ x - y = 3 \end{cases}$$

taken together, that is, can you find values of x and y which satisfy both these equations simultaneously?

Is there more than one such solution?

2 Solving simultaneous equations and inequalities

(*a*) Using graphs

(*a*) We already know one method of solving simultaneous equations such as

$$\begin{cases} 2x + y = 12 \\ x - y = 3. \end{cases}$$

Figure 1 should remind you of this method.

The graphs of $2x + y = 12$ and $x - y = 3$ intersect in the point $(5, 2)$. Therefore $x = 5$, $y = 2$ satisfies both the equation $2x + y = 12$ and the equation $x - y = 3$.

Do the graphs intersect in any other point?

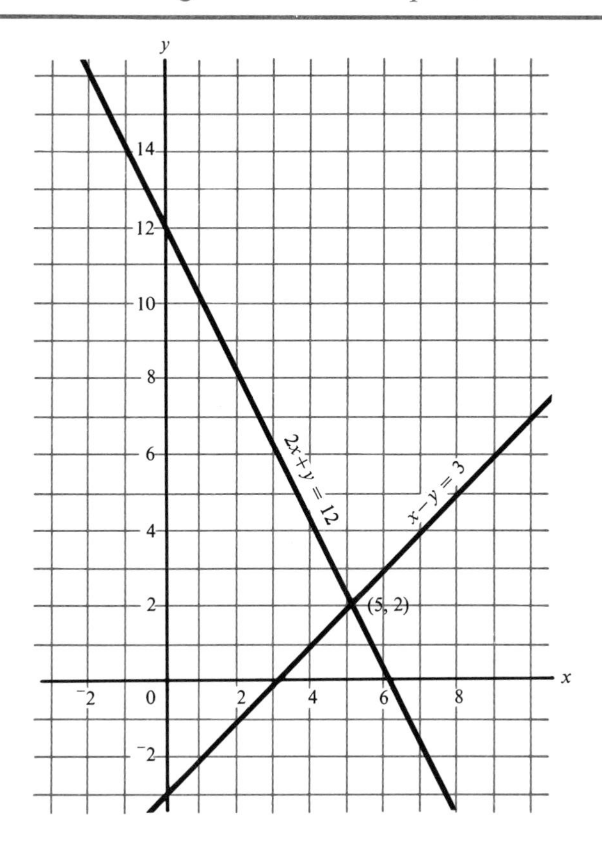

Fig. 1

(*b*) Figure 2 shows the graphs of the simultaneous inequalities

$$\begin{cases} 2x + y > 12 \\ x - y > 3. \end{cases}$$

The coordinates of any point in the unshaded region satisfy both inequalities.
Is there a solution such that (i) $x = 10$, (ii) $x = {}^{-}2$, (iii) $x = 5$?
Is there a solution such that (i) $y = 10$, (ii) $y = {}^{-}4$, (iii) $y = 100$?

Figure 2 shows that *every* solution is such that $x > 5$. There is no similar restriction on the value of y; solutions can always be found for any desired value of y.

(*c*) Sketch the graphs of the simultaneous inequalities

$$\begin{cases} 2x + y < 12 \\ x - y > 3. \end{cases}$$

Is it possible to find a solution for (i) any value of x, (ii) any value of y?

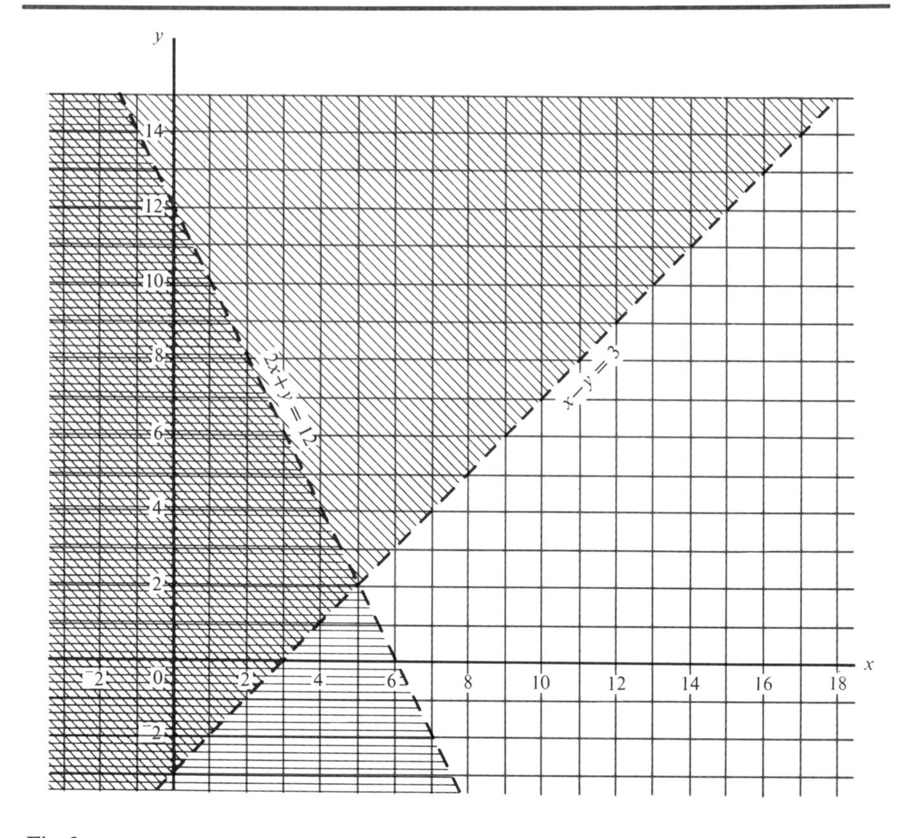

Fig. 2

Exercise A

1 Draw the graphs of $y = x + 5$ and $x + 2y = 1$ from $x = {}^{-}5$ to $x = 2$ on the same axes.

(*a*) Give the solution of the simultaneous equations

$$\begin{cases} y = x + 5 \\ x + 2y = 1. \end{cases}$$

(*b*) By shading out the unwanted regions, show the solution set of the simultaneous inequalities

$$\begin{cases} y > x + 5 \\ x + 2y < 1. \end{cases}$$

2 Use a graphical method to solve:

(*a*) $\begin{cases} y - 4x = 1 \\ 2x + y = 4; \end{cases}$ (*b*) $\begin{cases} 2x - y = 4 \\ x + 2y + 3 = 0. \end{cases}$

3 Sketch the graphs of the simultaneous inequalities:

$$(a)\ \begin{cases} y - x > 0 \\ y + x > {}^{-}2; \end{cases} \qquad (b)\ \begin{cases} y - x \leqslant 0 \\ {}^{-}2y - x \leqslant 3. \end{cases}$$

4 Sketch the graphs of the inequalities $\begin{cases} y < x + 1 \\ y > 1 - 4x. \end{cases}$

Is it possible to find a solution for (i) any value of x, (ii) any value of y?

5 Draw the graphs of the inequalities $\begin{cases} x - y \geqslant 2 \\ {}^{-}2x + y \geqslant {}^{-}2. \end{cases}$

For what values of x is it possible to find a solution?
For what values of y is it possible to find a solution?

(*b*) Using substitution

(*a*) Look again at the simultaneous equations

$$\begin{cases} 2x + y = 12 & (1) \\ x - y = 3. & (2) \end{cases}$$

If we rearrange equation (2) so that x is the subject of the equation, we have

$$x = y + 3. \qquad (3)$$

Since x and $y + 3$ are equal, we can substitute $y + 3$ for x in equation (1) and obtain

$$\begin{aligned} 2(y + 3) + y &= 12 \\ 2y + 6 + y &= 12 \\ 3y + 6 &= 12 \\ 3y &= 6 \\ y &= 2. \end{aligned}$$

Substituting 2 for y in equation (3), we have

$$x = 5.$$

Therefore the solution is $x = 5$, $y = 2$.
(*b*) Solve the simultaneous equations

$$\begin{cases} y - 2x = 7 \\ x + 2y = {}^{-}1 \end{cases}$$

by making y the subject of the first equation and then substituting for y in the second.

Check that your answer satisfies the equations.

Would it be equally sensible to make y the subject of the second equation and then substitute for y in the first?

Exercise B

Use the method of Section 2(b) to solve the simultaneous equations in Questions 1–6.

1 $\begin{cases} x+2y=10 \\ x-y=4. \end{cases}$ 2 $\begin{cases} x-y=2 \\ y={}^-x+6. \end{cases}$ 3 $\begin{cases} 2x+3y=7 \\ y={}^-3x. \end{cases}$

4 $\begin{cases} 2x+y=1 \\ 2x+5y=9. \end{cases}$ 5 $\begin{cases} x+y=10 \\ y+11x=35. \end{cases}$ 6 $\begin{cases} 2x+3y=1 \\ 3x-y=1. \end{cases}$

7 For each of the following simultaneous equations, make b the subject of one of the equations and then substitute for b in the other to obtain an equation connecting a and c.

(a) $\begin{cases} a=2+b \\ c=3b; \end{cases}$ (b) $\begin{cases} 2a=1+b \\ 3c=2b-4; \end{cases}$ (c) $\begin{cases} a=b^2 \\ c=1-b. \end{cases}$

8 By eliminating d from the simultaneous equations

$$\begin{cases} 4=\dfrac{d}{t} \\ d=3s, \end{cases}$$

obtain an equation connecting t and s.

9 By eliminating k from the simultaneous equations

$$\begin{cases} D=5k \\ P=14k, \end{cases}$$

obtain an equation connecting D and P.

(c) More graphs

(a) Figure 3 shows the graphs of $y=x^2$ and $y=2x+3$ for values of x from ${}^-4$ to 4.

What are the coordinates of the points where the graphs intersect?

Does $x={}^-1$, $y=1$ satisfy both the equation $y=x^2$ and the equation $y=2x+3$?

One solution of the simultaneous equations

$$\begin{cases} y=x^2 & (1) \\ y=2x+3 & (2) \end{cases}$$

is $x={}^-1$, $y=1$. There is another solution. What is it?

If we substitute $2x+3$ for y in (1), we obtain

$$2x+3=x^2.$$

What are the two solutions of this equation in x? Check that your answer is correct.

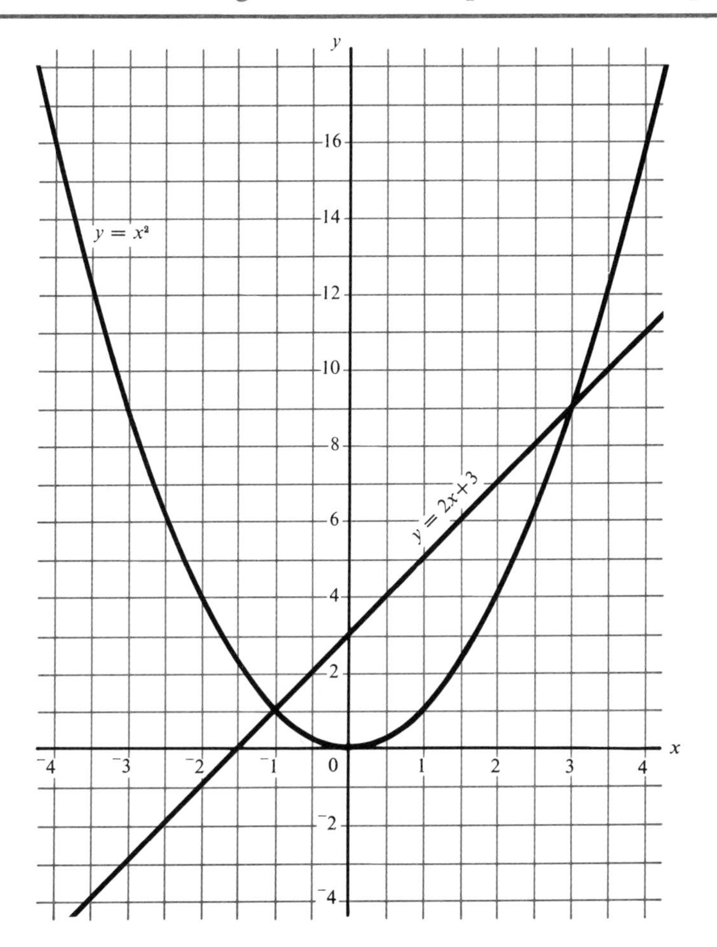

Fig. 3

(*b*) We can solve the equation

$$x^2 = 2 - 2x$$

by first drawing the graphs of the simultaneous equations

$$\begin{cases} y = x^2 \\ y = 2 - 2x. \end{cases}$$

Sketch these graphs to find the approximate position of the point(s) of intersection.

Now carefully draw a portion of these graphs which will include these points. (You should have found that it will be sufficient to draw the graphs for values of x from $^-4$ to 2.)

Use your graphs to find as accurately as you can the x-coordinates of the points of intersection.

What can you now say about the values of x which satisfy the equation

$$x^2 = 2 - 2x?$$

(*c*) What pairs of graphs would you draw in order to solve the following equations:

(i) $x^2 = x - \frac{1}{4}$; (ii) $x^3 = x + 6$; (iii) $\frac{1}{x} = 2x - 1$; (iv) $x^2 - x = 2$?

(*d*) Look at Figure 4. Write down the coordinates of some points in the shaded region. Do they satisfy the relation $y < x^2$ or $y > x^2$?

What relation is satisfied by points in the unshaded region?

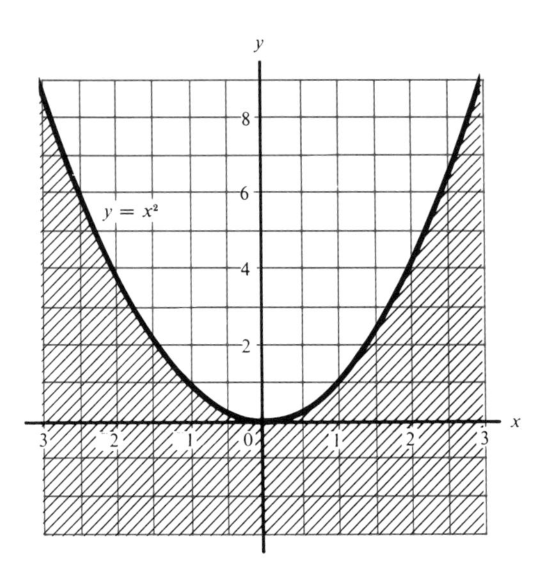

Fig. 4

(*e*) Make a neat sketch of the graphs of $y = x^2$ and $y = 2x + 3$ (see Figure 3). By shading out the regions which you do not want, show the solution set of the simultaneous inequalities

$$\begin{cases} y > x^2 \\ y < 2x + 3. \end{cases}$$

Exercise C

In Questions 1–4, remember to draw sketch graphs to find the approximate position of the point(s) of intersection.

1 Use a graphical method to solve the following simultaneous equations to 2 S.F.

(*a*) $\begin{cases} y = x^2 \\ y = x; \end{cases}$ (*b*) $\begin{cases} y = x^2 \\ y = \frac{3}{4} - x; \end{cases}$ (*c*) $\begin{cases} y = x^3 \\ y = 4x; \end{cases}$ (*d*) $\begin{cases} y = \frac{1}{2}x + 2 \\ y = x^2. \end{cases}$

2 By drawing suitable pairs of graphs, solve the following equations to 2 S.F.

(*a*) $x^2 = x - \frac{1}{4}$; (*b*) $x^2 - x = 3$;

(*c*) $x^3 = x + 6$; (*d*) $x^3 = 1 - x$.

3 Figure 5 shows the graph of $y = \frac{1}{x}$. Use a graphical method to solve the following equations to 2 S.F.

(*a*) $\frac{1}{x} = 3 - x$; (*b*) $\frac{1}{x} = 2x - 1$.

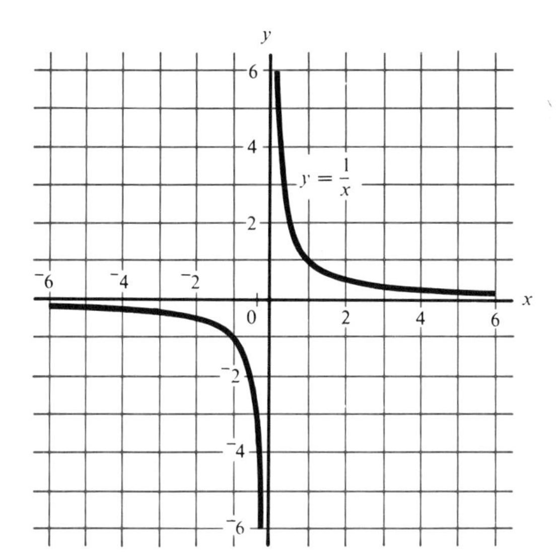

Fig. 5

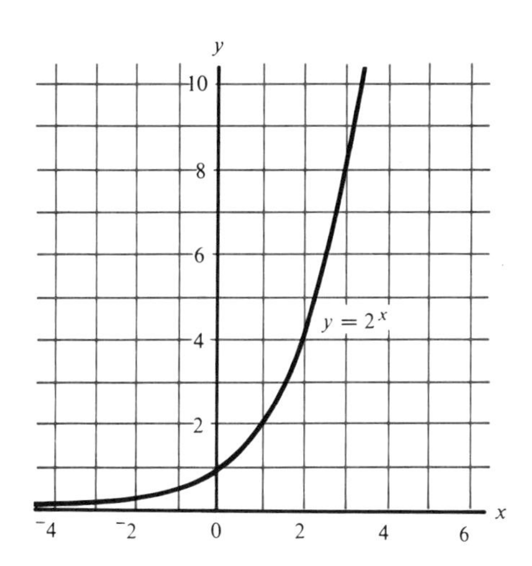

Fig. 6

4 Figure 6 shows the graph of $y = 2^x$. Use a graphical method to solve the following equations to 2 S.F.

(*a*) $2^x = \frac{1}{x}$; (*b*) $2^x = x^2$.

5 Sketch the graphs of the simultaneous inequalities:

(a) $\begin{cases} y < x^2 \\ y > x; \end{cases}$ (b) $\begin{cases} y \geqslant x^2 \\ y \leqslant 4 - 2x; \end{cases}$

(c) $\begin{cases} y < x^3 \\ y > 4x; \end{cases}$ (d) $\begin{cases} y < \dfrac{1}{x} \\ y > x - 2. \end{cases}$

(*d*) Adding and subtracting equations

(*a*) Once more consider the equations

$$\begin{cases} 2x + y = 12 & (1) \\ x - y = 3. & (2) \end{cases}$$

We know that we may add the same number to both sides of an equation. Therefore, since $x - y$ is equal to 3, we may add $x - y$ to the left-hand side of equation (1) and 3 to the right-hand side, that is, we may add equations (1) and (2).

$$2x + y = 12 \quad (1)$$

$$x - y = 3 \quad (2)$$

Adding,

$$3x + 0 = 15$$

$$3x = 15$$

$$x = 5.$$

Substituting for x in (2),

$$y = 2.$$

(*b*)

$$\begin{cases} 3x + 2y = 9 & (1) \\ {}^{-}x + 2y = 7. & (2) \end{cases}$$

We know that we may subtract the same number from both sides of an equation. Therefore, since ${}^{-}x + 2y$ is equal to 7, we may subtract ${}^{-}x + 2y$ from the left-hand side of equation (1) and 7 from the right-hand side, that is, we may subtract equation (2) from equation (1).

$$3x + 2y = 9 \quad (1)$$

$$^{-}x + 2y = 7 \quad (2)$$

Subtracting,

$$4x + 0 = 2$$

$$4x = 2$$

$$x = \tfrac{1}{2}.$$

Substituting for x in (2),

$$2y = 7\tfrac{1}{2}$$

$$y = 3\tfrac{3}{4}.$$

Therefore the solution is $x = \frac{1}{2}$, $y = 3\frac{3}{4}$.

(c) In (a) the coefficients of y in the two equations are numerically equal but opposite in sign, so adding the equations eliminates y and gives a linear equation in x which we are able to solve.

In (b) the coefficients of y in the two equations are numerically equal and equal in sign. This time, subtracting the equations eliminates y and gives a linear equation in x.

The following example shows how we can always arrange for the coefficient of one of the variables in two simultaneous equations to be numerically equal.

$$\begin{cases} 2x + 5y = 3 & (1) \\ 3x - 2y = 1. & (2) \end{cases}$$

We can multiply both sides of equation (1) by 3 to obtain $6x + 15y = 9$ and both sides of equation (2) by 2 to obtain $6x - 4y = 2$.

$$6x + 15y = 9$$
$$6x - 4y = 2$$

Subtracting,

$$0 + 19y = 7$$
$$19y = 7$$
$$y = \tfrac{7}{19}.$$

Substituting for y in (2),

$$3x = 1 + \tfrac{14}{19}$$
$$3x = \tfrac{33}{19}$$
$$x = \tfrac{11}{19}.$$

Therefore the solution is $x = \tfrac{11}{19}$, $y = \tfrac{7}{19}$.

Now solve the equations

$$\begin{cases} 2x + 5y = 3 & (1) \\ 3x - 2y = 1 & (2) \end{cases}$$

by multiplying (1) by 2 and (2) by 5 and then adding.

Do you obtain the same answer as before?

(d) We can eliminate x from the equations

$$\begin{cases} 3x - y = 7 & (1) \\ {}^{-}x + 2y = 5 & (2) \end{cases}$$

by multiplying (2) by 3 and then adding.

How would you eliminate x from each of the following pairs of equations:

(i) $\begin{cases} x + y = 8 \\ x - y = 3; \end{cases}$ (ii) $\begin{cases} 6x - 3y = {}^{-}1 \\ 2x + 5y = 10; \end{cases}$ (iii) $\begin{cases} 2x + y = 8 \\ 5x + 2y = 3? \end{cases}$

How would you eliminate y from each of the above pairs of equations?

Exercise D

Use the method of Section 2(d) to solve the simultaneous equations in Questions 1–8.

1 $\begin{cases} x+2y=7 \\ 3x-2y={}^-3. \end{cases}$ 2 $\begin{cases} 4x-3y=1 \\ x-2y=4. \end{cases}$ 3 $\begin{cases} 4x+3y=9 \\ 2x+5y=15. \end{cases}$

4 $\begin{cases} 5x+3y=1 \\ 2x+3y={}^-5. \end{cases}$ 5 $\begin{cases} 3x-2y=4 \\ 2x+3y={}^-6. \end{cases}$ 6 $\begin{cases} 3x=2y+1 \\ 5x=3y+3. \end{cases}$

7 $\begin{cases} 5x-3y=1 \\ 3x=y+5. \end{cases}$ 8 $\begin{cases} ax+by=c \\ x-y=1. \end{cases}$

(e) Using matrices

The simultaneous equations

$$\begin{cases} 2x+y=12 & (1) \\ x-y=3 & (2) \end{cases}$$

can be written in the form

$$\begin{pmatrix} 2 & 1 \\ 1 & {}^-1 \end{pmatrix}\begin{pmatrix} x \\ y \end{pmatrix}=\begin{pmatrix} 12 \\ 3 \end{pmatrix}.$$

The problem of solving the equations is therefore equivalent to that of looking for the point (x,y) of the domain which is mapped onto the point $(12,3)$ of the range by the one–one mapping

$$\begin{pmatrix} x \\ y \end{pmatrix}\rightarrow\begin{pmatrix} 2 & 1 \\ 1 & {}^-1 \end{pmatrix}\begin{pmatrix} x \\ y \end{pmatrix}.$$

Hence the inverse of this mapping applied to the point $(12,3)$ will give the required solution.

Check that the inverse mapping is

$$\begin{pmatrix} x \\ y \end{pmatrix}\rightarrow\begin{pmatrix} \frac{1}{3} & \frac{1}{3} \\ \frac{1}{3} & {}^-\frac{2}{3} \end{pmatrix}\begin{pmatrix} x \\ y \end{pmatrix}.$$

(If you have difficulty, look back at Chapter 7, Section 2.)

So

$$\begin{pmatrix} x \\ y \end{pmatrix}=\begin{pmatrix} \frac{1}{3} & \frac{1}{3} \\ \frac{1}{3} & {}^-\frac{2}{3} \end{pmatrix}\begin{pmatrix} 12 \\ 3 \end{pmatrix}=\begin{pmatrix} 5 \\ 2 \end{pmatrix},$$

that is,

$$x=5, \qquad y=2.$$

The inverse mapping could also be written in the form

$$\begin{pmatrix} x \\ y \end{pmatrix}\rightarrow{}^-\tfrac{1}{3}\begin{pmatrix} {}^-1 & {}^-1 \\ {}^-1 & 2 \end{pmatrix}\begin{pmatrix} x \\ y \end{pmatrix}$$

and you will find that the arithmetic is often simpler if division by the value of the determinant is delayed, thus:

$$\begin{pmatrix} x \\ y \end{pmatrix} = {}^-\tfrac{1}{3}\begin{pmatrix} ^-1 & ^-1 \\ ^-1 & 2 \end{pmatrix}\begin{pmatrix} 12 \\ 3 \end{pmatrix}$$

$$= {}^-\tfrac{1}{3}\begin{pmatrix} ^-15 \\ ^-6 \end{pmatrix} = \begin{pmatrix} 5 \\ 2 \end{pmatrix}.$$

Exercise E

Use the method of Section 2(*e*) to solve the simultaneous equations in Questions 1–10.

1 $\begin{cases} 2x + y = 1 \\ 5x + 3y = 2. \end{cases}$ 2 $\begin{cases} x + 2y = 10 \\ 2x + 3y = 13. \end{cases}$ 3 $\begin{cases} x + y = 2 \\ 5x + 7y = 4. \end{cases}$ 4 $\begin{cases} 3x + 2y = 1 \\ 7x + 3y = {}^-1. \end{cases}$

5 $\begin{cases} x + 4y = {}^-17 \\ 3x - 2y = 19. \end{cases}$ 6 $\begin{cases} 5x - 2y = 4 \\ 6x - y = 9. \end{cases}$ 7 $\begin{cases} 3x - 5y = 7 \\ 2x + 4y = 1. \end{cases}$ 8 $\begin{cases} 2x - 4y = 1 \\ x + 3y = 2. \end{cases}$

9 $\begin{cases} 3x = 2y \\ 4x = 5y + 7. \end{cases}$ 10 $\begin{cases} 4x + 3y = 4 \\ 2x = 5y + 15. \end{cases}$

3 Solution sets

(*a*) Several times in this chapter we have solved the simultaneous equations

$$\begin{cases} 2x + y = 12 \\ x - y = 3. \end{cases}$$

The solution set, which consists of a single pair of elements, is $\{(5, 2)\}$.

(*b*) The graphs of the simultaneous equations

$$\begin{cases} x + 2y = 3 \\ 2x + 4y = 10 \end{cases}$$

are shown in Figure 7. What do the graphs tell you about the number of pairs of elements which belong to the solution set?

What happens when you apply each of the methods of Sections 2(*b*), 2(*d*) and 2(*e*) to the equations

$$\begin{cases} x + 2y = 3 \\ 2x + 4y = 10? \end{cases}$$

Does each method lead you to the conclusion that the solution set is $\varnothing$?

(*c*) Investigate what happens when you apply each of the methods of Sections 2(*a*), 2(*b*), 2(*d*) and 2(*e*) to the simultaneous equations

$$\begin{cases} x + 2y = 3 \\ 2x + 4y = 6. \end{cases}$$

Do these equations have a solution?

What can you say about the number of pairs of elements in the solution set?

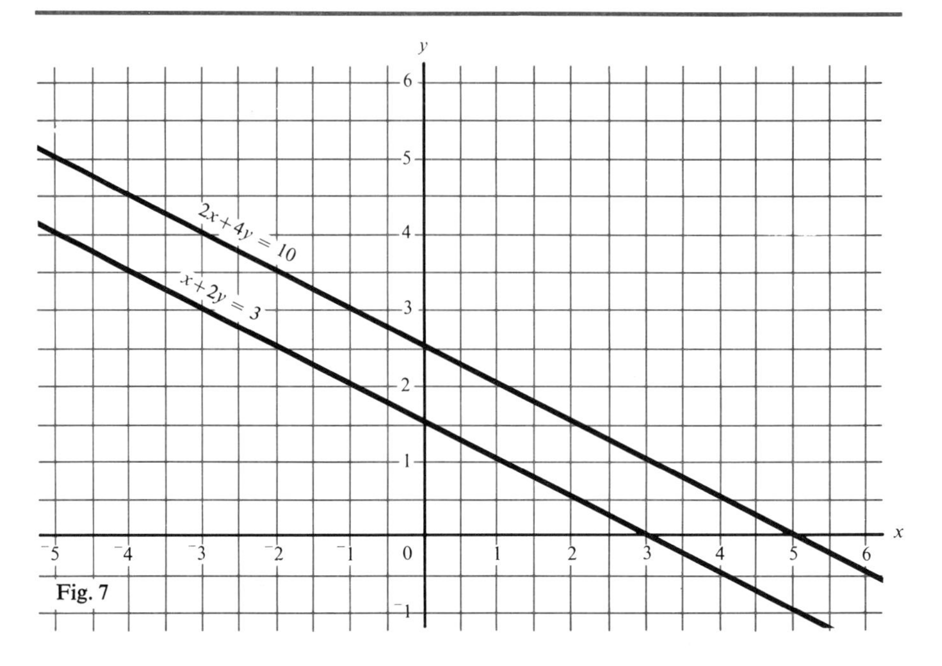

Fig. 7

Miscellaneous exercise F

1 Solve the simultaneous equations:

(a) $\begin{cases} x+y=14 \\ y-x=0; \end{cases}$ (b) $\begin{cases} 12x-10y=7 \\ 12x-6y=1. \end{cases}$

2 Sketch the graphs of the simultaneous inequalities:

(a) $\begin{cases} 2y \geqslant 1-x \\ y \leqslant \frac{1}{3}x+4; \end{cases}$ (b) $\begin{cases} y > \frac{1}{2}x \\ 3y > x-2. \end{cases}$

3 The values of x and y are connected by the equation $y = mx + c$. When $x = 3$, $y = 4$ and when $x = {}^-7$, $y = {}^-1$. Find m and c. What is the value of y when $x = {}^-1$?

4 The straight line $y = mx + c$ passes through the points (4, 5) and (1, 14). Find m and c.

5 The equation $x^2 + px + q = 0$ is satisfied by $x = {}^-1$ and $x = 2$. Find the values of p and q.

6 Discuss whether the following equations have a solution set with (i) no elements, (ii) one pair of elements, (iii) an infinite number of pairs of elements.

(a) $\begin{cases} x+y=1 \\ 2x+2y=2; \end{cases}$ (b) $\begin{cases} x+y=1 \\ 2x+2y=3; \end{cases}$ (c) $\begin{cases} x+y=1 \\ x-y=0; \end{cases}$ (d) $\begin{cases} 4x+6y=5 \\ 6x+9y=7\frac{1}{2}. \end{cases}$

7 Sketch the graphs of the simultaneous inequalities:

(a) $\begin{cases} x+2y>4 \\ x+2y<8; \end{cases}$ (b) $\begin{cases} x+2y>4 \\ x+2y>8; \end{cases}$ (c) $\begin{cases} x+2y<4 \\ x+2y<8; \end{cases}$ (d) $\begin{cases} x+2y<4 \\ x+2y>8. \end{cases}$

10 More mensuration

1 A reminder

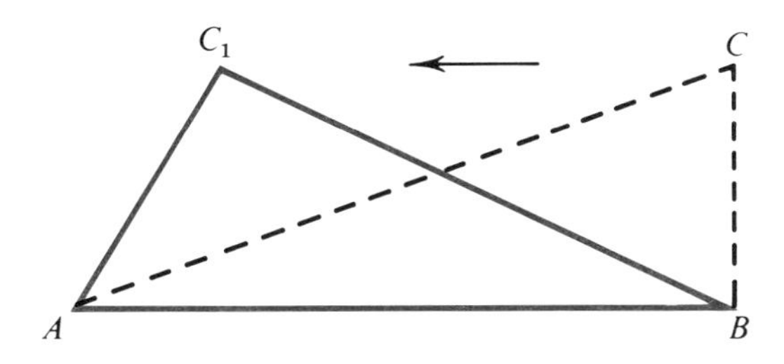

Fig. 1

(*a*) Figure 1 illustrates a shear in 2 dimensions under which the triangle ABC has been transformed into the triangle ABC_1.

Which line segment is invariant under this transformation?

What can you say about the areas of the two triangles?

(*b*) In two dimensions, a shear is a transformation which has a line of invariant points, and which preserves area.

2 Shearing in three dimensions

(*a*) Figure 2(*a*) shows a pack of playing cards.
Figure 2(*b*) shows the same pack after it has been sheared parallel to AB.

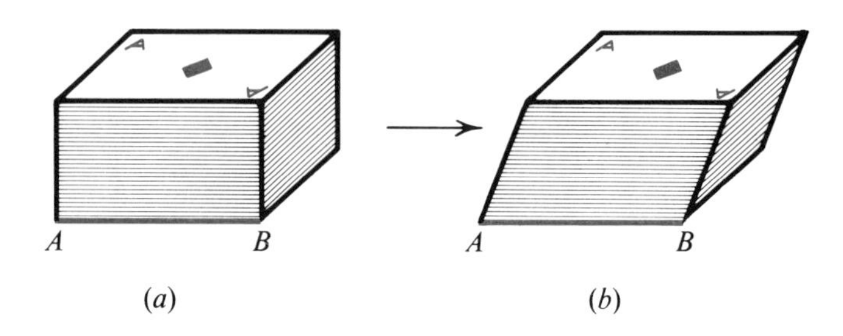

Fig. 2

Has the height of the pack changed?
Has the base area of the pack changed?
If the volume of the pack in Figure 2(*a*) is 50 cm³, what is the volume of the pack in Figure 2(*b*)?

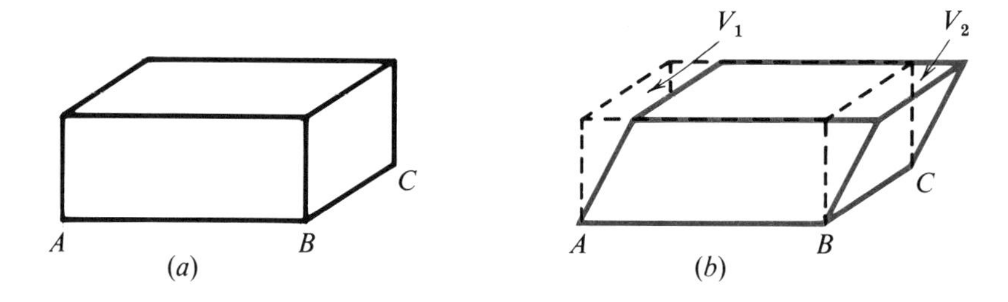

Fig. 3

(*b*) Figures 3(*a*) and 3(*b*) show a cuboid undergoing a shear parallel to AB.
Notice that the height and base area remain unchanged, and that all points on the base are invariant.

If you make a cuboid of plasticine and cut a wedge from one end, you should be able to reproduce the solid shown in Figure 3(*b*).

What can you say about the wedge-shaped volumes V_1 and V_2 in Figure 3(*b*)?

Can you explain why the volume of the solid in Figure 3(*a*) is the same as that of the solid in Figure 3(*b*)?

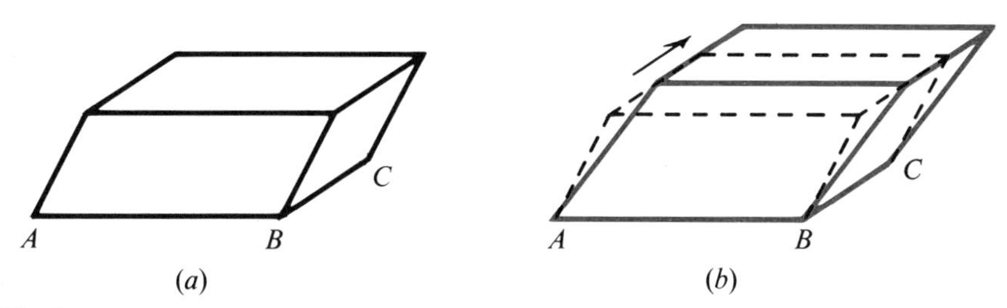

Fig. 4

(*c*) Figures 4(*a*) and 4(*b*) show the solid in Figure 3(*b*) undergoing a further shear parallel to *BC*.

You might like to try reproducing this with your plasticine.

Notice that all points of the base of the solid have remained invariant under both shears.

What other properties of the solid in Figure 3(*a*) have remained invariant?

If the volume of the cuboid in Figure 3(*a*) is 50 cm^3, what is the volume of the solid in Figure 4(*b*)?

Summary

A shear in three dimensions is a transformation which (*a*) leaves points in one plane invariant and (*b*) preserves volume.

Exercise A

1 By considering a shear of a simple solid find the volumes of each of the following:

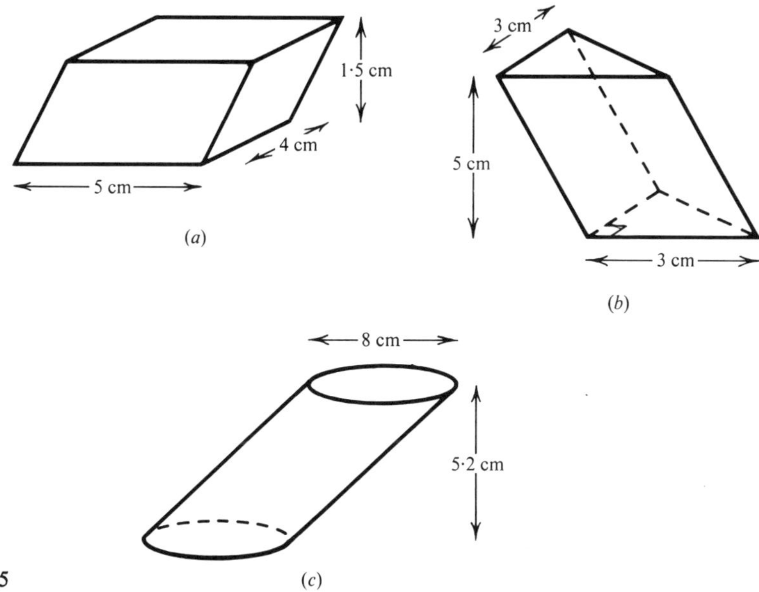

Fig. 5

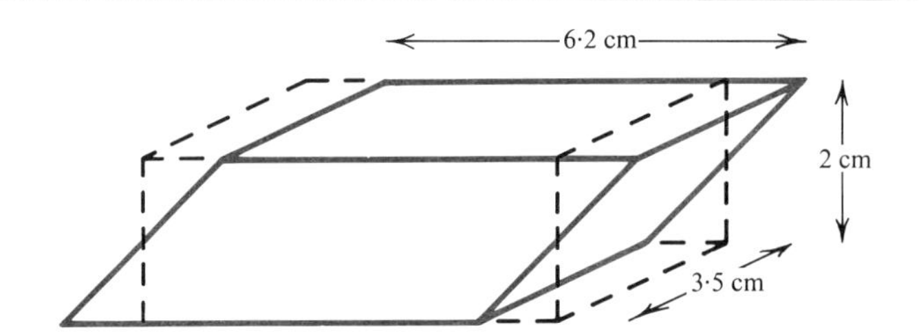

Fig. 6

2 Figure 6 shows a cuboid which has undergone a shear. Which plane is invariant under this transformation? What is the volume of the solid formed?

3 Do you think that surface area is invariant under shearing in three dimensions? Give an example to support your answer.

4 Figure 7 shows a cube with side length 6 cm, and illustrates how the cube can be divided into six congruent square-based pyramids. Figure 8 shows the net for such a pyramid.

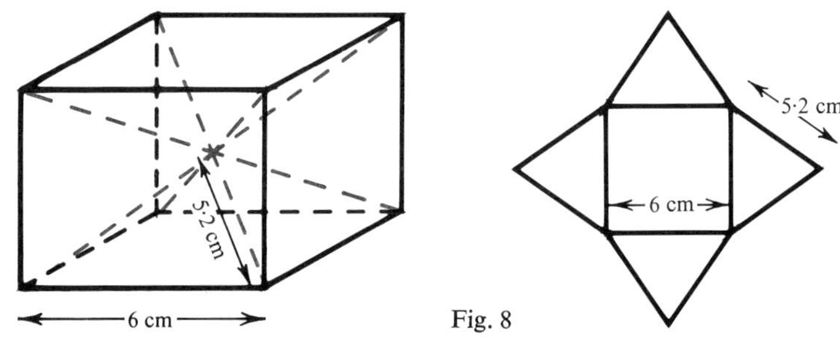

Fig. 7 Fig. 8

Make six pyramids and tape them so that they fold together to form the cube. What is the volume of one of these pyramids? Can you fold your model so that the vertices of the pyramids are outside the cube? What is this solid called?

3 Volume of a tetrahedron

(*a*) The properties of shearing discussed in Section 2 imply that if a solid can be transformed by a shear, or a succession of shears, into another solid, then the two solids have the same volume.

(*b*) Consider the tetrahedron $ABCD$ in Figure 9.

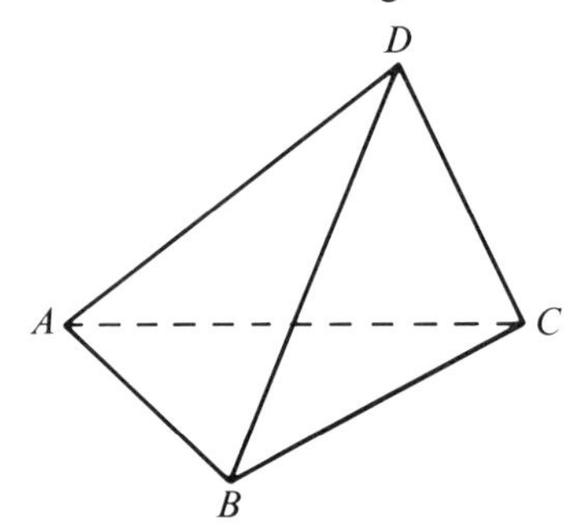

Fig. 9

We can now transform this as follows:

(i) Keeping the face ADC invariant (see Figure 10) shear so that B moves in the plane ABC to B_1, where $B_1AC = 90°$.

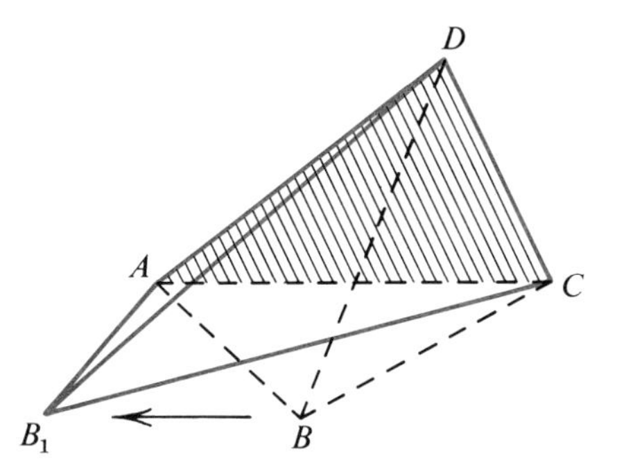

Fig. 10

Has the base area of the tetrahedron changed?

Has the height of the tetrahedron changed?

Do you agree that the volume of AB_1CD is the same as the volume of $ABCD$?

(ii) Keeping the face AB_1C invariant (see Figure 11) shear D to D_1, so that AD_1 is perpendicular to the plane AB_1C.

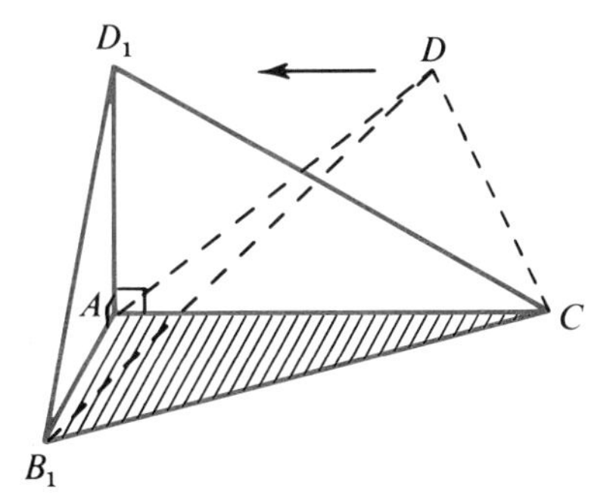

Fig. 11

Has the base area of the tetrahedron changed?

Has the height of the tetrahedron changed?

Do you agree that the volume of AB_1CD_1 is the same as the volume of $ABCD$?

(*c*) We have seen in Section (*b*) that we can transform any tetrahedron into a tetrahedron of the type shown in Figure 12(*b*), without changing its height, base area or volume.

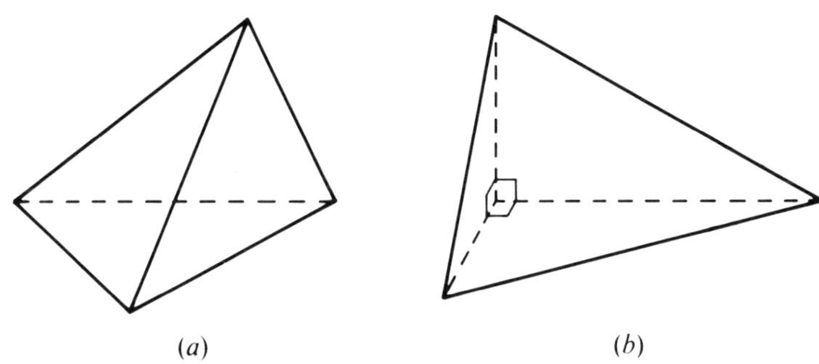

Fig. 12 (*a*) (*b*)

(*d*) Now consider the cuboid in Figure 13.

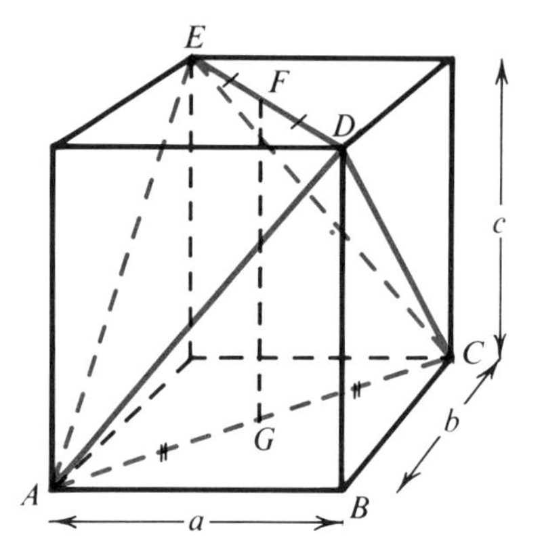

Fig. 13

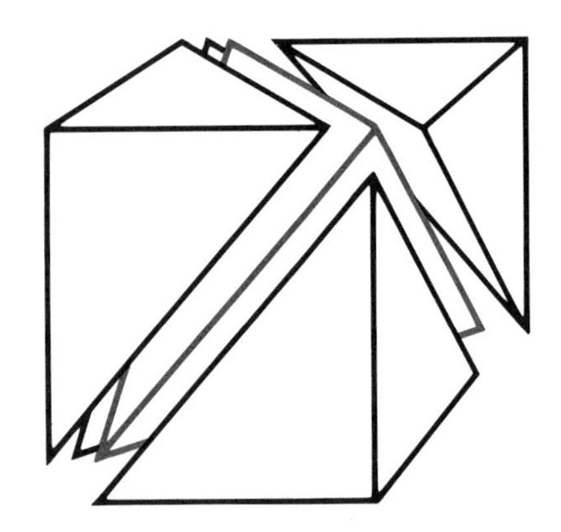

Fig. 14

If we cut from this four tetrahedra (see Figure 14) each congruent to the tetrahedron $ABCD$, then we are left with the solid shown in Figure 15.

(*e*) If we divide the solid in Figure 15 along the plane ACF, where F is the midpoint, we obtain the two tetrahedra shown in Figure 16. We can see that these tetrahedra are congruent since a half-turn about FG (see Figure 13) maps each tetrahedron onto the other.

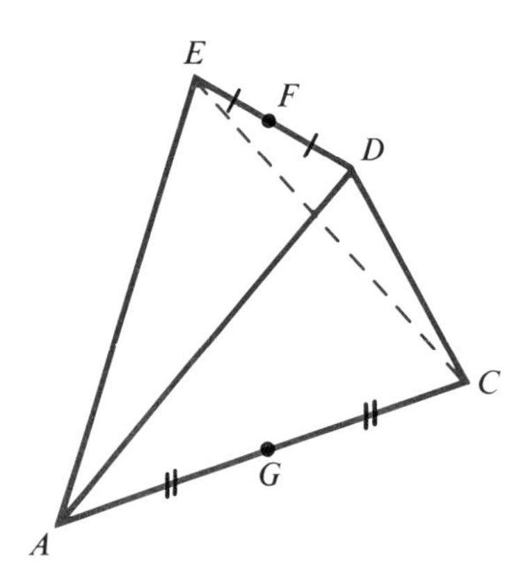

Fig. 15

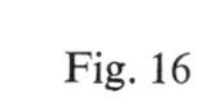

Fig. 16

Consider one of these tetrahedra $ACDF$. We can transform this as follows (see Figure 17).

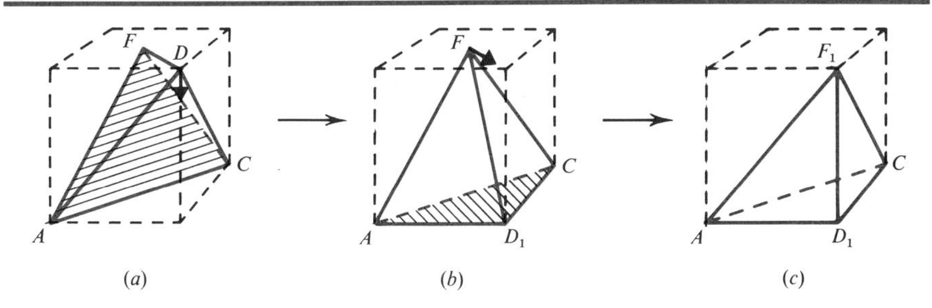

Fig. 17

(i) Keeping the face AFC invariant, shear D to D_1,
(ii) Keeping the face AD_1C invariant, shear F to F_1.

Do you agree that the volume of AD_1CF_1 equals the volume of $ADCF$?

What do you notice about AD_1CF_1 and the tetrahdron $ABCD$ in Figure 13? Into how many tetrahedra of equal volume have we now dissected the cuboid?

(*f*) Do you agree that the volume of the cuboid in Figure 13 is abc? You should have found that the cuboid has been divided into six tetrahedra of equal volume. Hence the volume of each tetrahedron is one-sixth of the volume of the cuboid, that is, $\frac{1}{6}abc$.

Look again at the tetrahedron $ABCD$ in Figure 13.

Do you agree that its base area is $\frac{1}{2}ab$, and its height is c?

The volume of the tetrahedron is

$$\begin{aligned}&\tfrac{1}{6}abc\\&=\tfrac{1}{3}\times(\tfrac{1}{2}ab)\times c\\&=\underline{\tfrac{1}{3}\times \text{base area}\times \text{height}.}\end{aligned}$$

(*g*) In Section 3(*b*) and 3(*c*) we found that any tetrahedron can be transformed into a tetrahedron of the above type, having the same height, base area and volume.

Can you now write down the formula for the volume of *any* tetrahedron?

Exercise B

1 Copy and complete the following table for volumes of various tetrahedra:

Base area (cm²)	Height (cm)	Volume (cm³)
20	15	
27	6·2	
8·9	2·7	
32		65
	17	39·2
0·53	0·16	

2 Obtain a carton of longlife milk. Measure it and calculate its volume. A pint is about 567 cm³. Compare this with your results.

3

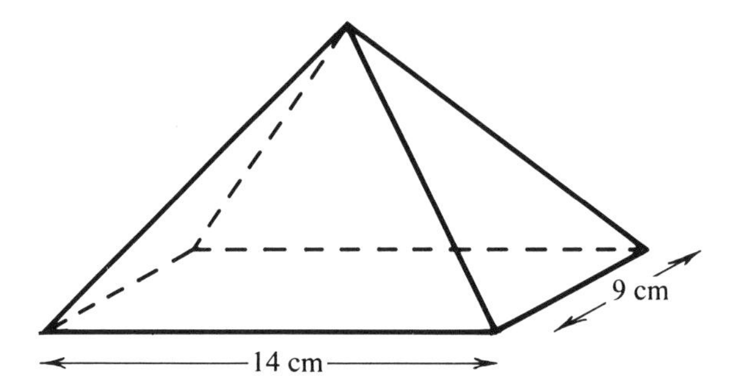

Fig. 18

Figure 18 shows a pyramid of height 6 cm having a rectangular base. The vertex is vertically above the centre of the rotational symmetry of the base (such a pyramid is called a right pyramid). By considering the pyramid divided into tetrahedra calculate its volume.

4 A tetrahedron has all edges of length 10 cm. Find its base area, height and volume.

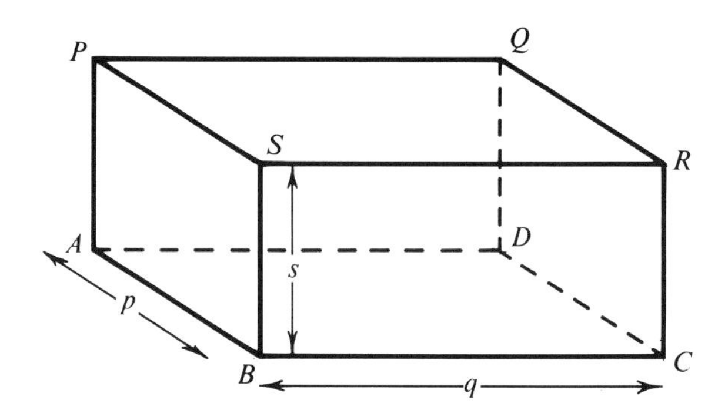

Fig. 19

5 $ABCDPQRS$ is a cuboid with $AB = p$ cm, $BC = q$ cm, $BS = s$ cm.
(i) Calculate the volume of tetrahedron $ABCS$.
(ii) Find as many tetrahedra as you can that have the same volume as $ABCS$.

6 $VABCD$ in Figure 20 is a right pyramid. Calculate its volume.

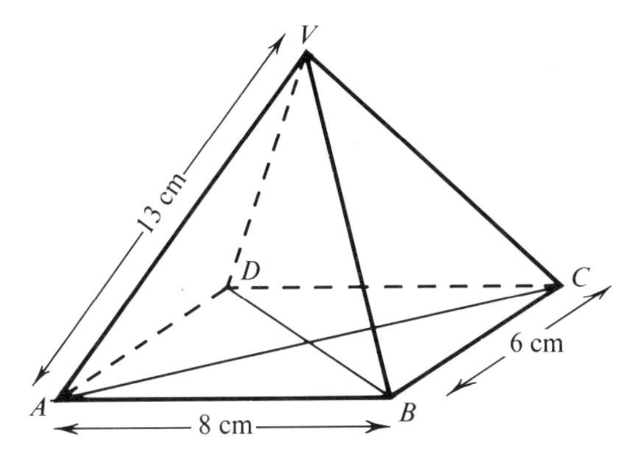

Fig. 20

4 Volume of a pyramid and cone

(*a*) Figure 21 shows a pentagonal-based pyramid, which has been divided into three tetrahedra $VPQR$, $VPRT$ and $VRST$.

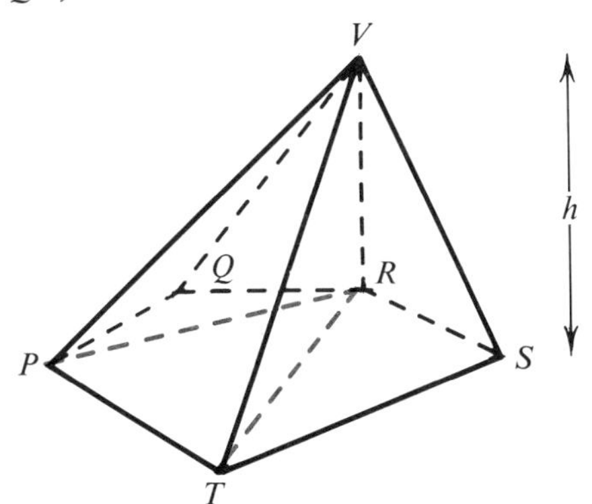

Fig. 21

Can any pyramid be divided into tetrahedra in this way?

If the base of the pyramid had six sides, how many tetrahedra would there be?

How many for seven sides?

How many for n sides?

(*b*) In Figure 21 we will call the areas of the triangles PQR, PRT and RTS, A_1, A_2, and A_3 respectively.

What is the base area of the pyramid in terms of A_1, A_2, A_3?

We can see that the volume of tetrahedron $VPQR = \frac{1}{3}A_1 h$,

the volume of tetrahedron $VPRT = \frac{1}{3}A_2 h$,

and the volume of tetrahedron $VRST = \frac{1}{3}A_3 h$.

Hence the volume of the pyramid $= \frac{1}{3}A_1 h + \frac{1}{3}A_2 h + \frac{1}{3}A_3 h$

$= \frac{1}{3}(A_1 + A_2 + A_3)h.$

But $A_1 + A_2 + A_3$ is the base area of the pyramid. So the volume of the pyramid

$= \frac{1}{3} \times$ base area $\times$ height.

Is this formula true for any pyramid? Why?

(*c*) We may consider a circle as the limit of a sequence of regular polygons (see Figure 22).

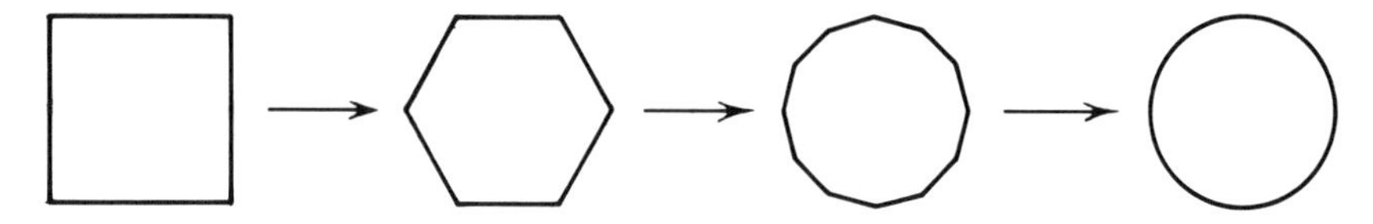

Fig. 22

Similarly, we may consider a cone as the limit of a sequence of pyramids (see Figure 23).

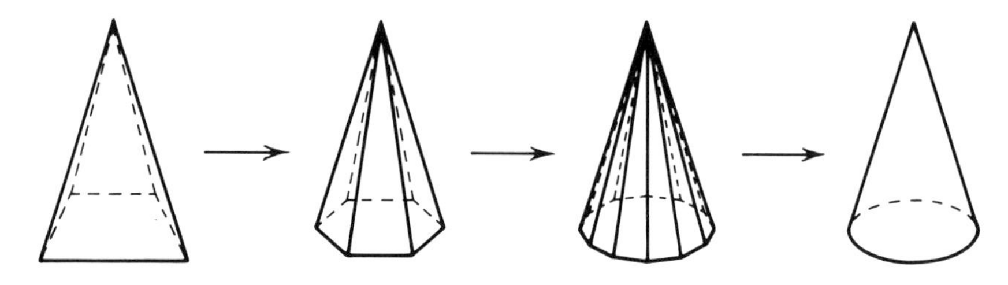

Fig. 23

Hence, the formula for the volume of any pyramid, $\frac{1}{3} \times$ base area $\times$ height, can be applied to a cone.

If a cone has base radius r and height h, what is the area of its base?

Write down the formula for the volume of the cone in terms of r and h.

(*d*) If a circular cone is cut along a plane parallel to the base, and the small cone removed, the remaining solid is called a frustum (see Figure 24). Example 1 explains how to find the volume of a frustum.

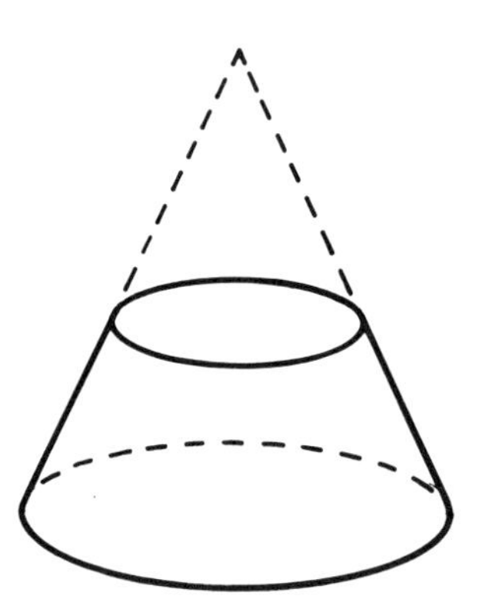

Fig. 24

Example 1

A frustum has base radius 16 cm, upper radius 6 cm and height 5 cm. Calculate its volume.

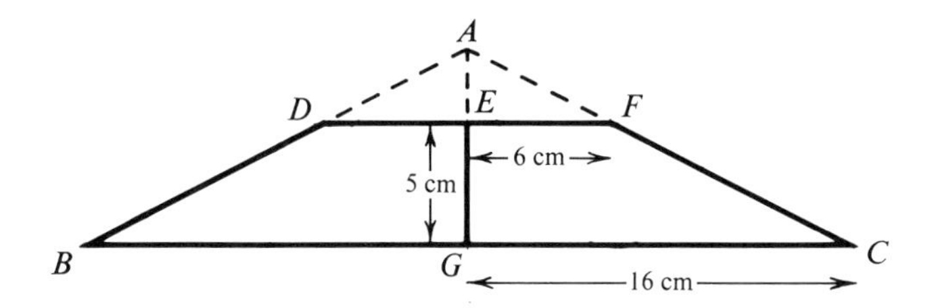

Fig. 25

Figure 25 shows a plane of symmetry of the frustum. What can you say about the triangles AEF and AGC?

The ratios $\frac{AE}{AG}$ and $\frac{EF}{GC}$ are equal. Can you see why?

If the height of the original cone is h,

then
$$\frac{AE}{AG}=\frac{EF}{GC},$$
so
$$\frac{h-5}{h}=\frac{6}{16}.$$

Solve this equation for h.
Did you find $h=8$?
Since the volume of frustum (v) is the volume of the larger cone minus the volume of the small cone we have:

$$\begin{aligned}v &= \tfrac{1}{3}\pi \times 16^2 \times 8 - \tfrac{1}{3}\pi \times 6^2 \times 3 \quad \text{cm}^3\\ &= \tfrac{1}{3}\pi(256 \times 8 - 36 \times 3) \quad \text{cm}^3\\ &= \frac{1940\pi}{3} \quad \text{cm}^3\\ &\approx 2030\ \text{cm}^3.\end{aligned}$$

Summary

1 The volume of any pyramid $= \frac{1}{3} \times$ base area $\times$ height.

2 The volume of a cone with base radius r and height h
$$= \tfrac{1}{3} \times \text{base area} \times \text{height}$$
$$= \tfrac{1}{3}\pi r^2 h.$$

Exercise C

1 Find the volume of a pyramid of height 7 cm having a rectangular base 10·3 cm long and 6·8 cm wide.

2 Find the volume of a pyramid of height 9 cm, having as base a regular hexagon with side length 3 cm.

3 The solid shown in Figure 26 has been obtained by removing the top 4 cm of a pyramid with a regular octagon as base. Find the height of the original pyramid, and the volume of the remaining solid.

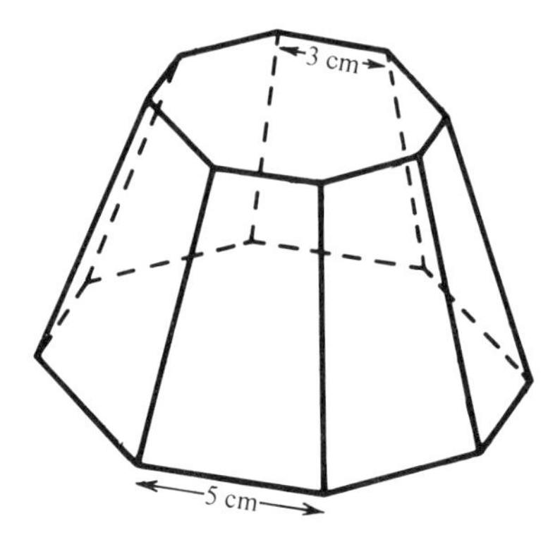

Fig. 26

4 Find the volume of a circular cone with base radius 4 cm and height 9 cm.

5 Find the height of a circular cone with base radius 1·5 cm and volume 8 cm^3.

6 Find the volume of a frustum of a circular cone with base radius 12 cm, top radius 5 cm and height 7 cm.

7 Justify the use of the formula $\frac{1}{3}\times$ base area $\times$ height in finding the volume of a cone with an elliptical base.

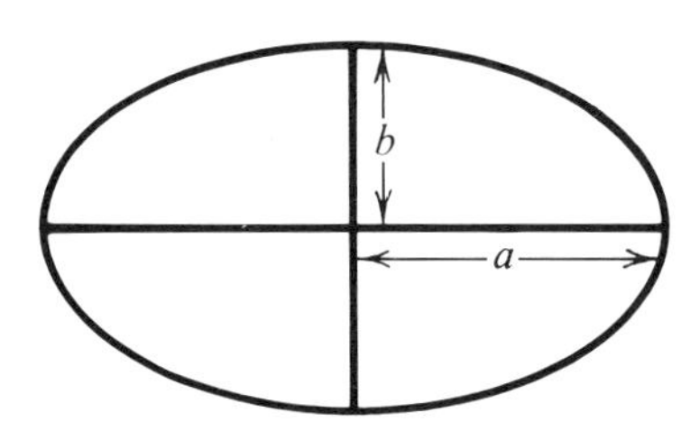

Fig. 27

Given that the area of the ellipse shown in Figure 27 is πab, find the volume of a cone of height 6 cm, having as base an ellipse with $a = 5$ cm, $b = 4$ cm.

5 Surface area of pyramid and cone

(*a*) The surface area of any pyramid can be found by calculating the area of each of its faces and adding the results. The process is explained in the following example.

Example 2

Find the total surface area of a right pyramid of height 10 cm having a square base with sides 6 cm (see Figure 28).

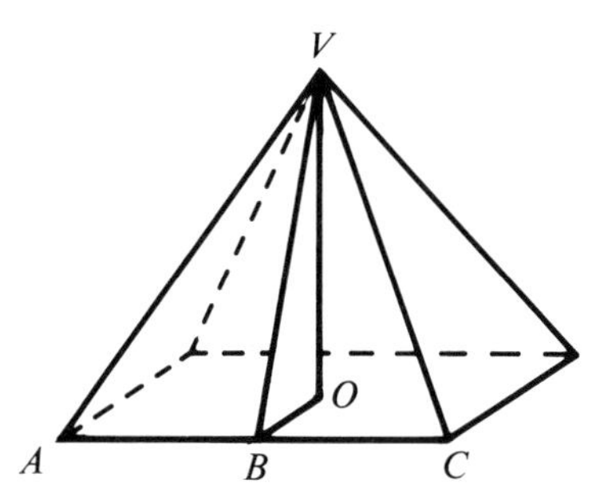

Fig. 28

The area of the base $= 6 \times 6 \text{ cm}^2 = 36 \text{ cm}^2$.

By Pythagoras' rule $VB = \sqrt{(100 + 9)} \text{ cm} = 10{\cdot}4 \text{ cm}$.

Hence the area of triangle $AVC = (\frac{1}{2} \times 6 \times 10{\cdot}4) \text{ cm}^2 = 31{\cdot}2 \text{ cm}^2$.

Hence total surface area $= (36 + 4 \times 31{\cdot}2) \text{ cm}^2$

$\approx \underline{160{\cdot}8 \text{ cm}^2}$

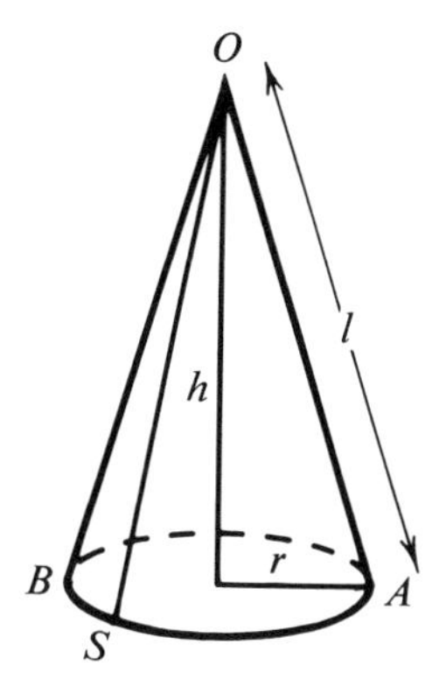

Fig. 29

Fig. 30

(*b*) If we slit the surface of the right circular cone shown in Figure 29 along a slant line OS we obtain the sector of the circle of radius OS shown in Figure 30.

By calculating the area of the sector we can find the curved surface area of the cone.

$$\text{The area of sector} = \frac{\alpha^\circ}{360^\circ} \times \text{area of circle}$$

$$= \frac{\alpha^\circ}{360^\circ} \times \pi l^2.$$

Arc $SABS$ is the circumference of the base of the cone and equals $2\pi r$.
So

$$2\pi r = \frac{\alpha^\circ}{360^\circ} \times 2\pi l$$

$$\frac{2\pi r}{2\pi l} = \frac{\alpha^\circ}{360^\circ} \text{ (dividing both sides by } 2\pi l)$$

and

$$\frac{r}{l} = \frac{\alpha^\circ}{360^\circ}.$$

Substituting for $\frac{\alpha^\circ}{360^\circ}$ in the expression obtained for the area of sector,

$$\text{area of sector} = \frac{r}{l} \times \pi l^2$$

$$= \pi r l.$$

That is, the curved surface area of a cone

$$= \underline{\pi \times \text{base radius} \times \text{slant height.}}$$

What is the base area of the cone? Write down a formula for the *total* surface area of the cone.

Exercise D

1 Find the curved surface area of a cone with base radius 6 cm and slant height 11 cm.

2 Find the height and curved surface area of a cone having base radius 2·5 cm and volume 36 cm^3.

3 Find the total surface area of a right pyramid of height 8 cm, having as its base a regular hexagon with side length 4 cm.

4 A cone has volume 400 cm^3 and height 12 cm. Find (*a*) its base area, (*b*) its base radius and (*c*) its total surface area.

5 A cone has base radius r and height h. Find a formula for its total surface area in terms of r and h.

6 Find the area of material needed to make the lampshade shown in Figure 31.

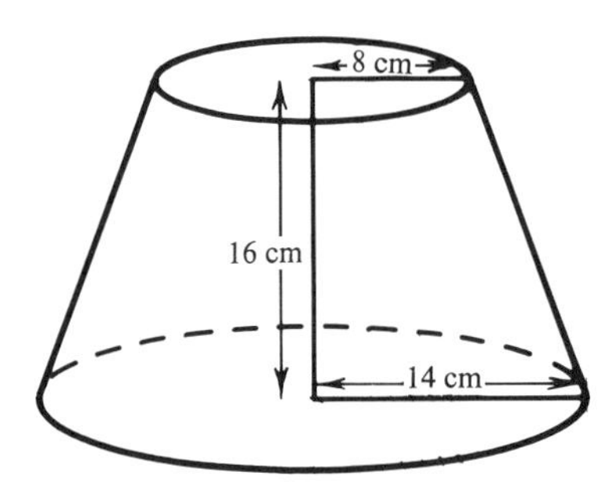

Fig. 31

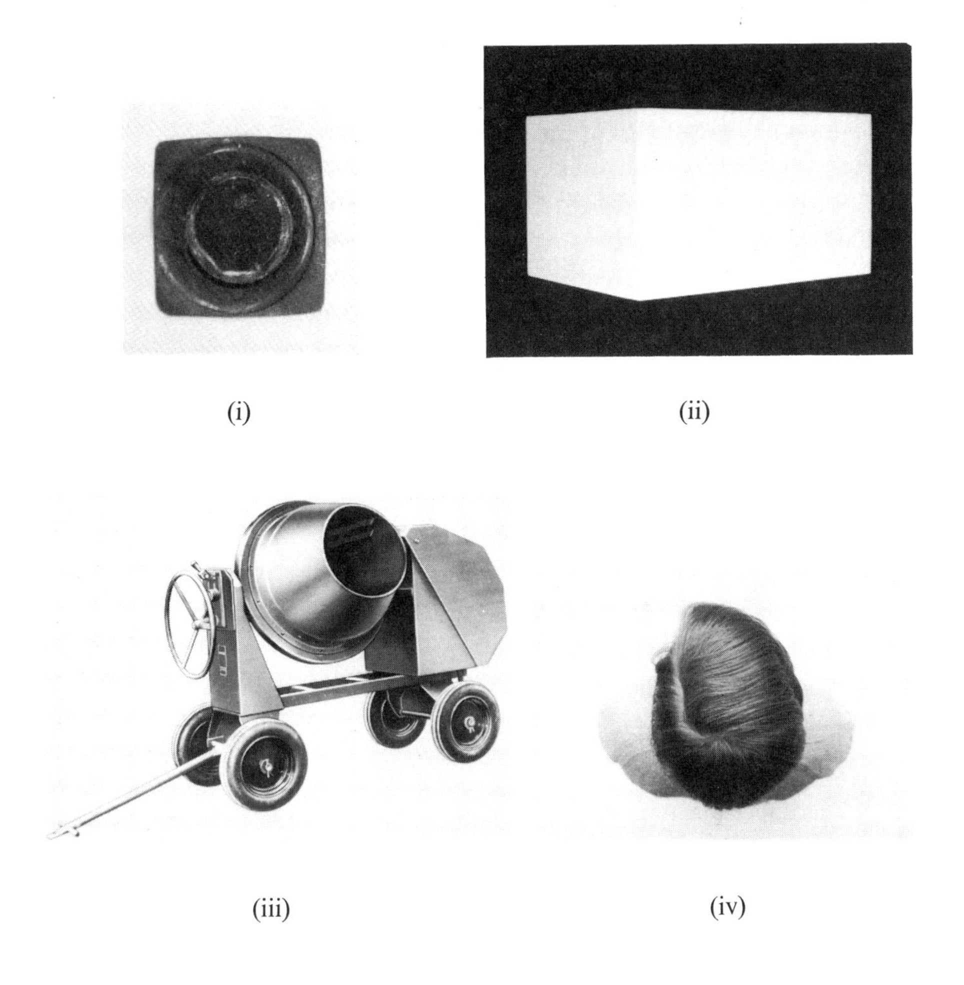

(i) (ii)

(iii) (iv)

11 Plans and elevations

1 Orthogonal projections

(*a*) The photographs at the beginning of this chapter are of four everyday objects. Can you guess what they are?

(*b*) Photograph 1 is of a square-headed bolt with the screw shaft pointing directly towards the camera. Suppose you are viewing the bolt from this angle. Try to visualize a transparent screen placed between you and the bolt as suggested by Figure 1.

By projecting parallel lines from the bolt to the screen, meeting the plane of the screen in a right angle, it would be possible to etch the view onto the screen. Figure 2 shows this projected view of the bolt. Such a view is said to be an *orthogonal projection* of the object – 'orthogonal' because the projection lines meet the plane of projection in a right angle.

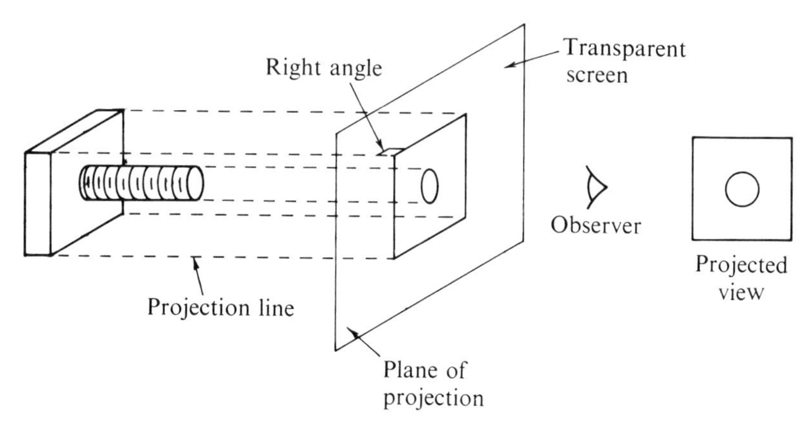

Fig. 1 Fig. 2

(*c*) The important thing about orthogonal projections is that they represent the 'true' shape of the object, in the sense that, if the plane of projection was inclined to the projection lines in other than a right angle, then the view would be distorted. (See Figure 3.)

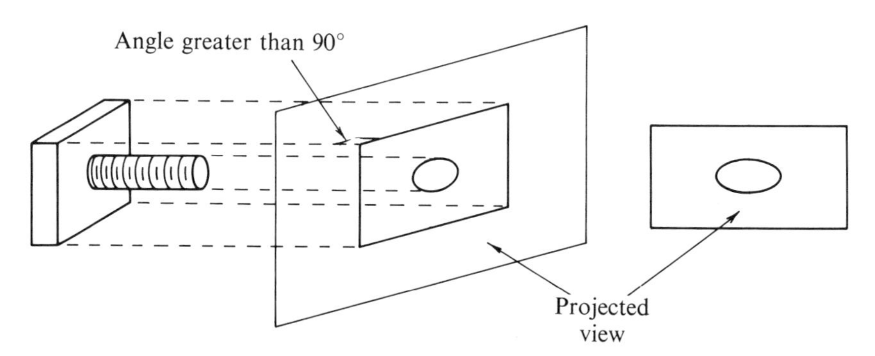

Fig. 3

Provided that the faces of the object we draw are parallel to the plane of projection we can use our drawing to measure otherwise unknown lengths and angles on these faces.

The length of side of the head of the bolt in Figure 2 is 2 cm. Measure the greatest distance across the head. Check your answer using Pythagoras' rule.

(*d*) Is the photograph of the bolt a true orthogonal projection? (Think about a bolt with a screw shaft 1 m long!)

Would you say that (i) maps of the world; (ii) contour maps are orthogonal projections? Study an atlas and see if you can decide how maps of the world have been produced from a globe.

(*e*) Figure 4 shows an orthogonal projection of one of the solids in Figure 5. Can you say which solid?

Fig. 4

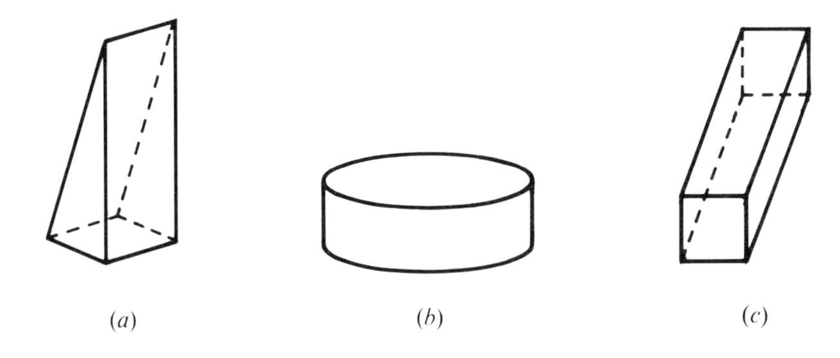

Fig. 5

(*f*) Figure 6 shows a second view of the same solid, viewed from a position orthogonal to the first view. Does this help you to decide which solid is being represented?

Fig. 6

(*g*) A third projected view of the solid is shown in Figure 7. The plane of projection is orthogonal to the planes of projection for the first two views. Only now can you be quite sure that it is (*b*) that we are drawing. Now draw three more solids which have two identical projections.

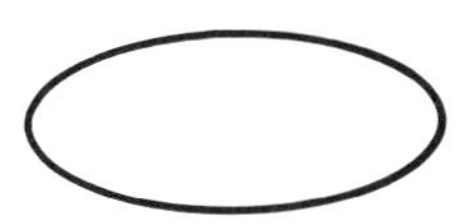

Fig. 7

(*h*) We can obviously draw as many orthogonal projections of a solid as we wish, but we usually find that three mutually orthogonal projections are sufficient. Two more views of the solid (*b*) are shown in Figure 8. Where do you think the planes of projection are situated?

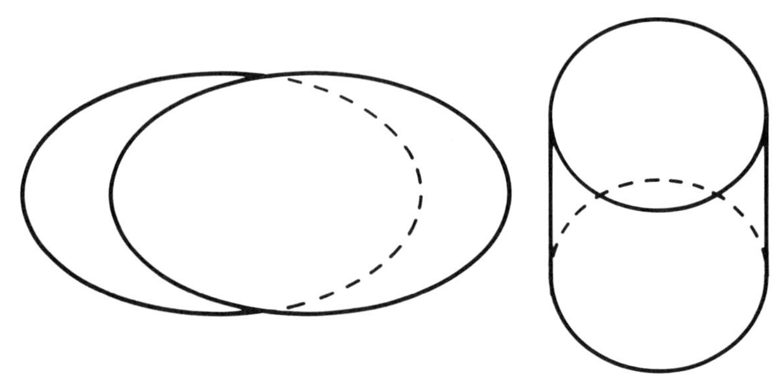

Fig. 8

Exercise A

1 Draw three orthogonal projections of each of the solids in Figure 9, viewed from the directions *A*, *B* and *C*.

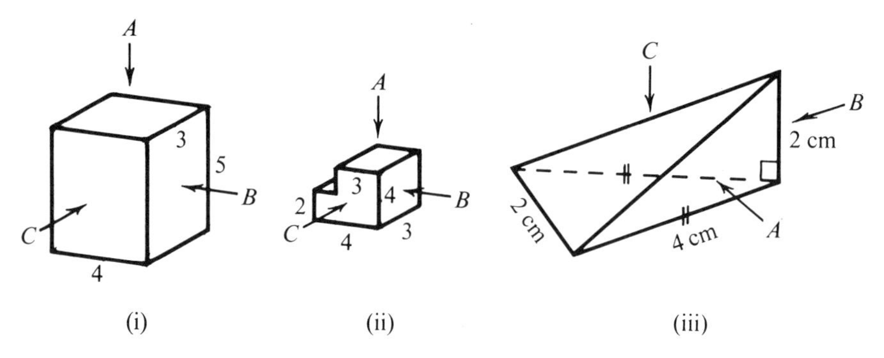

Fig. 9

2 The cone will slot exactly through the two holes in the piece of wood represented by Figure 10.

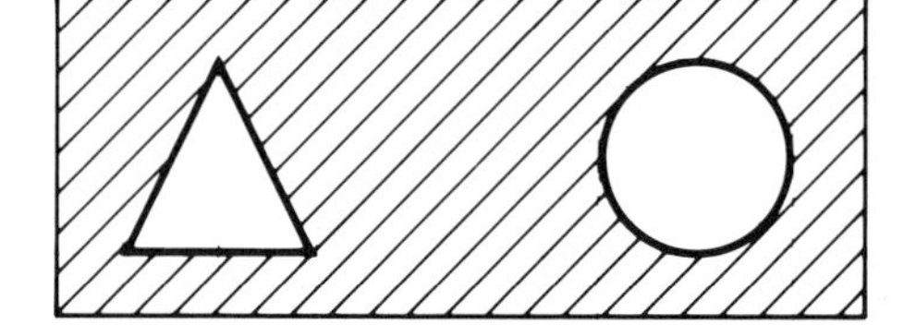

Fig. 10

Draw solids which will fit exactly through each hole for the following:

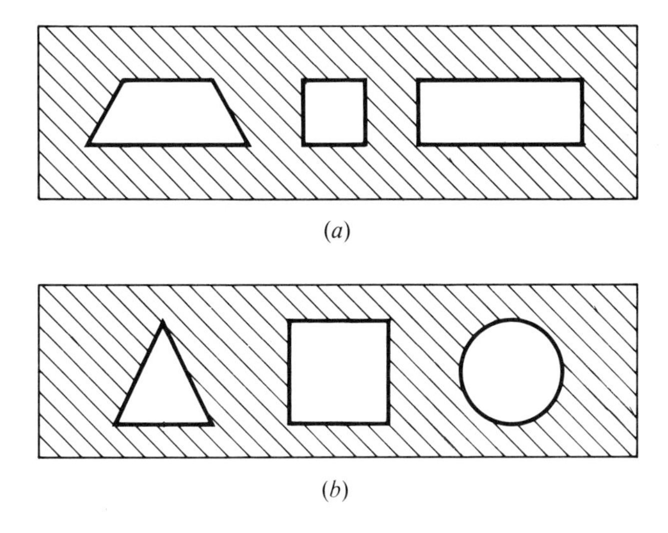

(*a*)

(*b*)

Fig. 11

3 Which of the drawings in Figure 12 do you think *could* be orthogonal projections of a cuboid? The broken lines represent hidden features.

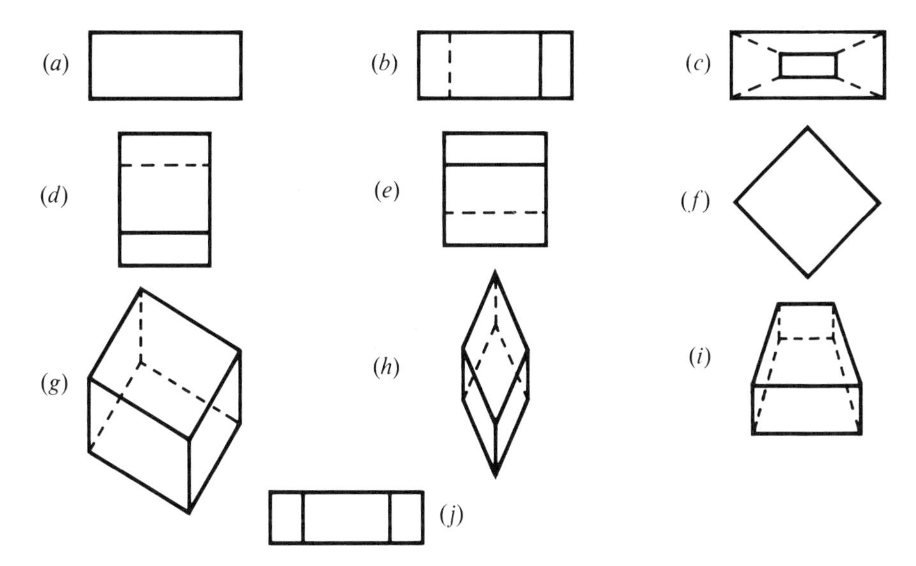

Fig. 12

4 Considering orthogonal projection as a transformation of 3D space into 2D space, which properties of figures are invariant?

5 Does the distance of the plane of projection from an object have any effect on the orthogonal projection of the object? Is the same principle true of (i) a photograph; (ii) an artist's view of an object?

6 If a triangle ABC is an orthogonal projection of a triangle XYZ is XYZ necessarily an orthogonal projection of ABC? Draw a diagram to explain your answer.

7 When is the orthogonal projection of a line segment onto a plane (i) equal in length to the line segment itself; (ii) a point; (iii) half the actual length of the line segment?

2 Standardized drawings

(*a*) Figure 13 shows three orthogonal projections of a solid. Try to draw a perspective view of the solid (ignore the two red lines for the moment).

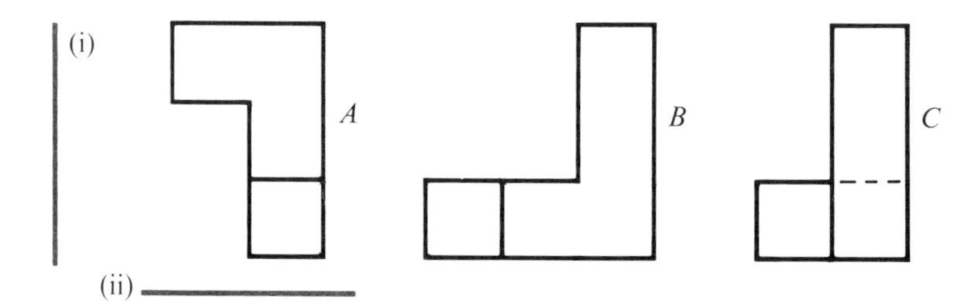

Fig. 13

(*b*) Figure 13 may have left you somewhat confused. If you are now told that the plane of projection for A is directly above the object, the plane of projection for B is in the position suggested by the red line (i) and for C is that suggested by the red line (ii), does this make your task any easier? The solid is shown in Figure 15.

(*c*) Obviously, if we have some idea of the positions of the planes of projection relative to an object, then we will find it far easier to interpret the drawings. We therefore position the projected views of an object on paper according to the standard procedure described below.

(*d*) Study Figure 14 which shows a solid partially enclosed by three mutually orthogonal planes of projection – the Front Vertical Plane (FVP), the Horizontal Plane (HP) and the Left Auxiliary Vertical Plane (LAVP). The planes meet in the lines XO, X_1O and Y_1O.

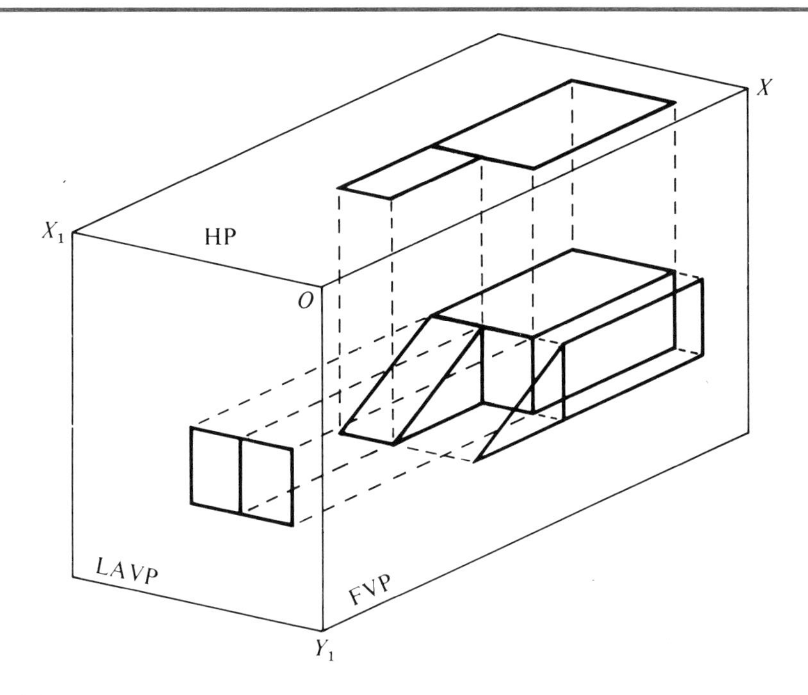

Fig. 14

If we project the object onto each of these planes and then 'open' the planes out so that they all lie in the same plane as FVP (see Figure 16) the projections will finally be positioned as in Figure 17.

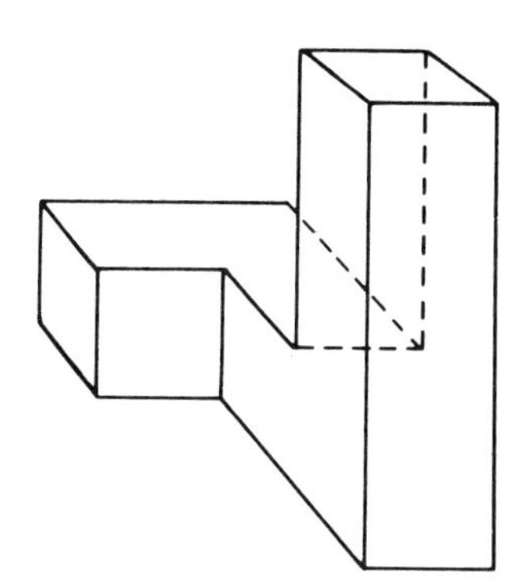

Fig. 15

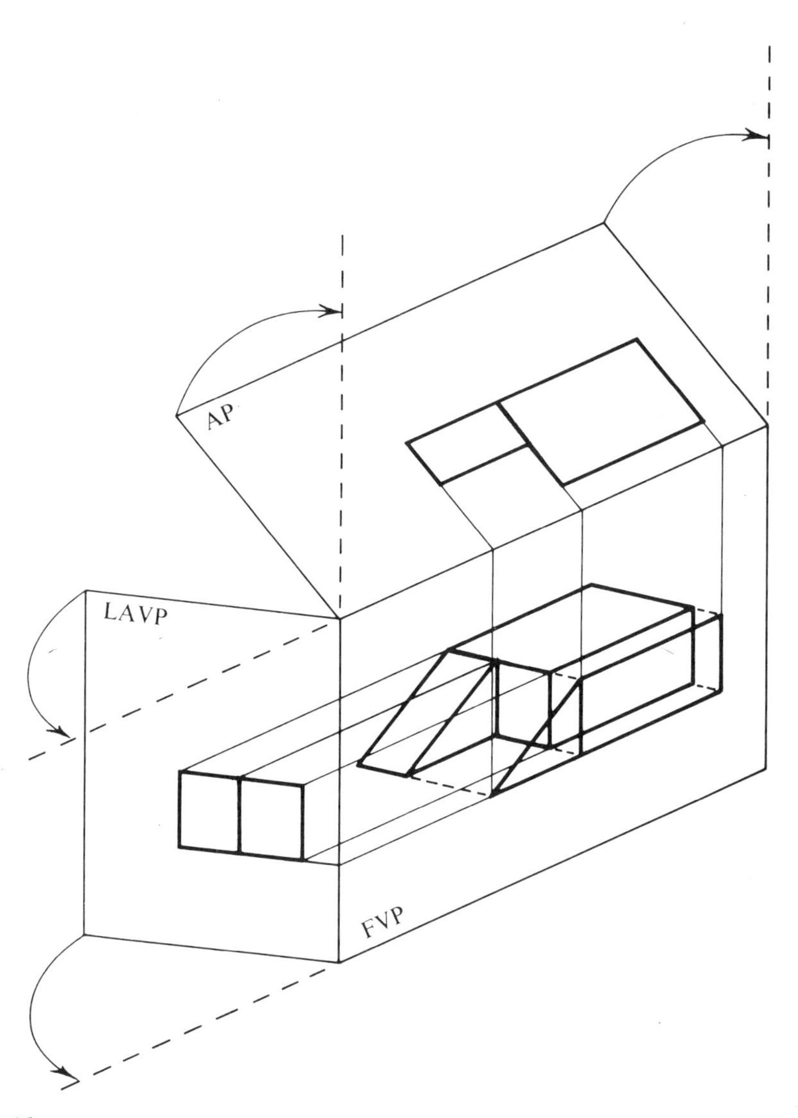

Fig. 16

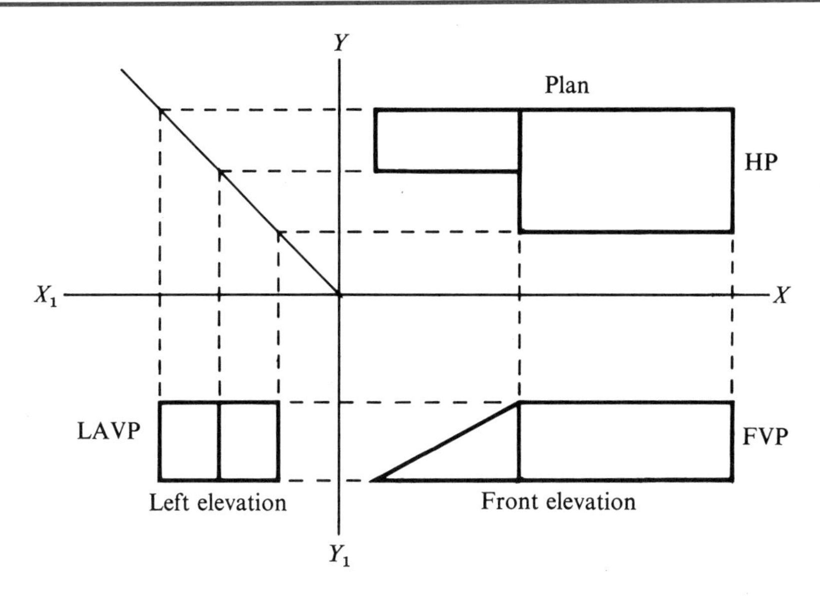

Fig. 17

Projections onto the vertical planes are called ELEVATIONS, and those onto the horizontal plane, PLANS. The particular system of standard planes of projection which leads to the plan being drawn directly above the *front elevation* and the auxiliary elevations (*left and right elevations*) to the left and right of the front elevation is called *third-angle projection*. The system was originally devised in America and is now almost universally approved. Figure 18 will suggest to you the reason for calling it third-angle projection.

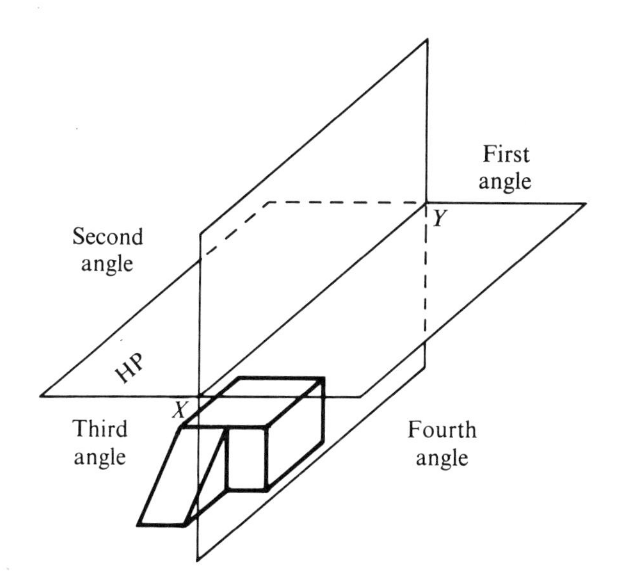

Fig. 18

(*e*) Draw a right elevation of the solid in Figure 14. Where would this view be positioned in Figure 17?

(*f*) Study Figure 17 closely. The first step in drawing orthogonal projections is to decide upon the relative position of the FVP. Once this has been done the HP and LAVP (or RAVP) can be positioned accordingly. One of the views can then be drawn, given the necessary dimensions (in Figure 17 we will assume that the plan has been drawn first). By projecting down and perpendicular to the $X-Y$ lines we can now position the front elevation. Now notice the construction line at 45 degrees to the $X-Y$ lines. Can you see how the left elevation has been produced using this? Were any measurements required? Must the construction line always be at 45 degrees to the $X-Y$ lines?

Exercise B

1 Draw in third-angle projection three views of each of the solids shown in Figure 19. Draw the front elevation from the direction shown by the arrows, and choose your own dimensions. Did you have to draw the views for (*c*) in any particular order?

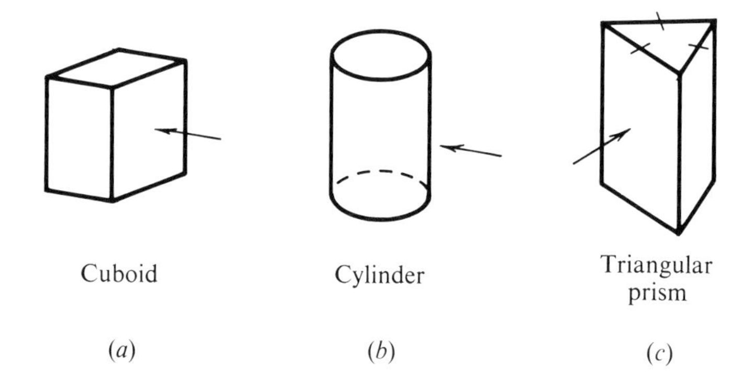

Fig. 19

2 The drawings in Figure 20 show a third-angle plan and elevation of a number of solids. Sketch, or describe the object in each case, giving an 'everyday' example where possible. [For example, (*i*) could be a roof.]

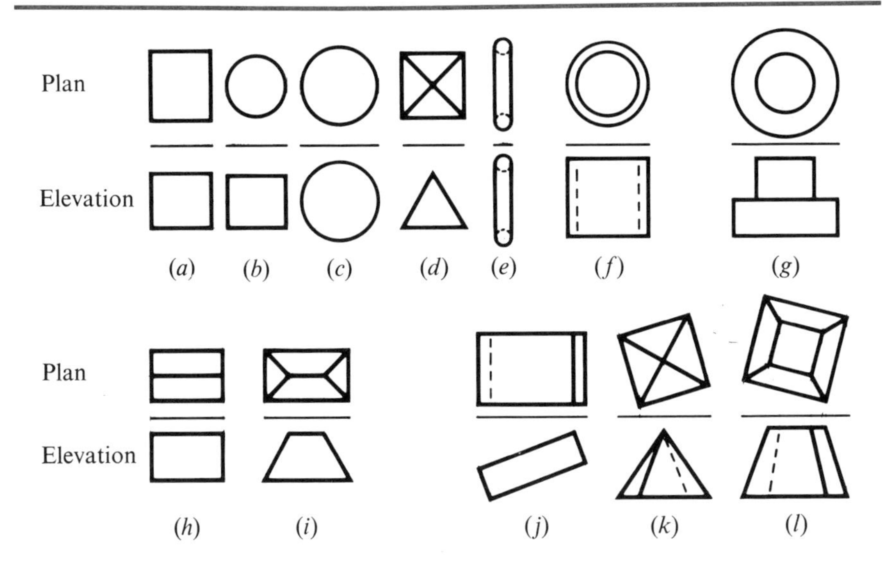

Fig. 20

3 In Figure 21, one view out of three has been omitted. Copy what is given and sketch the missing view.

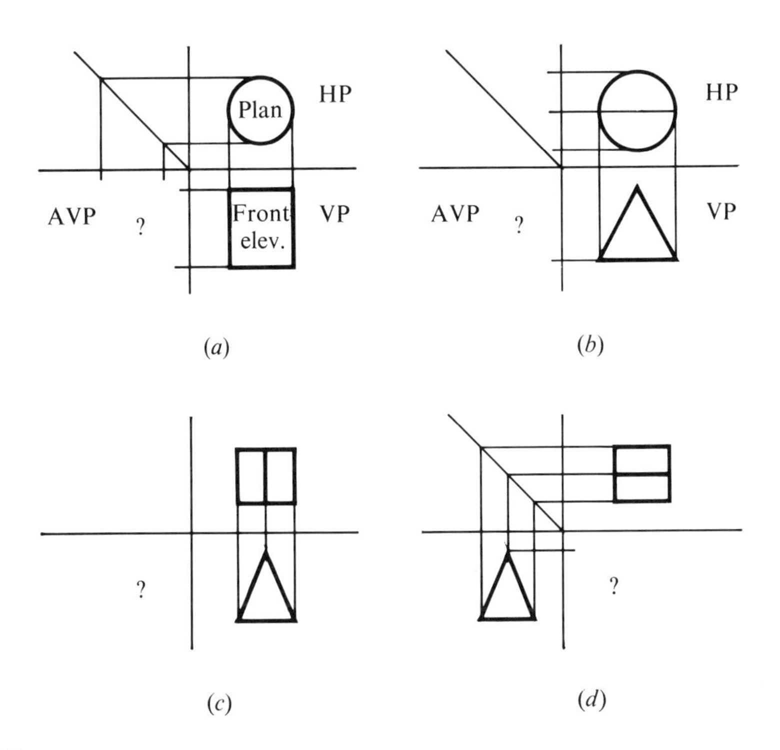

Fig. 21

4 Another system of standard planes of projection is called *first-angle projection*. Figure 22 shows the solid in Figure 14 drawn in first-angle projection. Draw diagrams to help you explain how each view has been projected.

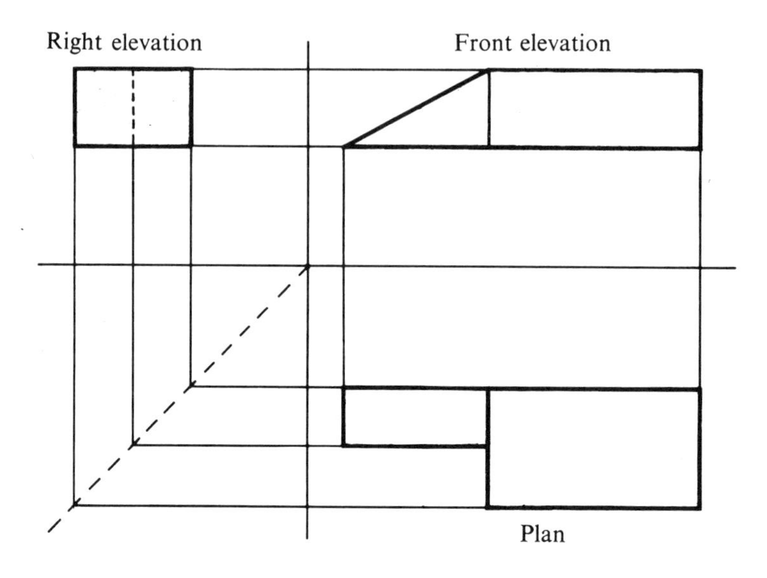

Fig. 22

3 Solids with faces inclined to a plane of projection

(*a*) Photograph (ii) is of a cuboid. Hold a cuboid in this position. Could you draw an orthogonal projection of the cuboid from this viewpoint?

(*b*) Figure 23 shows a plan of a cuboid of height 3 cm with one of its vertical faces inclined at an angle 60 degrees to the FVP. Unless you knew the distances *AB*, *BC*, and *CD* you would find it impossible to draw the front elevation of the cuboid without first drawing another view. Which other view is this?

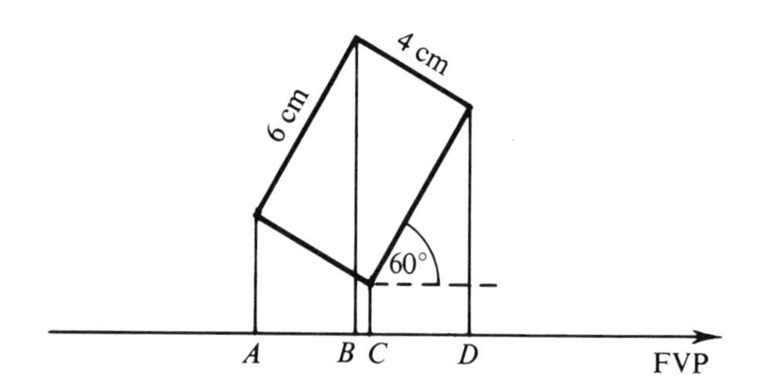

Fig. 23

(*c*) Figure 24 shows that by first drawing the *plan* of the cuboid the front elevation can be produced immediately. The plan is easily drawn because it projects a 'true' shape onto the horizontal plane.

Whenever we wish to draw a view of an inclined solid we must always first draw the view which projects such a 'true' shape.

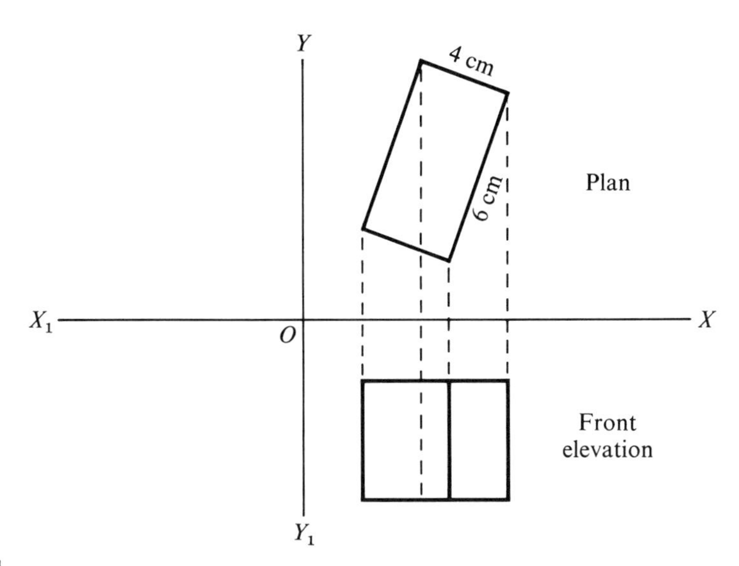

Fig. 24

Exercise C

1 Draw the left elevation of the cuboid in Figure 24.

2 The solid in Figure 25 is shown in either plan or elevation in Figures 26 (*a*)–(*c*). In each case copy what is drawn and project the missing view.

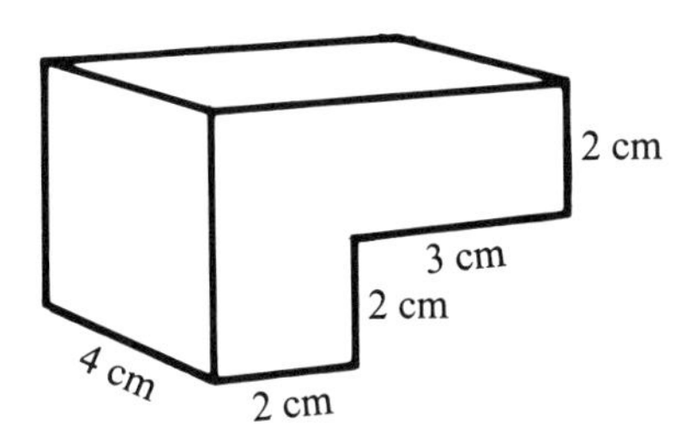

Fig. 25

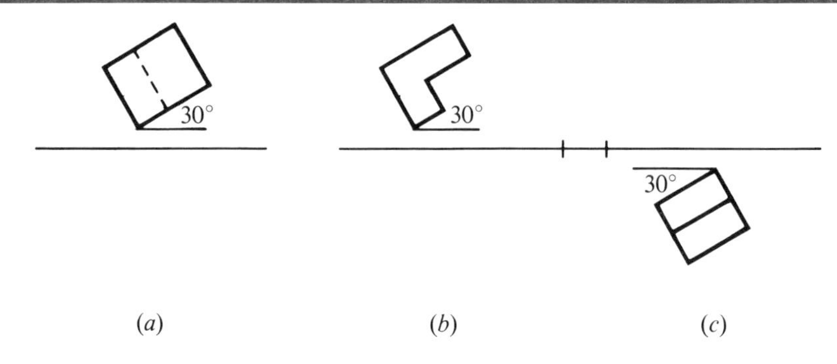

Fig. 26

3 The angle between a line and its orthogonal projection onto a plane is 30 degrees. Find, by drawing, the length of the orthogonal projection of a segment of the line 8 cm long.

4 The triangular faces of a prism are equilateral triangles of side 3 cm. The length of the prism is 5 cm. Draw a plan and one elevation of the prism, when one rectangular face is parallel to the FVP and the long edges are inclined at 30 degrees to the HP.

4 Solving 3D problems by drawing

In Exercise D you will be asked to find unknown lengths and angles of solids by drawing. Each of the problems can be solved using

(i) orthogonal projections, and
(ii) scale drawings.

Your main problem will be that of deciding which particular projections you should draw to enable you to make the necessary measurements. Remember that you can only make a 'true' measurement from a view which projects a 'true' shape onto the plane of projection.

Exercise D

1 Draw the plan and one elevation of a cube, side 8 cm, with its vertical faces inclined at 45 degrees to the FVP. Hence find the length of the diagonals of the cube.

2 $VABCD$ is the square-based pyramid shown in Figure 27. $AB = 6$ cm, $XA = 1$ cm, $CY = 2$ cm, $VB = 8$ cm. By drawing the triangles VAB and VDC and the square base find the length of:

(i) VX; (ii) VY; (iii) XY.

Hence find the angle YVX.

3 In Figure 27, find by drawing:

(i) the height of the pyramid;

(ii) the angle between VC and VA.

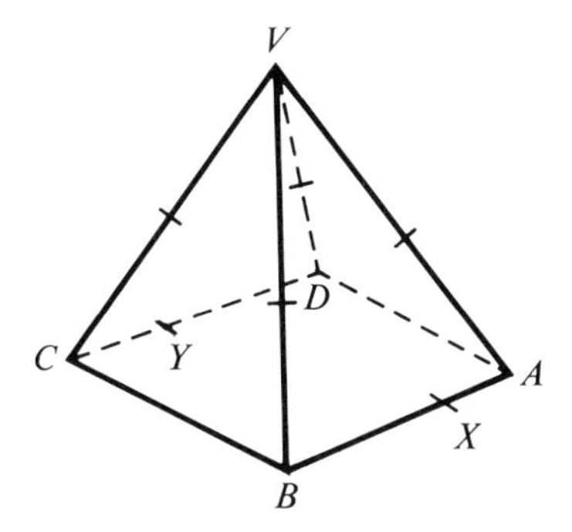

Fig. 27

4 Figure 28 shows a roof section of a house (the section has two planes of symmetry). Find by scale drawing:

(i) BC; (ii) angle BCD.

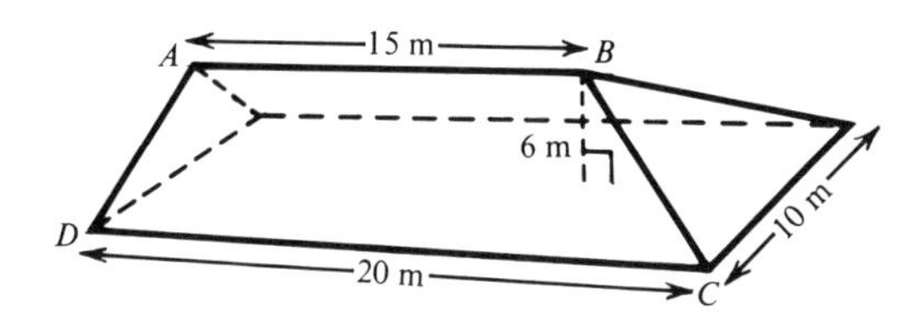

Fig. 28

5 Find, by drawing, the radius of the smallest sphere which will accommodate a right squared-based pyramid of height 6 cm, and length of base 4 cm.

6 Find, by drawing, the magnitude of the vector $\begin{pmatrix} 2 \\ 1 \\ 3 \end{pmatrix}$.

5 Another method of solving 3D problems

(*a*) If we can reduce the problem of finding unknown angles and lengths of solids to that of finding the angles and lengths of right-angled triangles then we can use

(i) Pythagoras' rule, and

(ii) trigonometrical ratios

to help us calculate the answers. In general, they will be more accurate than those obtained by drawing.

The following example shows how Question 4 in Exercise D can be solved using this method.

Example 1

Find (i) the length BC; (ii) the angle BCD, of the roof section shown in Figure 28.

(i) To calculate BC we can use the right-angled triangles BXZ and BZC shown in Figure 29.

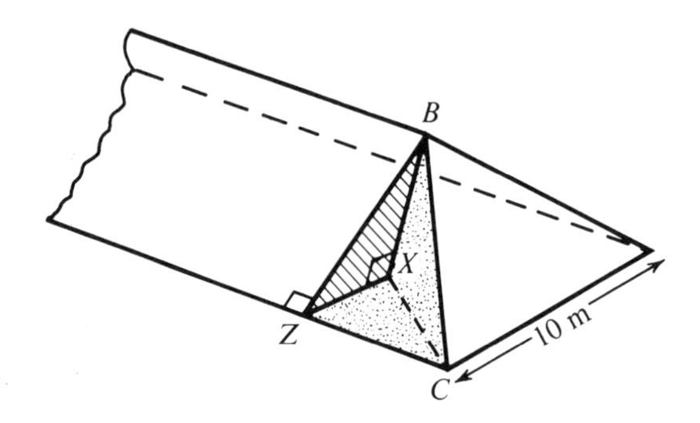

Fig. 29

By studying the symmetry of the roof section we can see that $XZ = 5$ m. Since $BX = 6$ m and BXZ is a right-angled triangle (see Figure 30) then

$$BZ^2 = BX^2 + XZ^2 = (25 + 36)\ \text{m}^2$$
$$= 61\ \text{m}^2.$$

Hence

$$BZ = \sqrt{61}\ \text{m} = 7{\cdot}81\ \text{m (3 s.f.)}.$$

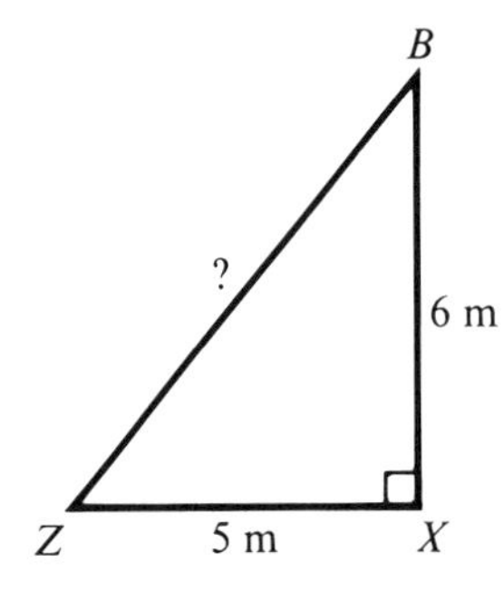

Fig. 30

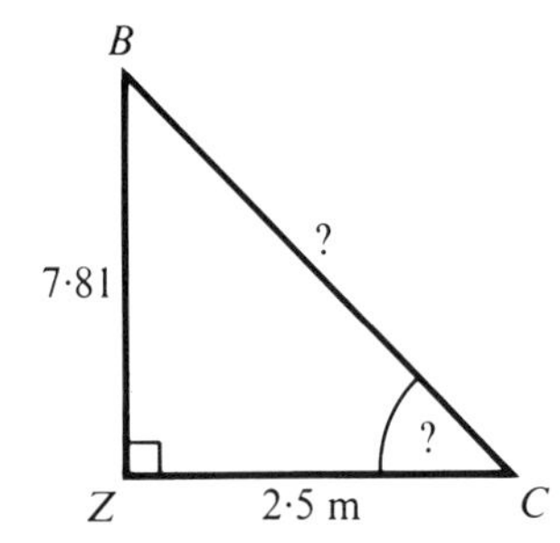

Fig. 31

Again using the symmetry of the roof section, $ZC = 2{\cdot}5$ m, and using triangle BZC (see Figure 31);

$$BC^2 = ZC^2 + BZ^2 = (2{\cdot}5^2 + 61)\ \text{m}^2$$
$$= 67{\cdot}25\ \text{m}^2.$$

(Why did we use $BZ^2 = 61$ and not $7{\cdot}81^2$?)

Hence

$$BC = \sqrt{67{\cdot}25}\ \text{m} = 8{\cdot}20\ \text{m (3 s.f.)}.$$

(ii) To calculate angle BCD we can use triangle BCZ (Figure 31).
We have

$$\tan \angle BCD = 7{\cdot}81/2{\cdot}5 = 3{\cdot}12 \text{ (3 S.F.)}$$
$$\text{angle } BCD = 72{\cdot}3^\circ.$$

Did you obtain approximately these answers by drawing?
(*b*) When you are solving 3D problems by calculation:

(i) sketch the solid and decide upon the right-angled triangles you should use to help you solve the problem;
(ii) if necessary draw each right-angled triangle separately and mark on the diagram the lengths of sides and angles you already know;
(iii) use Pythagoras' rule and your knowledge of trigonometrical ratios to calculate the answers.

Exercise E

1 For the cuboid in Figure 32 calculate:
(i) DB; (ii) AE; (iii) angle DAC; (iv) angle EAB.

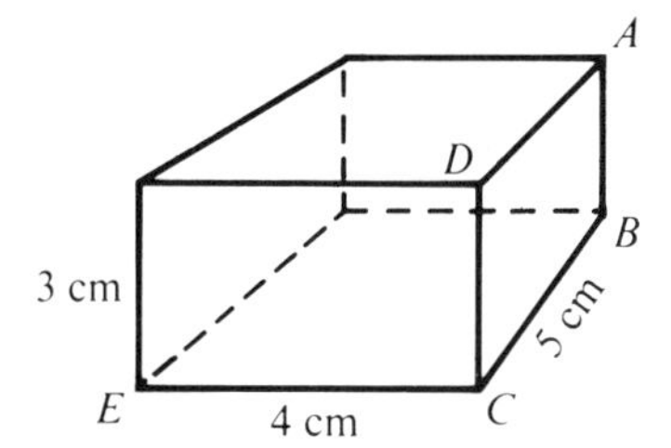

Fig. 32

2 Figure 33 represents a beam of light from a torch. Calculate the area of a circle of light cast upon a wall 6 m away.

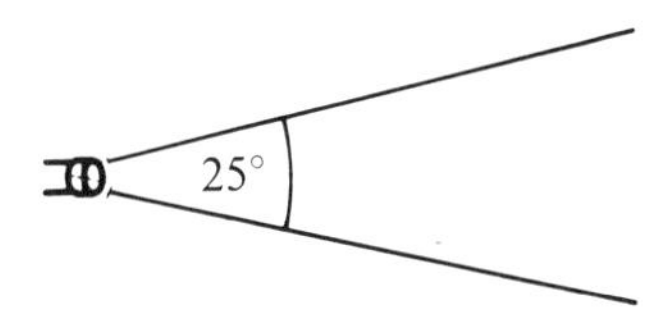

Fig. 33

3 A goldfish bowl in the form of a truncated sphere (Figure 34) has diameter 40 cm. The base and the opening at the top each have a radius of 10 cm. Calculate the height of the bowl.

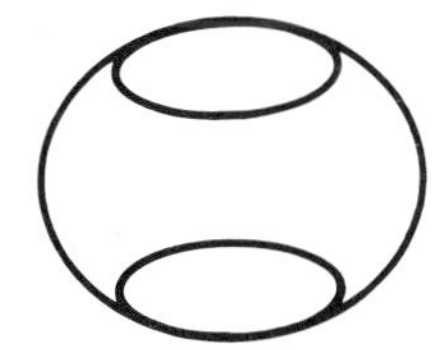

Fig. 34

4 Figure 35 shows a tetrahedron $ABCD$ in which $\angle ACB = \angle ACD = 90°$. CBD is an equilateral triangle of length of side 4 cm. $AC = 3$ cm. Calculate

(i) AB;
(ii) the length of the perpendicular from A to BD;
(iii) $\angle ABD$.

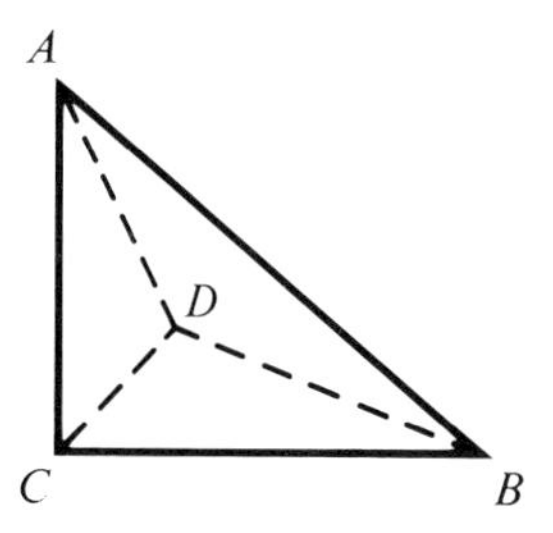

Fig. 35

5 Calculate the magnitude of the vector $\begin{pmatrix} 2 \\ 1 \\ 3 \end{pmatrix}$.

6 Figure 36 represents a piece of wire, of length 8 cm, which has been bent into three mutually orthogonal directions. Calculate the distance between the ends of the wire.

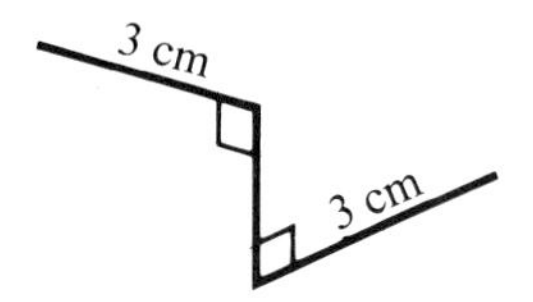

Fig. 36

7 Will a right pyramid, length of sloping side 8 cm, base 4 cm, fit inside a sphere of radius 5 cm?

8 The framework in Figure 37 has two planes of symmetry. $AC = 20$ m, $DF = AF = DE = 8$ m and $DB = 30$ m. Calculate (i) AB; (ii) $\angle AEC$.

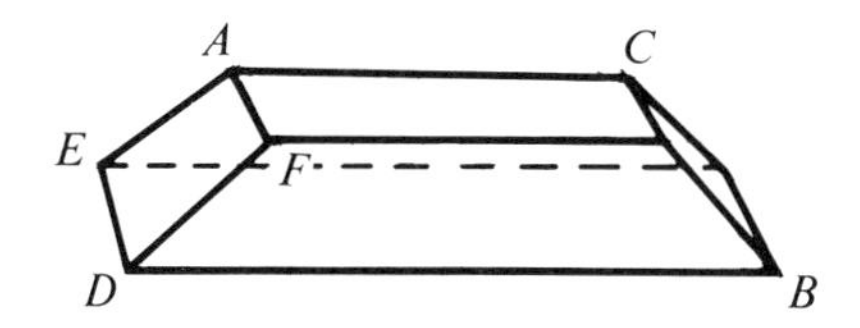

Fig. 37

9 A church spire is in the form of a hexagonal pyramid (Figure 38). The sides of the hexagon are 20 m, and the sloping faces of the tower are isosceles triangles with the two equal sides 80 m long. Calculate

(i) the height of the tower;
(ii) the angle at which each face of the tower slopes to the horizontal;
(iii) the area of lead needed to cover the exterior of the tower.

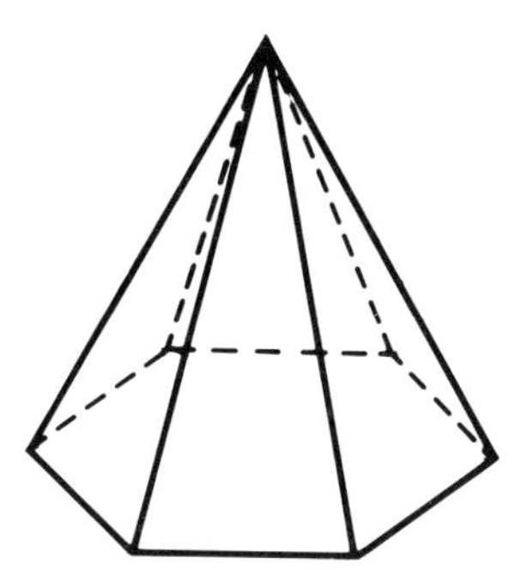

Fig. 38

10 Three vertical poles of height 60 m, 50 m and 40 m are situated in flat country at the vertices of an equilateral triangle of side 100 m. The tops of the poles are joined by straight wire cables. Calculate (i) the length of each cable; (ii) the angle between the plane in which the cables lie and the horizontal.

11 Two planes P_1 and P_2 meet in an angle of 30° (see Figure 39). $ABCD$ is a square drawn on plane P_1 with AD parallel to the line of intersection of the two planes. What kind of figure is the orthogonal projection of $ABCD$ onto P_2? Calculate the area of this figure if $AB = 4$ cm.

12 If the side AD of a square as in Question 11 was produced and met the line of intersection of the two planes in an angle of 45° what kind of quadrilateral would the orthogonal projection onto P_2 be? What would be the area of this quadrilateral?

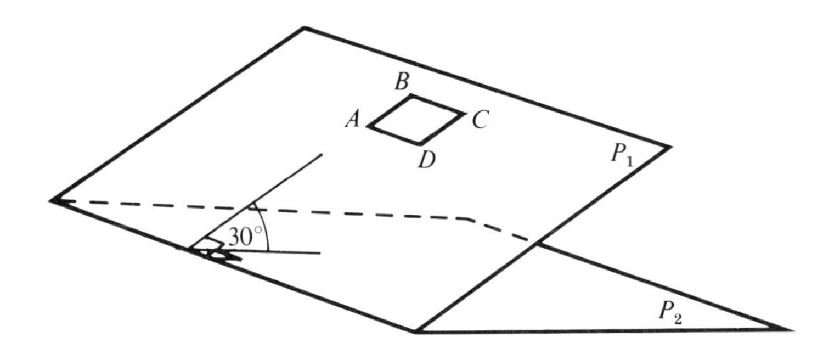

Fig. 39

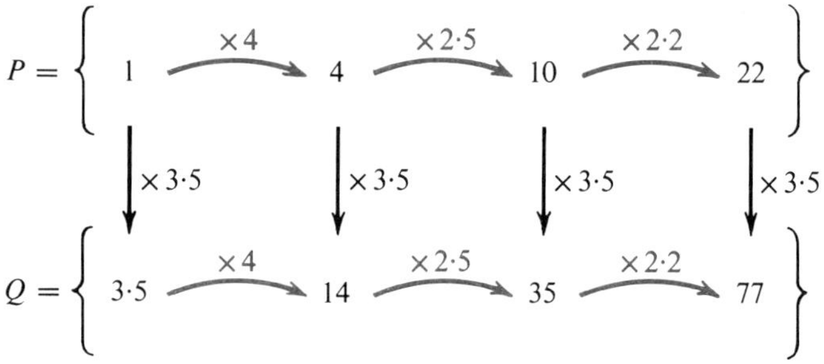

$$P = \left\{ 1 \xrightarrow{\times 4} 4 \xrightarrow{\times 2\cdot 5} 10 \xrightarrow{\times 2\cdot 2} 22 \right\}$$

$$\downarrow \times 3\cdot 5 \qquad \downarrow \times 3\cdot 5 \qquad \downarrow \times 3\cdot 5 \qquad \downarrow \times 3\cdot 5$$

$$Q = \left\{ 3\cdot 5 \xrightarrow{\times 4} 14 \xrightarrow{\times 2\cdot 5} 35 \xrightarrow{\times 2\cdot 2} 77 \right\}$$

12 Looking for functions

1 The linear rule

(*a*) The diagram above reminds us that proportional sets have the following properties:

(i) corresponding pairs of numbers are related by a constant scale factor;
(ii) sets of multipliers are identical.

In this case the scale factor is 3·5 and

$$M_P = M_Q = \{4, 2\cdot 5, 2\cdot 2\}.$$

(*b*) Let us look at the ordered sets

$$A = \{1, 2\cdot 1, 4\cdot 2, 5\},$$
$$B = \{3, 6\cdot 3, 12\cdot 6, 15\}.$$

Are A and B proportional sets? Does the table of multipliers confirm your answer?

Members of A	Multipliers for A	Members of B	Multipliers for B
1·0		3·0	
	2·1		2·1
2·1		6·3	
	2·0		2·0
4·2		12·6	
	1·2		1·2
5·0		15·0	

Corresponding members of A and B are related by the rule $x \to 3x$. This function is shown in the arrow diagram [Figure 1(a)] and graph [Figure 1(b)].

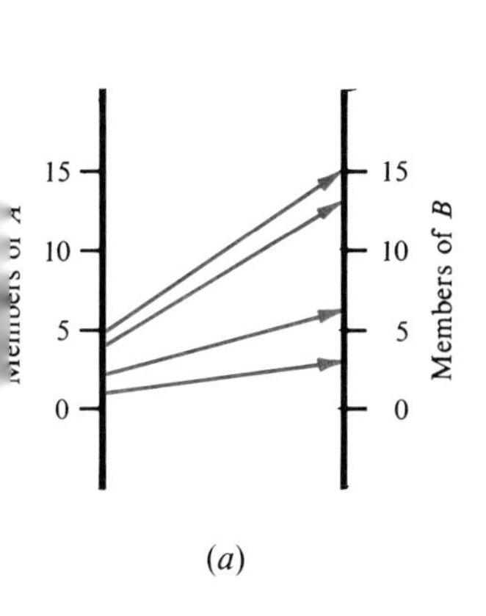

(a)

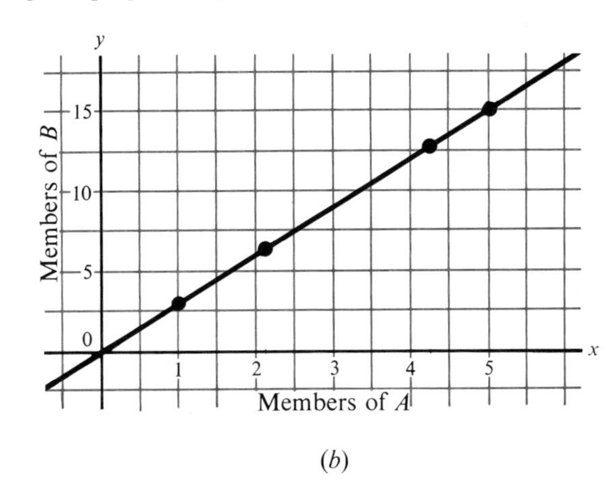

(b)

Fig. 1

The line through the four points in Figure 1(b) passes through the origin and has gradient 3. Do you agree that its equation is $y = 3x$? Notice that in this case sets A and B are proportional with scale factor 3.

(c) Let us now consider the ordered sets

$$C = \{1{\cdot}4, 3{\cdot}0, 3{\cdot}9, 4{\cdot}6\}$$
$$D = \{3{\cdot}8, 7{\cdot}0, 8{\cdot}8, 10{\cdot}2\}.$$

The table of multipliers for C and D shows that they are not proportional sets.

Members of C	Multipliers for C	Members of D	Multipliers for D
1·4		3·8	
	2·14		1·84
3·0		7·0	
	1·30		1·26
3·9		8·8	
	1·18		1·16
4·6		10·2	

But if we graph the members of C and D we obtain a straight line which does not pass through the origin (see Figure 2).

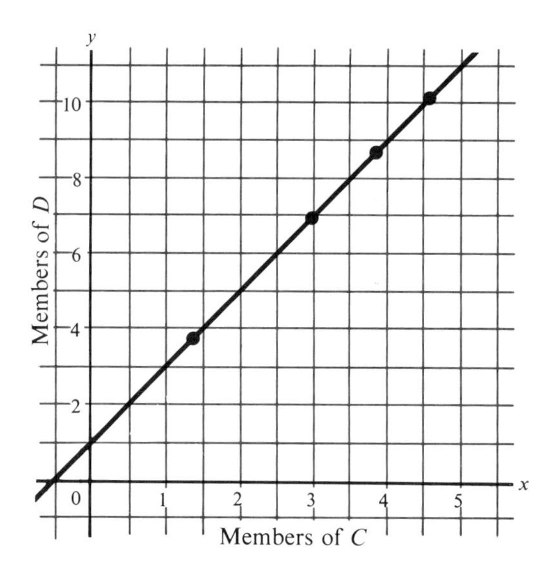

Fig. 2

What is the gradient of the line and where does it meet the y-axis?
Do you agree that the equation of the line is

$$y = 2x + 1?$$

(*d*) Copy and complete the multipliers table for the sets *E* and *F* shown below.

Members of *E*	Multipliers for *E*	Members of *F*	Multipliers for *F*
0·8		1·6	
	1·75		
1·4		1·3	
2·0		1·0	
			0·4
3·2		0·4	

Are *E* and *F* proportional sets?
Corresponding members of *E* and *F* are graphed in Figure 3.

The graph is again a straight line which does not pass through (0,0). Check that its equation is

$$y = {}^{-}\tfrac{1}{2}x + 2.$$

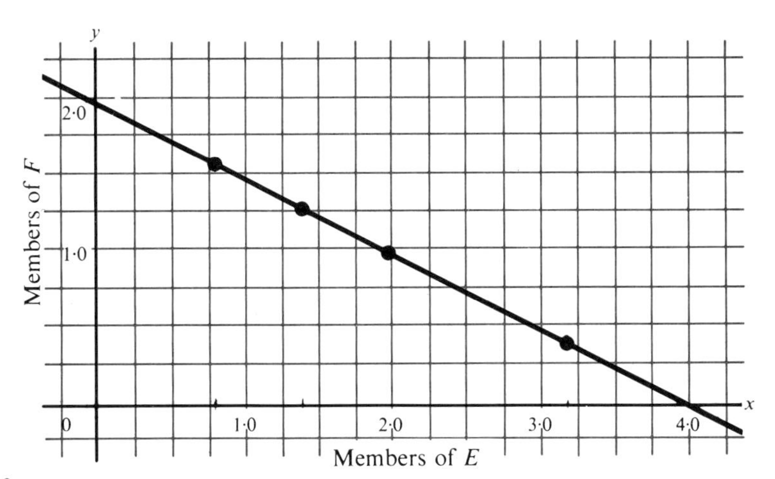

Fig. 3

(*e*) In sections (*b*), (*c*) and (*d*) we have found the following rules relating members of pairs of sets:

(i) $y = 3x$;
(ii) $y = 2x + 1$;
(iii) $y = {}^{-}\frac{1}{2}x + 2$.

These are all of the form $y = mx + c$ and we call them *linear* rules. Can you explain why this name is used? Rule (i) is a special case and describes the relation between proportional sets. When a rule is of the form $y = mx$ we sometimes write it as $y \propto x$.

Exercise A

1 R and S are proportional sets and $R = \{1, 2{\cdot}5, b\}$, $S = \{4, a, 15\}$.

(*a*) Write down the scale factor.
(*b*) Find the values of a and b.
(*c*) List the members of M_R and M_S.

2 This question refers to the sets C and D of Section 1(*c*).

(*a*) List the set D_1 whose members are each one less than the corresponding members of D.
(*b*) Complete the multipliers table for sets C and D_1.
(*c*) Are C and D_1 proportional sets?

3 The following table was produced in an experiment:

s:	1·2	1·4	1·6	1·8	2·0	2·2
f:	34	39·6	45·3	51	56·6	62·3

Make a table showing the multipliers for each set. What is the rule which relates f and s?

4 The annual cost of running a particular make of car for different mileages is given in the table:

Distance (km) d:	5000	10 000	15 000	20 000
Cost (£) c:	80	110	140	170

Show by a multipliers table that the sets are not proportional. Draw a graph of the data and use it to find the rule which relates c and d.

5 The prices of ladders of different lengths are given in the table:

Length (m) l:	4	5	6	6·6	7·3
Price (£) p:	9·00	11·70	14·40	16·20	18·00

Find graphically the rule relating p and l.

2 Scientific experiments

Many experiments which are performed in school science laboratories and elsewhere, involve taking readings of two quantities and comparing the sets of data in an attempt to find a simple relation between them. Here are some examples:

Length and time of swing of a pendulum.
Object and image distance of a lens.
Voltage and current in an electrical circuit.
Age and mass of rabbits.
Height and diameter of base of stem (of seedling).

Can you think of others?

In some cases the rule will be a linear one and confirmation of this will appear when the data is graphed. 'Real life' experiments however do not produce perfectly straight lines. Here is a table obtained by suspending different masses on a spring:

Mass (kg) x:	1	2	3	4	5
Length of spring (cm) y:	22·4	27·6	29·8	35·0	38·4

Graph the results and draw the straight line which you think is suggested by the five marked points. What is the gradient of your line and where does it meet the y axis? Write down the equation of your line. What length of spring do you think would result if a mass of 3·5 kg were suspended? Compare your answers with those obtained by others. Do you expect them to be the same?

Many experiments on the other hand will produce sets of results which are not even approximately related by a linear rule. Here is an example. The table shows the distance travelled by a freely falling object at 1-second intervals for the first 5 seconds.

Time of fall (seconds) t:	1	2	3	4	5
Distance travelled (metres) d:	5	20	45	80	125

The data is graphed in Figure 4 which shows that the rule is not a linear one. Can you suggest a name for the shape of the graph?

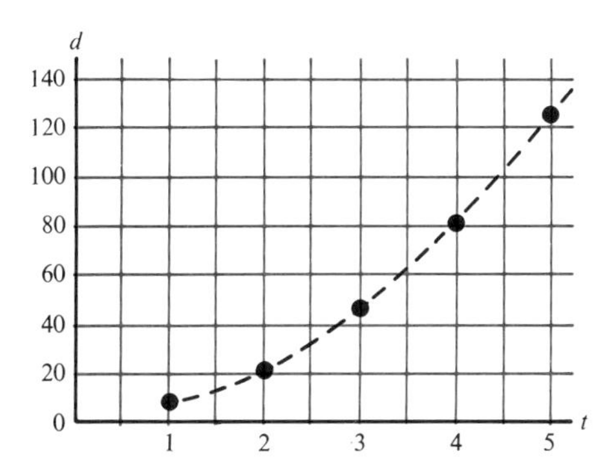

Fig. 4

We now look more closely at the two sets of data. In the multipliers table the squares of multipliers for t and the multipliers for d are identical showing that d is proportional to t^2.

t	Multipliers for t	Squares of multipliers for t	d	Multipliers for d
1			5	
	2·0	4·0		4·0
2			20	
	1·5	2·25		2·25
3			45	
	1·33	1·78		1·78
4			80	
	1·25	1·56		1·56
5			125	

Corresponding values of t^2 and d are:

t^2:	1	4	9	16	25
d:	5	20	45	80	125

What is the scale factor?

Do you agree that the rule is $d = 5t^2$ and that the curve in Figure 4 is a *parabola* whose equation is $d = 5t^2$?

Notice that when d is plotted against t^2 a straight line is obtained (see Figure 5). What is its gradient?

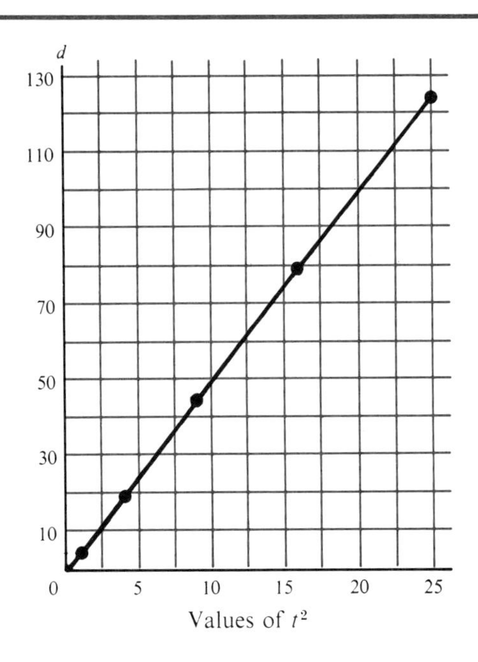

Fig. 5

Summary

1 If the function rule connecting two sets of numbers is of the form $y = ax^2$ it is called a square rule.

2 The graph of y against x^2 in this case is a straight line through the origin.

3 The value of a is measured by the gradient of this line.

4 The graph of $y = ax^2$ is a parabola.

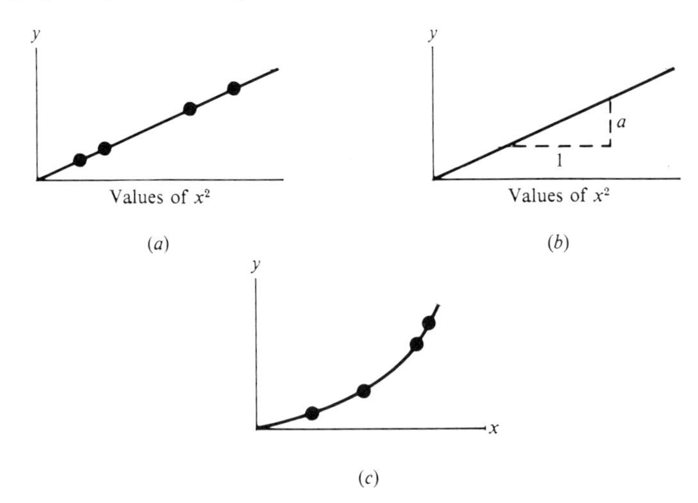

Fig. 6

Exercise B

1 Here are two corresponding sets of experimental data:

e:	4	7	10	13	16	19
c:	15	20	24	27·4	30·4	33

Show by a table of multipliers that the sets are approximately related by a square rule.

2 Figure 7 shows a curve which looks like part of a parabola. Take readings from the graph and complete the table:

x:	5	10	15	20	25	30
y:						

Make a table of the sets of multipliers for x and y and the squares of multipliers for x. Is the curve a parabola? What is its equation?

3 Figure 8 shows the graph of A against r^2 where A is the area of a circle and r is its radius (r is measured in cm and A in cm^2). What should the gradient of the line be? Check your answer by measurement. Sketch the graph of A against r.

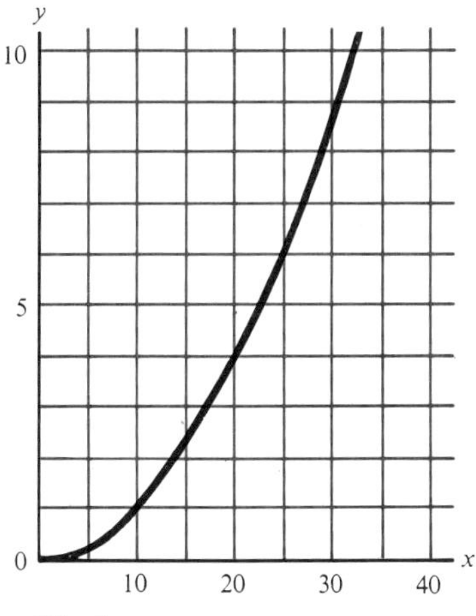

Fig. 7

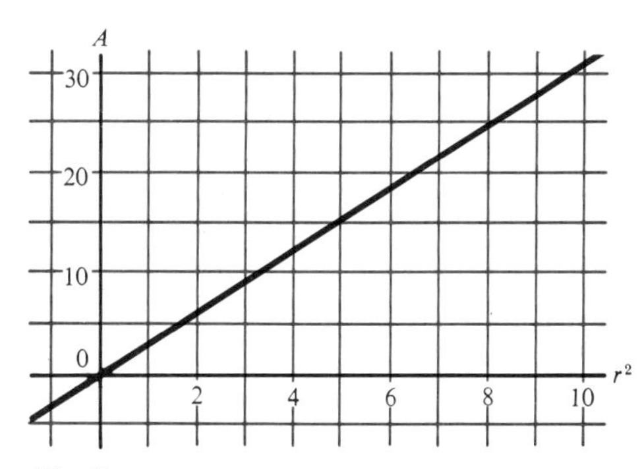

Fig. 8

3 The reciprocal rule

The dial of a transistor set is marked in metres and kilohertz. Here are some corresponding numbers:

Wave-length l:	300	500	600	1500
Frequency f:	1000	600	500	200

The multipliers table has two identical columns showing that l is proportional to $\frac{1}{f}$.

l	Multipliers for l	f	Multipliers for f	Reciprocals of multipliers for f
300		1000		
	1·67		0·60	1·67
500		600		
	1·20		0·83	1·20
600		500		
	2·50		0·4	2·50
1500		200		

Here is the table of values of l and $\frac{1}{f}$:

l:	300	500	600	1500
$\frac{1}{f}$:	0·001	0·0017	0·002	0·005

Figure 9 shows the graphs obtained by plotting l against f and l against $\frac{1}{f}$.

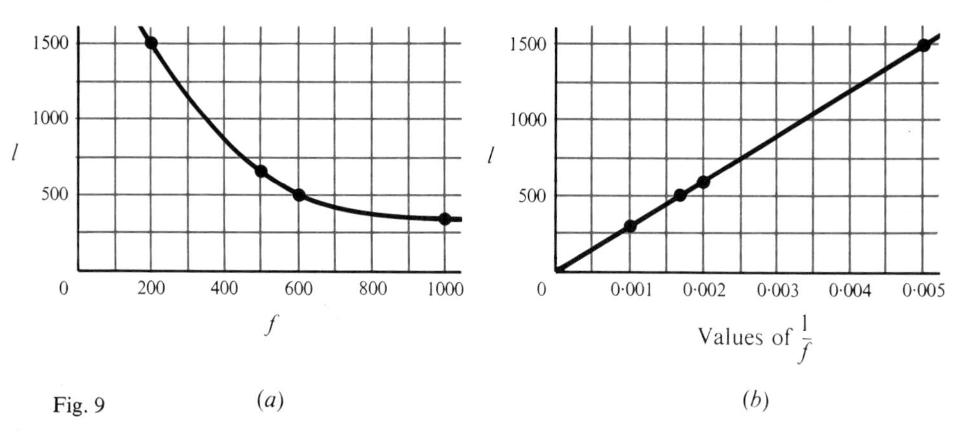

Fig. 9

The graph in Figure 9(a) is called a *hyperbola*.
What is the gradient of the straight line in Figure 9(b)?
Do you agree that values of l and f are related by the rule $l = \frac{300\,000}{f}$?

Each value of l is increased by 100 to give the following table:

l_1:	400	600	700	1600
f:	1000	600	500	200

Check that l_1 and f satisfy the relation $l_1 = \frac{300\,000}{f} + 100$.

Summary

1 If the rule describing the relation between two sets of numbers has the form $y = \frac{a}{x}$, it is called a *reciprocal rule* and the numbers are said to be *inversely proportional*.

2 The graph of y against $\frac{1}{x}$ is a straight line through the origin with gradient a.

3 The graph of $y = \frac{a}{x}$ is a hyperbola.

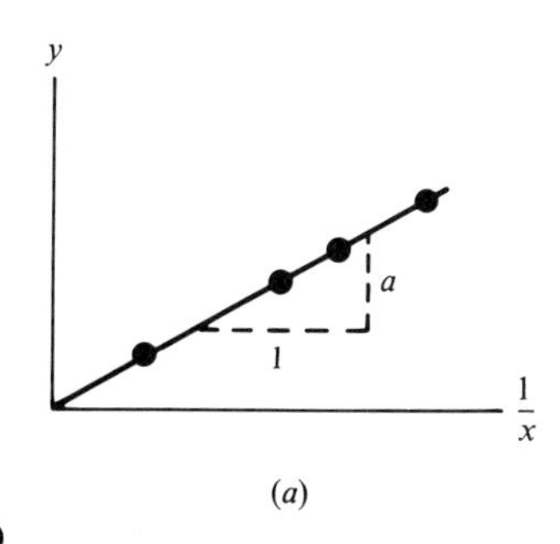

(*a*)

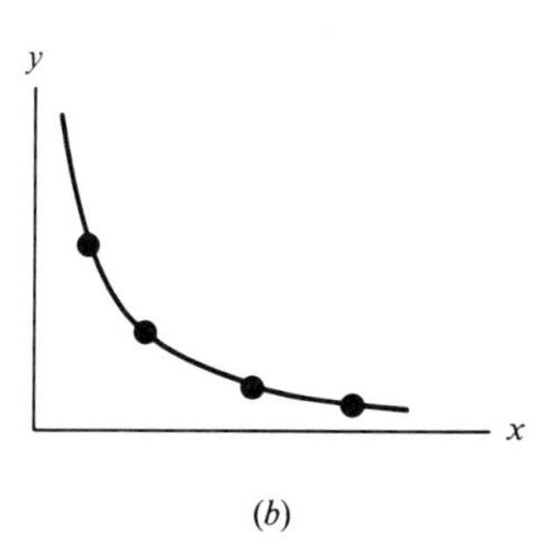

(*b*)

Fig. 10

Exercise C

1 In an experiment to investigate how the volume of a quantity of air varies under different pressures, the following table of results was obtained:

Pressure (N/cm²) p:	20	25	30	35	40	45
Volume (cm³) v:	158	125	105	90	79	70

Make a table showing the multipliers for p and v and the reciprocals of the multipliers for v. Calculate the corresponding values for $\frac{1}{v}$ and plot p against $\frac{1}{v}$ in a graph. Use your graph to find the rule relating p and v.

2 Figure 11 shows a curve which looks like part of a hyperbola. Make a table of six corresponding pairs of values of x and y. Calculate the sets of multipliers for x and y and also the reciprocals of the multipliers for x. Is the curve confirmed as a hyperbola? Find its equation by plotting a graph of values of y against $\frac{1}{x}$.

3 For photographic flash work, the table relates distance and aperture setting:

Distance, d:	1·00	1·40	2·00	2·75	4·00	5·50
Aperture, A:	22	16	11	8	5·6	4

Find an approximate rule relating d and A.

4 The following table of values is known to come from a reciprocal rule function.

x:	3	4	5	6	7
y:	105	87·5	63	52·5	45

One value of y is incorrect. Draw a suitable graph to find which it is and correct it. If $y = \frac{a}{x}$ what is the value of a?

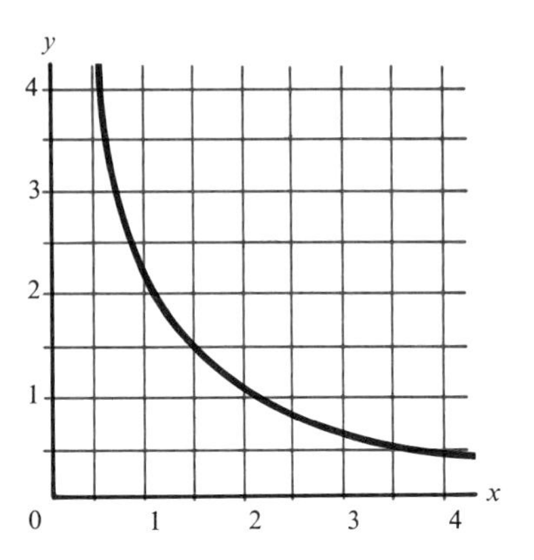

Fig. 11

4 Finding function rules in general

So far the ordered sets of data we have considered have been related by one of the following rules:

$$y = mx + c \text{ (linear)}$$
$$y = ax^2 \text{ (square)}$$
$$y = \frac{a}{x} \text{ (reciprocal)}$$

There are, of course, many other types of rule which relate experimental data. Finding the rule which applies in a particular case requires care both in computation and graph plotting. A calculating aid is almost a necessity.

Example 1

p:	0·32	0·68	1·28	2·12	3·20
t:	0·1	0·2	0·3	0·4	0·5

The graph of the data shown in Figure 12 suggests that the rule is not a linear one.

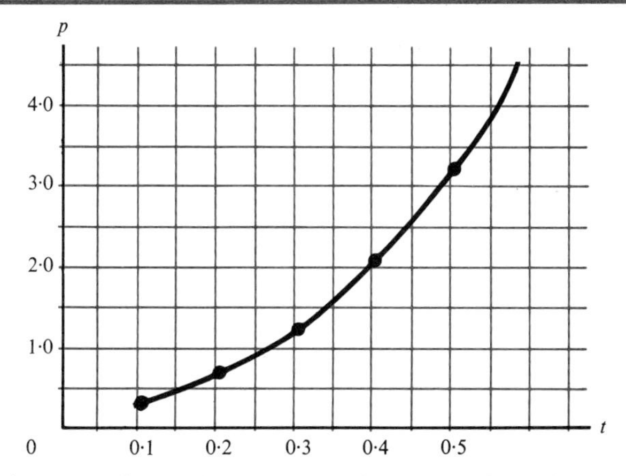

Fig. 12

Since plotting p against t does not produce a straight line, let us consider values of t^2 and $\frac{1}{t}$.

t^2:	0·01	0·04	0·09	0·16	0·25
$\frac{1}{t}$:	10·0	5·0	3·3	2·5	2·0

Figure 13 shows that a straight line graph is obtained when p is plotted against t^2. Do you think that plotting p against $\frac{1}{t}$ will produce a straight line? See if your prediction is correct by drawing a graph of p against $\frac{1}{t}$.

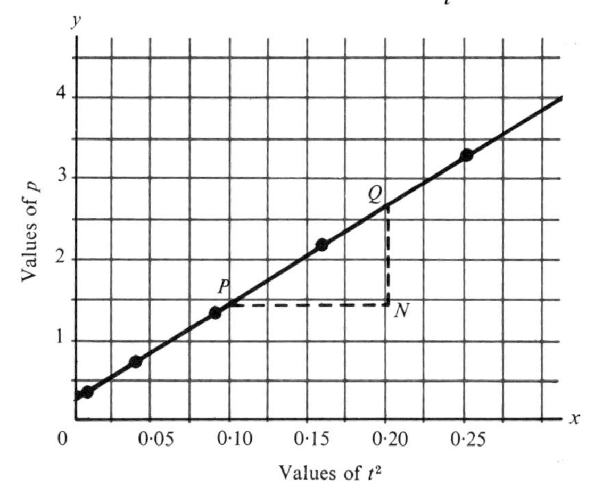

Fig. 13

Looking again at Figure 13 we see that the line crosses the y axis at $y = 0{\cdot}2$. By considering triangle PQN we obtain the value of the gradient as $\frac{2{\cdot}6 - 1{\cdot}4}{0{\cdot}20 - 0{\cdot}10}$ or 12. Do you agree that the equation of the graph in Figure 13 is

$$y = 12x + 0{\cdot}2?$$

Since values of p are shown on the y-axis and values of t^2 on the x-axis, the rule relating p and t is $p = 12t^2 + 0{\cdot}2$.

Summary

A systematic approach to finding function rules is given in the flow diagram (see Figure 14). It refers to two ordered sets X and Y and their corresponding multiplier sets M_X and M_Y.

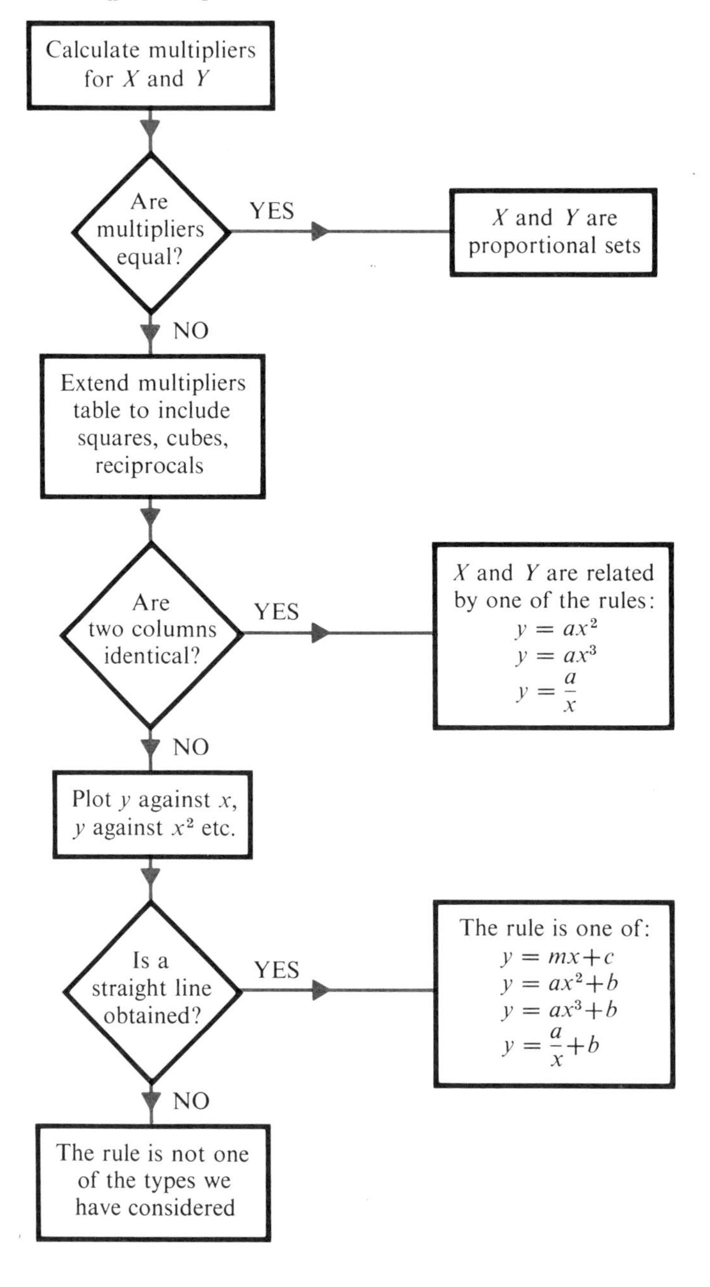

Fig. 14

Exercise D

1 The prices of fibre-glass paddling pools of different diameter are given in the table:

Diameter (m) d:	2	2·5	3	4	5
Cost (£) c:	12	13·8	16	21·6	28·8

The rule connecting c and d is of the form $c = ad^2 + b$ where a and b are constants. Draw a suitable graph to find the values of a and b.

2 Values of x and y are related by the rule $y = \frac{a}{x^2}$. Copy and complete the following table:

x	Multipliers for x	Reciprocals of squares of multipliers for x	y	Multipliers for y
2			5	
	?	?		?
?			1·25	
	?	?		?
10			?	

What is the value of a?

3 It is believed that a rule of the form $y = ax^2 + b$ connects values of x and y. The following results were obtained experimentally:

x:	0	1	2	3	4
y:	2·5	5·2	14·1	29·8	52·6

Find graphically, approximate values of a and b.

4 The following results are connected by a relation of the form $y = \frac{a}{x} + b$:

x:	1	2	4	7	10
y:	5·5	4·5	4	3·8	3·7

Plot values of $\frac{1}{x}$ against y and use your graph to find values of a and b.

5 Verify by a graph that the following figures satisfy approximately an equation of the form $y = ax^3 + b$, and find a and b as accurately as you can.

x:	4	5	6	7	8
y:	5·2	6·6	8·7	11·6	15·4

5 The growth function

The egg of a frog consists of a single cell. Once it has been fertilized, it divides into two. These two cells subdivide again giving four cells in all. If we assume that this process continues, the following sequence of numbers results:

$$1, 2, 4, 8, 16, 32 \ldots$$

If, further, we assume that the division of cells takes place at equal intervals of time, we obtain the following table:

Time	0	1	2	3	4	5
Number of cells	1	2	4	8	16	32

The function rule has a form which is quite different from any of the preceding examples in this chapter. Check that the rule is in fact

$$x \rightarrow 2^x.$$

If we call this function f, what is

$$f(6), f(10), f^{-1}(128), f^{-1}(2048)?$$

What value does the table suggest for 2^0?

The domain of the function f is the non-negative integers. It will prove worthwhile to extend it to include negative numbers. Copy and complete the following table:

$^-6$	$^-5$	$^-4$	$^-3$	$^-2$	$^-1$	0	1	2	3	4
					$\frac{1}{2}$	1	2	4	8	16

What are the values of $2^{^-3}$, $2^{^-1}$, $2^{^-5}$? What is the connection between 2^n and $2^{^-n}$?

The example we have considered is a growth function based on 2. What is the rule of the following table?

$^-4$	$^-3$	$^-2$	$^-1$	0	1	2	3	4
				1	5	25		625

Copy it and fill in the missing numbers.

Exercise E

1 If g is the growth function $g: x \rightarrow 4^x$, find:

(*a*) $g(2)$; (*b*) $g(3)$; (*c*) $g(5)$;
(*d*) $g^{-1}(4^7)$; (*e*) $g^{-1}(256)$.

2 Figure 15 is the graph of a growth function $h: x \rightarrow A^x$. Use the graph to find:

(*a*) $h(2)$; (*b*) $h(5)$; (*c*) $h^{-1}(2{\cdot}2)$; (*d*) $h^{-1}(4)$.

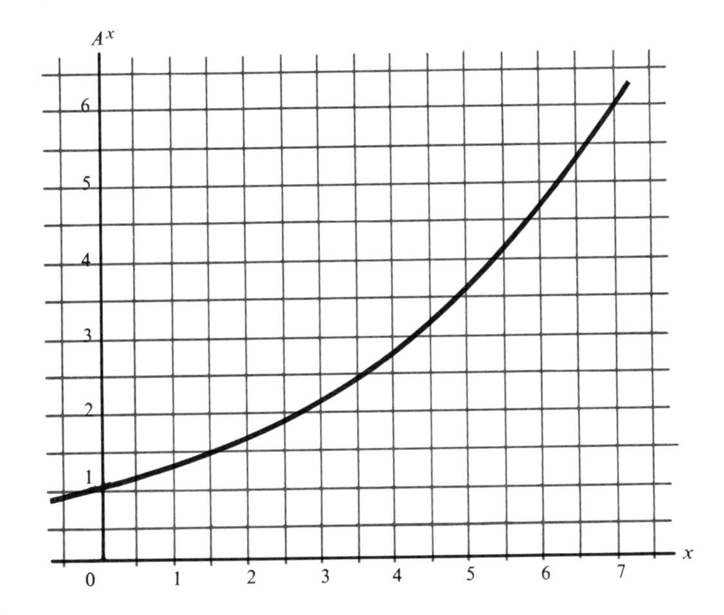

Fig. 15

What is the value of A?

3 The following table refers to the amounts of oxygen collected during a chemistry experiment:

Time (min) t:	1	2	3	4	5	6
Volume (ml) V:	20	24	29	35	42·5	51·5

Show this information in a graph.

For each interval of one minute, work out the fraction

$$\frac{\text{volume at end of interval}}{\text{volume at beginning of interval}}.$$

For example, the fraction for the first minute interval is $\frac{24}{20} = 1{\cdot}2$. Does the volume increase in a similar way to the frog cells in Section 5? Explain your answer carefully in your own words. Assuming the pattern of growth continues, estimate the volume at the end of the seventh minute.

4 f is the growth function $f: x \rightarrow 2^x$. Find the values of a, b, c, d, e, t in the following:

(*a*) $f(3) = f(2) \times f(a)$; (*b*) $f(5) = f(b) \times f(3)$;
(*c*) $f(2) = f(2) \times f(c)$; (*d*) $f(^-3) = f(^-2) \times f(d)$;
(*e*) $f(^-2) = f(e) \times f(1)$; (*f*) $f(t) = f(4) \times f(5)$.

If $f(p) = f(m) \times f(n)$, how do you think p is related to m and n?

Units and dimensions

(*a*) Measurement – the basic units

Cooking and car-maintenance are two common domestic activities which involve a certain amount of measurement. Here are some examples:

oven temperatures, tyre pressures, amounts of recipe ingredients, plug gaps.

Can you think of any others? What units are used for each of these measurements?

The need for well-defined and accurate units of measurement arose mainly as a result of developments in industry and science. Until the Middle Ages, fairly imprecise and often local units of measurement were normally sufficient for the typical community. Nowadays, however, scientists and technologists require very accurate units for their work in medicine, space travel, etc.

There are four *basic* quantities which are measured; other quantities are related to the basic four in a way which will be described in a later section. The four, shown in Table 1, are length, time, mass and temperature.

TABLE 1

Quantity	Standard metric unit	Comment
Length	Metre	
Time	Second	
Mass	Kilogramme	Mass is not the same as weight; the weight of an astronaut can vary but his mass in a sense remains constant.
Temperature	Degree Celsius	The word 'centigrade' is sometimes used in-instead of Celsius.

Investigation 1

Find out about the origins of the metric system and the methods of defining the basic units.

Investigation 2

Recently, more accurate methods of defining the metre and second have been found. What can you discover about these developments?

(*b*) Measurement – derived units

Apart from the basic four, many other quantities are measured – area, volume, speed for example. What others can you think of? The units for these quantities are *derived* from the basic units. Table 2 shows this in detail.

TABLE 2

Quantity	Unit	Symbol
Area	Square metre	m^2
Volume	Cubic metre	m^3
Speed	Metres per second	m/s or ms^{-1}

We can extend this idea and use the symbols M (mass), L (length), T (time) to show precisely how quantities such as area, volume, and speed are derived from the basic ones. For example, speed is a length divided by a time or $\frac{L}{T}$ for short.

We say that *speed has the dimensions* $\frac{L}{T}$. Do you agree with Table 3?

TABLE 3

Quantity	Unit	Symbol	Dimensions
Area	Square metre	m^2	L^2
Volume	Cubic metre	m^3	L^3
Speed	Metres per second	m/s or ms^{-1}	$\frac{L}{T}$ or LT^{-1}

Notice that the last two columns of Table 3 are closely related.

Investigation 3

Find out about the units and dimensions of acceleration, force, work, pressure.

Investigation 4

Find out all you can about the following electrical units:

volts, amperes, watts, ohms.

What do you know about the relationships between them?

(*c*) Checking the dimensions of a formula

Do you ever confuse $2\pi r$ and πr^2? Which is used to find the area of a circle? It is easy to decide using the idea of dimension. Since area has dimensions L^2, it must be $A = \pi r^2$ (π is a number and has no dimensions).

Here are two further examples of 'checking by dimensions'.

Example 1

A class has been asked to find a formula, with p as the subject, relating p, q, r, s, the lengths shown in Figure 1.

Two suggested answers are

(i) $p = \frac{rs}{q}$; (ii) $p = \frac{q}{rs}$.

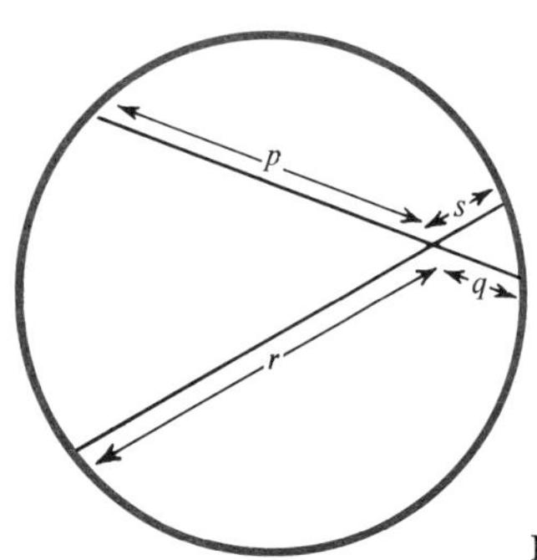

Fig. 1

$p = \frac{q}{rs}$ cannot be right because the quantities are all lengths and so $\frac{q}{rs}$ has dimensions $\frac{L}{L^2}$ or $\frac{1}{L}$ or L^{-1}. What can you say about the answer $p = \frac{rs}{q}$?

Example 2

The following two formulas are suggested for the area of the trapezium in Figure 2:

(i) $A = \frac{hab}{2}$; (ii) $A = \frac{h}{2}(a+b)$.

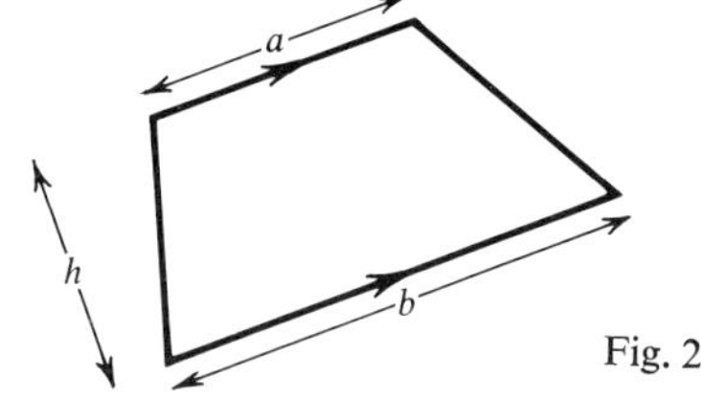

Fig. 2

(i) is obviously incorrect because $\frac{hab}{2}$ has dimensions $L \times L \times L$ or L^3 and so cannot be a measure of area.

(ii) could be correct: $a + b$ is a length and so is h. Hence $\frac{h}{2}(a+b)$ has dimensions L^2. Is $A = \frac{h}{2}(a+b)$ the correct formula for the area of a trapezium?

Exercise A

1 Look at the list of formulae for area and volume. Which ones are obviously wrong when you check the dimensions? Correct them and say which shapes they refer to.

(*a*) $A = \pi rl$; (*b*) $A = \pi r^2 h$; (*c*) $V = 2\pi r(r+h)$;
(*d*) $V = \frac{1}{3}\pi r^2 h$; (*e*) $A = 6a^2$.

2 The density of a substance is found by dividing its mass by its volume. Suggest a suitable unit for density. What are its dimensions?

3 Here are some answers given when a class was asked to find a formula for H in terms of the other lengths (see Figure 3).

(a) $H = \frac{h}{R-r}$; (b) $H = \frac{hR}{R-r}$;

(c) $H = \frac{h-r}{R-r}$; (d) $H = \frac{h}{Rr}$.

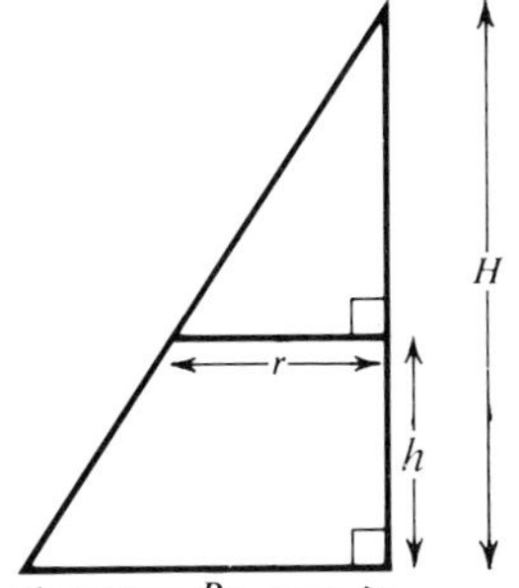

Fig. 3

Check the dimensions of each formula. Which could be correct?

4 The momentum of a moving object can be obtained by multiplying its mass by its velocity. State a suitable unit for momentum and find its dimensions.

5 The quantity 71 g/m^2 is printed on a box of typing paper. What information does it give about the paper? What are the dimensions of this quantity? Can you suggest a name for it?

6 An inflated rubber bathing ring has the measurements r cm and R cm shown in Figure 4. State the dimensions of each of the following quantities and say which could be a formula for the volume of the ring.

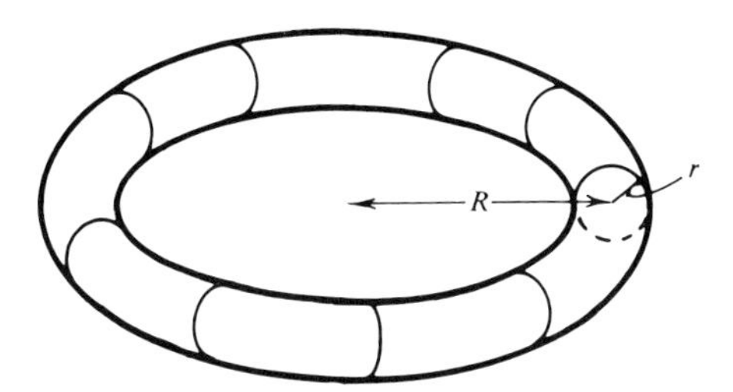

Fig. 4

(a) πrR; (b) $2\pi^2 r^2 R$; (c) $2\pi \frac{r}{R}$; (d) $\frac{\pi r}{R^2}$.

7 If A and B are areas and h is a length, what are the dimensions of the quantity

$$\frac{h}{3}\,(A + \sqrt{(AB)} + B)?$$

Can you suggest the shape associated with this formula?

8 The Ångström unit and the parsec are units of length used in atomic theory and astronomy respectively. Find out how each is defined.

Revision exercises

Computation 4

Here is a list of some of the aids which we employ to do computations when they are too difficult to be done exactly in our heads:

(*a*) guesswork; (*b*) paper and pen;
(*c*) printed tables (e.g. ready reckoner, square roots, etc.);
(*d*) slide rule; (*e*) logarithms;
(*f*) desk calculating machines; (*g*) electronic computers.

Say which aid or aids would be most appropriate if you were computing:

1 67×14p.

2 354×21.

3 The value of π to 1000 decimal places.

4 How long it would take you to drive from London to Edinburgh.

5 The density of copper, in a physics experiment.

6 7586^3.

7 The instant at which a moon rocket would reach its destination.

8 $\sqrt{496}$.

9 $2{\cdot}1 \times 3{\cdot}7 \times 5{\cdot}5$.

10 How many pencils you are going to need next term.

Computation 5

Find the answers to the following as accurately as you can. You are allowed complete freedom of method.

1 2345×3456.
2 $56{\cdot}7^2$.
3 $0{\cdot}065 \times 67$.
4 $0{\cdot}873^2$.
5 888×9898.
6 $66\,990 \div 154$.
7 $1\,917\,747 \div 333$.
8 $67 \div 23$.
9 $354 \div 9{\cdot}7$.
10 $\dfrac{231 \times 441}{21}$.

Exercise K

Calculate the following:

1 $\frac{64}{10}-\frac{32}{5}$.
2 $\frac{1}{5}+\frac{1}{15}$.
3 $\frac{1}{7}-\frac{4}{49}$.
4 $\frac{1}{13}+\frac{1}{2}+\frac{2}{3}$.
5 $(\frac{8}{9}\times\frac{3}{24})+\frac{1}{9}$.
6 $3\frac{1}{2}\times 5\frac{1}{3}$.
7 $\frac{2}{7}\div\frac{3}{5}$.
8 $5\frac{1}{3}-3\frac{5}{8}$.
9 $\dfrac{2\frac{1}{2}+3\frac{3}{4}}{1\frac{1}{3}-\frac{7}{8}}$.
10 $\dfrac{\frac{3}{8}\times\frac{2}{15}}{\frac{5}{8}\times\frac{7}{15}}$.

Exercise L

State the letter(s) corresponding to the correct answer(s).

1 Figure 1 shows two cylinders both full of oil. The smaller one contains 7 kg of oil. What is the mass of the oil in the larger cylinder?

(*a*) $10\frac{1}{2}$ kg; (*b*) 21 kg; (*c*) 28 kg; (*d*) 42 kg.

The ratio of the areas of the curved surfaces of the cylinders is:

(*a*) 2:3; (*b*) 1:2; (*c*) 1:3; (*d*) 1:6.

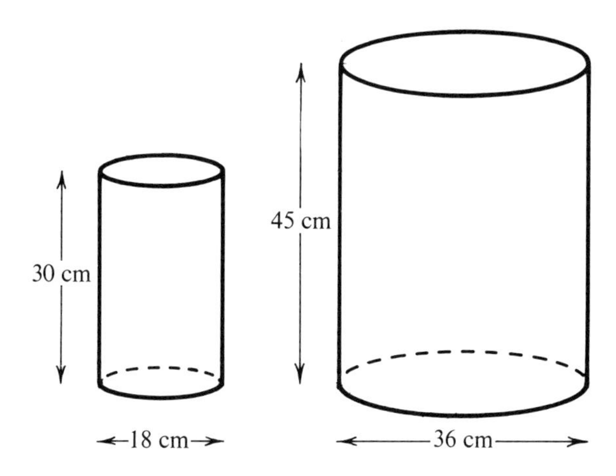

Fig. 1

2 $\sqrt{3}\approx 1{\cdot}73$. Which of the following square roots have the same significant figures as $\sqrt{3}$ (that is, differ only in the position of the decimal point)?

(*a*) $\sqrt{30}$; (*b*) $\sqrt{3000}$; (*c*) $\sqrt{0{\cdot}0003}$; (*d*) $\sqrt{300}$; (*e*) $\sqrt{0{\cdot}3}$.

3 The inverse of the matrix $\begin{pmatrix}3 & 2\\ 5 & 4\end{pmatrix}$ is:

(*a*) $\begin{pmatrix}2 & ^-1\\ ^-2\frac{1}{2} & 1\frac{1}{2}\end{pmatrix}$; (*b*) $\begin{pmatrix}^-3 & 5\\ 2 & ^-4\end{pmatrix}$; (*c*) $\begin{pmatrix}4 & ^-2\\ ^-5 & 3\end{pmatrix}$; (*d*) none of these.

4 Figure 2 shows a cube. There is a line in the plane $EFGH$ which:

(*a*) meets AB;
(*b*) is parallel to AB;
(*c*) is perpendicular to AB;
(*d*) is none of these.

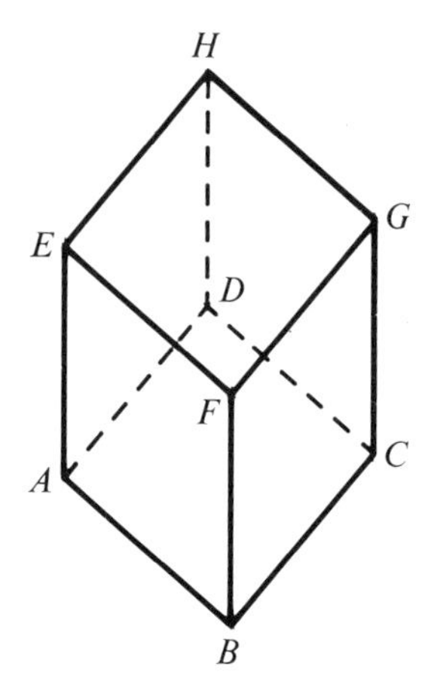

Fig. 2

5 Which of the following operations leave the cube (Figure 2) as a whole unchanged?

(*a*) Reflection in the plane $ACGE$;
(*b*) translation through the vector **AB**;
(*c*) a turn through 120° about BH as axis;
(*d*) a half-turn about BC.

6 Let us call a matrix of the form $\begin{pmatrix} p & 0 \\ 0 & q \end{pmatrix}$ a P-matrix, and one of the form $\begin{pmatrix} 0 & r \\ s & 0 \end{pmatrix}$ a Q-matrix, where no one of p, q, r, s is zero.

Which of the following are true, which false?

(*a*) The unit matrix is a Q-matrix.
(*b*) The square of a P-matrix is a Q-matrix.
(*c*) The product of a P-matrix and a Q-matrix can never be the zero matrix.
(*d*) The multiplicative inverse of a Q-matrix is a P-matrix.
(*e*) The additive inverse of a Q-matrix is a Q-matrix.

True: *a b c d e*
False: *a b c d e*

7 Let $\mathbf{P} = \begin{pmatrix} -1 & 0 \\ 0 & 1 \end{pmatrix}$ and $\mathbf{Q} = \begin{pmatrix} 0 & -1 \\ 1 & 0 \end{pmatrix}$. Which of the following are true, which false?

(*a*) $\mathbf{P}^2 = \mathbf{I}$, where $\mathbf{I}$ is the unit matrix.
(*b*) $\mathbf{PQ} = \mathbf{QP}$.
(*c*) $|\mathbf{P}| = |\mathbf{Q}|$.
(*d*) $\mathbf{Q}$ represents reflection in $x = y$.
(*e*) $\mathbf{Q}$ is its own multiplicative inverse.

True: *a b c d e*
False: *a b c d e*

8 You are given the following table showing values of x and y:

x:	5	15
y:	20	180

With which of the following statements are these data consistent?

(*a*) $y \propto x$;
(*b*) $y \propto x^2$;
(*c*) y is not proportional to any power of x;
(*d*) $y = 16x - k$, for some constant value of k.

Exercise M

State the letter(s) corresponding to the correct answer(s).

1 Of 16 students, 12 take economics, 8 take philosophy and all take at least one of these subjects. What is the probability that two students, chosen at random, take economics only?

(*a*) $\frac{1}{8}$; (*b*) $\frac{7}{30}$; (*c*) $\frac{1}{4}$; (*d*) $\frac{7}{16}$; (*e*) $\frac{1}{2}$.

2 If O stands for any odd number and E for any even number, then the matrix product $\begin{pmatrix} O & E \\ E & O \end{pmatrix}\begin{pmatrix} E & O \\ O & E \end{pmatrix}$ is:

(*a*) $\begin{pmatrix} E & E \\ E & E \end{pmatrix}$; (*b*) $\begin{pmatrix} O & O \\ E & E \end{pmatrix}$; (*c*) $\begin{pmatrix} E & E \\ O & O \end{pmatrix}$; (*d*) $\begin{pmatrix} O & E \\ E & O \end{pmatrix}$; (*e*) $\begin{pmatrix} E & O \\ O & E \end{pmatrix}$.

3 The value of $\sqrt{0{\cdot}009}$ is:

(*a*) 0·3; (*b*) 0·03; (*c*) 0·095 approx.; (*d*) none of these.

4 A price is increased by 20% to £96. The original price was:

(*a*) £76; (*b*) £116; (*c*) £80; (*d*) none of these.

5 Which of these is a fraction lying between $\frac{4}{5}$ and $\frac{5}{6}$?

(*a*) $\frac{9}{13}$; (*b*) $\frac{3}{4}$; (*c*) $\frac{6}{7}$; (*d*) none of these.

6 $3x + 5 > 11 - x$ implies:

(*a*) $x > 3$; (*b*) $x > 4$; (*c*) $x < 1\frac{1}{2}$; (*d*) none of these.

7 The gradient of the line $3x - 4y = 6$ is:

(*a*) $\frac{3}{4}$; (*b*) $\frac{4}{3}$; (*c*) 6; (*d*) none of these.

8 Two transformations have matrices

$$\mathbf{A} = \begin{pmatrix} ^-1 & 0 \\ 0 & 1 \end{pmatrix} \quad \text{and} \quad \mathbf{B} = \begin{pmatrix} 0 & ^-1 \\ 1 & 0 \end{pmatrix}.$$

Then:

(*a*) $\mathbf{A}^2 = \mathbf{I}$ (the identity matrix);
(*b*) $\mathbf{AB} = \mathbf{BA}$;
(*c*) $\mathbf{B}$ is the matrix for reflection in $x = y$;
(*d*) $\mathbf{B}$ is its own inverse.

Exercise N

1 Find a and b if $\begin{pmatrix} ^-2 & a \\ 4 & 1 \end{pmatrix}\begin{pmatrix} 3 \\ b \end{pmatrix} = \begin{pmatrix} 0 \\ 4 \end{pmatrix}$.

2 Write down any pair of positive integers x and y which satisfy *both* the inequalities:

$$x + 2y > 20; \qquad 2x - y > 30.$$

3 Solve the equations

$$2x + 3y = 2$$
$$^-3y = 4.$$

4 Find the equation of the straight line joining $A(0,3)$ and $B(2,7)$.
The line AB meets the line $x + 2y = 9$ at C. Calculate the coordinates of C.

5 $ABCD$ is a parallelogram. A is the point (2,2) and B is the point (3,4). The diagonals AC, BD meet at (4,3). What are the coordinates of C and D?

6 Show on a sketch the set of points

$$\{(x,y)\colon x(y - 2) = 0\}.$$

7 A certain kind of biscuit is made from a cylindrical disc of dough, whose radius is 3 cm and thickness $\frac{1}{2}$ cm.
Find how many biscuits you could make out of a lump of dough of volume 300 cm^3.

8 Calculate the volume of the solid in Figure 3.

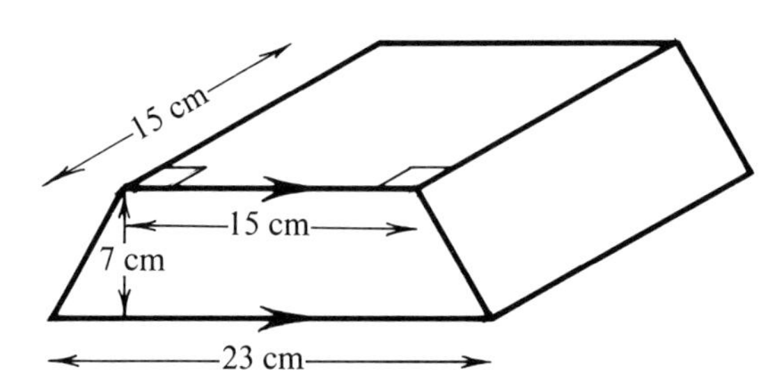

Fig. 3

Exercise O

1 If $4x + 5y > 8$ and $3x - 5y > 6$, deduce an inequality involving x but not y.

2 Find x and y if $\begin{pmatrix} 3 & 2 \\ ^-4 & 1 \end{pmatrix}\begin{pmatrix} x \\ y \end{pmatrix} = \begin{pmatrix} 6 \\ 14 \end{pmatrix}$.

3 Find x and y if $(x, y)\begin{pmatrix} 2 & 1 \\ ^-5 & 3 \end{pmatrix} = (20, 21)$.

4 Find x and y if $\begin{pmatrix} 1 \\ 2 \end{pmatrix} = \begin{pmatrix} 2 & ^-5 \\ ^-1 & 3 \end{pmatrix}\begin{pmatrix} x \\ y \end{pmatrix}$.

5 If $\mathbf{A} = \begin{pmatrix} 3 & 2 \\ 4 & 3 \end{pmatrix}$ and $\mathbf{B} = \begin{pmatrix} 7 & 6 \\ ^-2 & 5 \end{pmatrix}$, write down $\mathbf{A}^{-1}$ and hence find the 2×2 matrix $\mathbf{C}$ such that $\mathbf{AC} = \mathbf{B}$.

Find also the 2×2 matrix $\mathbf{D}$ such that $\mathbf{DA} = \mathbf{B}$.

6 Let $\mathbf{X} = \begin{pmatrix} 2 & 0 \\ 3 & 1 \end{pmatrix}$ and $\mathbf{Y} = \begin{pmatrix} 3 & 1 \\ 4 & 2 \end{pmatrix}$.

(*a*) If $\mathbf{a} = \begin{pmatrix} 2 \\ ^-5 \end{pmatrix}$ and $\mathbf{b} = \begin{pmatrix} 3\frac{1}{2} \\ ^-6\frac{1}{2} \end{pmatrix}$, show that $\mathbf{Yb} = \mathbf{Xa}$.
(*b*) Write down $\mathbf{Y}^{-1}$.
(*c*) Use your answers to (*a*) and (*b*) to help you find $\mathbf{P}$ such that $\mathbf{b} = \mathbf{Pa}$.
(*d*) Find $\mathbf{Q}$ such that $\mathbf{Xb} = \mathbf{Qa}$.

7 P is the point $(1,0)$, Q is $(4,6)$ and R is $(5,2)$.

Triangle PQR is enlarged with centre of enlargement $(4,0)$ and scale factor 3. What are the coordinates of P', Q', R'?

8 a and b are the binary numbers 10001·111 and 101·1. Find:

(i) $a + b$; (ii) $a - b$; (iii) $a \div b$ to 1 binary place.

Index

Published by the Press Syndicate of the University of Cambridge
The Pitt Building, Trumpington Street, Cambridge CB2 1RP
32 East 57th Street, New York, NY 10022, USA
296 Beaconsfield Parade, Middle Park, Melbourne 3206, Australia

ISBN 0 521 20078 4 hard covers
ISBN 0 521 08621 3 paperback

First published 1973
Reprinted 1974 1975 1978 1979 1980 1983

First printed in Great Britain by William Clowes & Sons Ltd.,
London, Colchester and Beccles
Reprinted in Great Britain at the University Press, Cambridge